COLLECTED WORKS OF A.M. KLEIN

NOTEBOOKS: SELECTIONS FROM THE A.M. KLEIN PAPERS

Much of A.M. Klein's finest prose is to be found in the mass of uncompleted work that he abandoned at the time of his breakdown, and that became accessible only when his papers were deposited in the National Archives. *Notebooks* offers a generous selection of this work, revealing previously unsuspected facets of Klein's character and artistry.

The fiction, criticism, and memoirs collected here focus on Klein's exploration of the role of the artist. The works illuminate crucial periods of his career, especially the early 1940s, when he was transforming himself into a modernist, and the early 1950s, when he was struggling to overcome the misgivings about his art that were to lead to his final breakdown.

The semi-autobiographical text which Klein referred to as 'Raw Material' and the unfinished novel of prison life entitled 'Stranger and Afraid' cast a new light on Klein's often frustrating relationship with the Montreal Jewish community. In 'Marginalia' he discusses poetic form and technique and makes observations on the nature of poetry, thereby providing insights into his own concerns as a writer. In The Golem,' a profoundly ambiguous treatment of the act of creation, a selfportrait emerges of a storyteller who has lost faith in the power and value of his story. The volume includes a critical introduction, which places the material in the context of Klein's other works, as well as textual and explanatory notes.

(The Collected Works of A.M. Klein)

ZAILIG POLLOCK is professor in the Department of English, Trent University, and chairman of the A.M. Klein Research and Publication Committee. He is editor of *A.M. Klein: Complete Poems.*

USHER CAPLAN is editor with the National Gallery of Canada. He is co-editor, with M.W. Steinberg, of *Beyond Sambation: Selected Essays and Editorials, 1928–1955* and *A.M. Klein: Literary Essays and Reviews.*

A.M. KLEIN

Notebooks: Selections from the A.M. Klein Papers

EDITED BY
ZAILIG POLLOCK AND USHER CAPLAN

UNIVERSITY OF TORONTO PRESS
Toronto Buffalo London

Toronto Buffalo London
Reprinted in paperback 2014

ISBN 978-0-8020-2990-4 (cloth)
ISBN 978-1-4426-2305-7 (paper)

Printed on acid-free paper

Canadian Cataloguing in Publication Data

Klein, A.M. (Abraham Moses), 1909–1972
Notebooks : selections from the A.M. Klein papers

(Collected works of A.M. Klein)
Includes bibliographical references.
ISBN 978-0-8020-2990-4 (bound)
ISBN 978-1-4426-2305-7 (pbk.)

1. Klein A.M. (Abraham Moses), 1909–1972 – Notebooks, sketchbooks, etc. I. Pollock, Zailig, 1948– II. Caplan, Usher, 1947– . III. Title. IV. Series: Klein, A.M. (Abraham Moses), 1909–1972. Collected works of A.M. Klein.

PS8521.L45Z53 1994 C818′.5203 C94-930645-2
PR9199.3.K48Z47 1994

Frontispiece: Photograph of A.M. Klein. Courtesy Colman and Sandor Klein.

University of Toronto Press acknowledges the financial assistance to its publishing program of the Canada Council and the Ontario Arts Council.

This book has been published with the help of a grant from the Canadian Federation for the Humanities, using funds provided by the Social Sciences and Humanities Research Council of Canada.

Dedicated to the memory of Tom Marshall

Contents

INTRODUCTION ix
EDITORIAL PROCEDURES xxi
ACKNOWLEDGMENTS xxv
BIOGRAPHICAL CHRONOLOGY xxvii

From the 'Raw Material' File 3
'Stranger and Afraid' 51
Diary (1944) 90
Diary (1945) 95
'The Contemporary Poet' 99
'Marginalia' 103
'Towards a Psychoanalysis of G.M. Hopkins: The Art of the Rorschach' 125
Untitled Novel 129
'The Golem' 142
Selected Notes and Fragments 182

ABBREVIATIONS 193
TEXTUAL NOTES 195
EXPLANATORY NOTES 209
APPENDIX: KLEIN'S INVENTORY OF HIS LITERARY MANUSCRIPTS 255

Introduction

The present volume consists of a selection of prose writings from the literary manuscripts in the A.M. Klein Papers at the National Archives of Canada. These manuscripts, whose dates of composition range mainly from the early forties to the mid-fifties, contain some of Klein's most adventurous and accomplished writing. They also provide us with a fresh and, at times, surprising portrait of the poet in the final and most productive period of his career.

The Klein Papers were acquired by the National Archives of Canada from Klein's family in 1973. In addition to Klein's literary manuscripts, the Papers include hundreds of letters (mostly letters to Klein, but also some drafts and carbon copies of letters from him); speech and lecture notes on a wide range of Jewish and literary topics; personal records and memorabilia, including material from his 1949 election campaign; a large number of files relating to Klein's work for Samuel Bronfman; press clippings of various sorts; and selected items from Klein's personal library, including his working copies of *Ulysses*.[1]

The literary manuscripts constitute a small part of the Klein Papers as a whole, approximately a quarter of their thirty-five volumes. Usher Caplan has characterized these manuscripts as mostly consisting of 'the working papers of a writer at a particular moment in his career ... [Klein] certainly was not saving them for the archives, which he seems to have looked down upon as a kind of literary graveyard.'[2] Towards the very end of his career Klein put together a detailed inventory of his literary manuscripts (reproduced in the Appendix to this volume), in an apparent attempt to impose some order on them. But the impression remains of a haphazard and at times bewildering mass of writings in a variety of genres – diaries, poems, stories, plays, critical essays, and translations – and at every conceivable stage of completion, from rough notes and drafts to typescripts clearly intended for publication.

The Collected Works of A.M. Klein as a whole exclude a large portion of this material, for the most part on the grounds of literary value. A sweeping exception has been made for the poetry and short fiction: the *Complete Poems* and the *Short Stories* include all of the unpublished pieces that were judged to be in a relatively advanced state of completion. In addition, an ample selection of Klein's letters is slated to appear in the not-too-distant future. Among the more notable unpublished writings that have been excluded from the series on literary grounds are 'That Walks like a Man,' a thriller inspired by the Igor Gouzenko affair; 'Worse Visitors We Shouldn't Have,' a script for a musical based on Yiddish motifs; and 'The Icepick,' an unfinished play about the death of Trotsky. Also omitted are Klein's extensive translations of Hebrew and Yiddish prose, on the grounds that they are less central to his achievement and of less general interest than the material which has been chosen for inclusion.

Most of Klein's best unpublished prose is to be found, not in the pieces that were rejected for publication, but rather in the uncompleted work that remained tucked away in his file cabinets – handwritten material which he evidently never submitted to a typist and which he perhaps was saving, in the way a painter hangs on to his old sketchbooks, for later use. The present volume offers a generous selection of these uncompleted and somewhat private writings. In making our choices, we decided to focus on a relatively small number of texts which, in our opinion, could stand on their own as works of literature. All are fairly substantial and, in most cases, highly 'finished' pieces of writing. Taken together, they form a remarkably coherent body of work, strikingly different from the published writings of the period, yet complementary to them.

The texts fall into several distinct groups: autobiographical fictions kept in a file which Klein labelled 'Raw Material' (c. 1942–c. 1944), and a closely related unfinished novel 'Stranger and Afraid' (c. 1944); two small sets of diary entries from the mid-forties, the first dealing with Klein's plan (soon after abandoned) to run as a candidate for the CCF in 1944, the second with his decision, in 1945, to accept a lectureship at McGill University; a body of literary criticism from the late forties, growing directly out of his work as a lecturer at McGill; two chapters of an untitled novel dealing with the events leading up to the declaration of the State of Israel in 1948 and possibly dating, at least in part, from as late as 1950; and two chapters and extensive notes for a historical novel on the legend of the golem, probably begun in 1953 and abandoned by the mid-fifties. In addition to these more substantial texts, some typical examples of the notes and fragments which are scattered throughout the Klein Papers have been selected for inclusion.

'RAW MATERIAL' AND 'STRANGER AND AFRAID'

'Raw Material' and 'Stranger and Afraid' represent Klein's most ambitious and most revealing work at a crucial period in his career, the period between *The Hitleriad* and 'Portrait of the Poet as Landscape.'

By the end of 1942, Klein had grown increasingly frustrated with the direction his career was taking. In the late thirties, after a silence of several years, he had returned to poetry, beginning with a number of political satires of a vaguely leftist cast. Soon, however, he turned to what was to be his central theme over the next few years, the Nazi threat to humanity, in general, and to the Jewish people, in particular. 'Childe Harold's Pilgrimage,' '*In Re* Solomon Warshawer,' the psalms and ballads, and, finally, *The Hitleriad* all reflect this new concern. After completing *The Hitleriad*, Klein clearly felt the need to reassess his sense of himself as a poet, and, specifically, his relationship with the Jewish community to which most of the work of the preceding few years had been addressed. This reassessment is the central concern of a group of prose texts which Klein gathered together in a file he labelled 'Raw Material.'

'Raw Material' presents, especially in its later sections, a portrait of a profoundly frustrated poet, named Kay, whose poetry is of no interest to his community, which values only his hack work as a speech-writer and lecturer. Klein's anger at his community for failing to appreciate the true value of his work is expressed in a number of sardonic portraits of his family, his associates, and the Montreal Jewish community as a whole, revealing a side of him which one would hardly suspect from his published writings.

But as important as 'Raw Material' is for the insights it offers into Klein's troubled relationship with his community, it is more than just a collection of thinly disguised autobiographical documents. 'Raw Material' consists of a variety of texts, some of which are not at all 'raw,' but highly polished works of literature, foreshadowing 'Portrait of the Poet as Landscape' in their symbolic and allusive exploration of the role of the poet in the modern world, and foreshadowing, as well, *The Second Scroll*, in their testing of the boundaries separating diary, memoir, fable, fiction, poetry, and poetic prose.

Sometime in 1945, Klein decided to approach the issues explored in 'Raw Material' from an entirely new perspective. The result was an attempt at a prison novel, 'Stranger and Afraid.' There is evidence that Klein was already beginning to consider such a novel while he was still at work on 'Raw Material,'[3] and the close connection between 'Raw Material' and 'Stranger and Afraid' is reflected in the similarity between their central characters, Kay in the former and Drizen in the latter. (Drizen was actually named Kay in an early version of 'Stranger and Afraid.') As a convict imprisoned for a mysterious, unnamed crime, Drizen shares Kay's sense of impotence and vulnerability; and, in his prison recollections of the city which has cast him out, he also shares Kay's stance as an ironic social commentator.

'Stranger and Afraid' shows even closer links than 'Raw Material' to Klein's poetry of the mid-forties. Drizen's nightmarish prison experiences are echoed in 'Portrait of the Poet as Landscape,' with its account of the poet as a 'convict on parole,' who

> ... suspects that something has happened, a law
> been passed, a nightmare ordered. Set apart,
> he finds himself, with special haircut and dress ...

And Drizen's vivid evocations of Montreal from his prison cell, which constitute the most elaborate description of the city in Klein's work, have their counterpart in the Montreal poems of *The Rocking Chair.*

DIARIES

Like 'Raw Material,' 'Stranger and Afraid' was never completed. Klein clearly saw no way out of the frustrations which these texts so vividly express, and was unable to conceive of an artistically satisfactory resolution of the tensions which they so powerfully dramatize. In two fragmentary sets of diary entries from 1944 and 1945, we see him attempting to overcome this sense of frustration, not through his art, but through major changes in his life.

On the evidence of the Klein Papers, Klein does not seem to have kept a diary on a regular basis. Apart from one section in 'Raw Material' [pp. 4–19], the two diaries included in this edition are the only examples of the form in the Papers. Whether they are, in fact, genuine diaries or more or less fictionalized narratives, as is clearly the case with the diary entries in 'Raw Material,' they provide an invaluable record of Klein's state of mind at a critical turning-point in his career.

In the spring of 1944, Klein was approached by his long-time friend David Lewis, who was then the national secretary of the CCF, to run for the party in the federal riding of Cartier. He accepted Lewis's offer but, although he had always been generally sympathetic to the socialist aims of the CCF, he had serious misgivings about actually running for office. These misgivings continued to grow as time went by. On 21 April 1944, soon after the events recorded in the diary, Klein wrote to E.K. Brown:

> Under ordinary circumstances, albeit I cherish certain desiderata in the social order, I would never have thought to fling myself into a type of battle which is repugnant to me. Even now I would much rather hold a minor lectureship in a university which would provide me with a minimum of congenial work

> and a maximum of leisure to work upon the hundred 'projects' which agitate me.

Towards the end of the year, he withdrew from the race.

Klein was now at something of a loss. Continuing with a full-time law practice seemed out of the question, and he considered various alternatives, including moving to New York. But Samuel Bronfman, who depended on Klein as a speech-writer and adviser, wanted him to stay in Montreal. Klein had told Bronfman, as recorded in the 1944 diary, that he 'would prefer [a] professorship at McGill to [a] House of Commons seat,' and, perhaps as a way of ensuring that Klein would remain in Montreal, Bronfman arranged for part of his annual contribution to McGill to be used for Klein's salary as a lecturer in the English Department. In May of 1945 Klein attended the meeting described in the 1945 diary with the principal of McGill, F. Cyril James, at which the details of the appointment were worked out. As the account in the diary makes clear, Klein was uneasy about his status at McGill – 'A Jew teaching English poetry!' – but he proved to be a very successful teacher, and his three years at McGill, beginning in the fall of 1945, coincided with the most creative period of his poetic career.

LITERARY CRITICISM

The years at McGill also coincided with the beginning of Klein's most intense period of activity as a literary critic. The Klein Papers contain hundreds of pages of notes from Klein's courses on forms and techniques of poetry, sixteenth- and seventeenth-century literature, and modern British and American poetry, which show him to have been a highly conscientious, well-prepared lecturer. In general, however, these notes reveal little about his personal views on poetry. The most important exception is a set of notes for a lecture entitled 'The Contemporary Poet,' which he delivered on 10 April 1946 in his course on modern British poetry. Along with 'Portrait of the Poet as Landscape,' which had been published a year earlier, this lecture represents Klein's most complete overview of the situation of the poet in the contemporary world.

A substantial body of literary criticism on a wide range of topics soon followed. Earlier in his career, Klein had written book reviews and literary essays, mostly on Jewish themes, but in the late forties there was a substantial increase in the quantity and scope of his literary criticism. Klein's most important critical project of the period was his commentary on Joyce's *Ulysses*, of which three chapters were published in the late forties and early fifties. Other substantial works of literary criticism which Klein published at this time are 'Annotation on Shapiro's *Essay on Rime*,' 'A Definition of Poetry?'

and the satire on literary criticism 'And the Mome Raths Outgrabe.' But the best evidence of the range of Klein's literary interests is to be found in a group of mostly shorter texts, which Klein filed under the heading 'Marginalia.'[4]

All of the 'Marginalia' texts in the Klein Papers deal with poetry: some are detailed explications of works which Klein had lectured on at McGill; others are more general discussions of poetic form and technique; still others are observations on the nature of poetry, themselves frequently cast in highly poetic terms. Whatever their ostensible subjects, these texts, like most of Klein's literary criticism, are valuable primarily as expressions of Klein's own concerns as a writer.

The relevance of Klein's literary criticism to these concerns is particularly obvious in the most interesting of the unpublished literary essays of the period, 'Towards a Psychoanalysis of G.M. Hopkins: The Art of the Rorschach.' Klein's interest in the poetry of Gerard Manley Hopkins dated back at least to 1940.[5] This interest seems to have increased in the mid-forties, when he lectured on Hopkins at McGill; and it is reflected in much of Klein's poetry of the period.[6] Significantly, among the 'heroes' listed in 'The Contemporary Poet' [p. 101], Hopkins is the only English poet to be included.

Klein's account of the specifics of Hopkins's poetic theory and practice borrows heavily from a few obvious sources. The originality of the essay lies elsewhere, in its claim that *all* aspects of Hopkins's life and work can be seen as expressions of a single unifying principle, symbolized by the Rorschach blot, 'the model of internal symmetry frayed with peripheral ambiguity.' In notes for a lecture on Hopkins which he gave some years later, Klein replaced the symbol of the Rorschach blot with another one – 'the seraphic wings' – but the main thrust of his argument remains the same: 'to unify, to discover the pattern, to make all aspects cohere' [MS 6942].

Klein's conviction that there is a single all-encompassing unity underlying the variety of Hopkins's life and work reflects, to some extent, the assumptions of the New Criticism, which was at the height of its influence when he wrote the essay. But in his single-minded attempt 'to make all aspects cohere,' Klein goes much further than the New Critics ever did. This obsessive emphasis on unity and coherence, which is characteristic of Klein's literary criticism in general, tells us less about Hopkins than it does about Klein himself.

UNTITLED NOVEL

Klein's struggle, throughout the forties, to find alternatives to his increasingly frustrating role as a Jewish poet achieved its greatest success in the Quebec poems of *The Rocking Chair*, published in 1948. But, as Klein explained in a letter which he drafted that year to the American poet Karl Shapiro, recent historical events had convinced him that he no longer required his 'Gallic prototype's beatific vision' [MS 424]:

> Now the continuation of our own culture stands before the Jewish writer as *the* challenge. The hiatus of the Diaspora has been closed – closed even for those who still remain therein. We do not write any longer *in vacuo*; we write in the aftermath of a great death, European Jewry's, and in the presence of a great resurrection. Our miracle, moreover, owns to a miracle's greatest virtue – contemporaneity. [MS 423]

The new direction in Klein's career is evident in an unfinished and untitled novel in which he explores the aftermath of the Holocaust and the events immediately preceding the establishment of the Jewish state.

Although the novel marks a new direction in Klein's career, it also continues an old one, for, like much of Klein's writings of the forties – 'Stranger and Afraid'; the short stories 'A Detective Story, or A Likely Story' and 'The Trail of "Clupea Harengus" '; the unpublished novel 'That Walks like a Man'; and even 'Portrait of the Poet as Landscape' – it is shaped by the conventions of the detective genre. What differentiates the novel from earlier exercises in the genre is the application of these conventions to Jewish themes: 'Urim & Thummim [are] equated with modern detective work' [MS 7266]; and Pimontel, the narrator and protagonist of the novel, is a detective from an Orthodox background, trained in the techniques of rabbinical commentary, for whom the 'hermeneutics' of his profession are 'like Torah and like Talmud' [p. 136].

From a rather sketchy set of notes, it is clear that the novel would have involved Pimontel, along with a wide range of other types of Diaspora Jews, in a 'pilgrimage' [MS 4443], 'in [the] style of Canterbury' [MS 7588], to a Palestine on the verge of statehood. There he would have applied his skills as a 'master-commentator' [MS 4470] to solving an unspecified crime, linked, in some way, to the explosion of an atomic bomb near the Dead Sea, 'the New Sinai ... enunciating the new *Mono*logue: Kill' [MS 7539].

The first, vividly autobiographical, chapter of the novel, 'Hapaxlegomenon,' traces the events in Pimontel's life leading up to the visit of a mysterious stranger who summons him on his pilgrimage. The second chapter, 'Adloyada,' follows immediately on the events of the first. After the visit of the stranger, Pimontel goes to the synagogue which he had attended as a child to participate in the Purim service, celebrating the salvation of the Jews of Persia from the evil demagogue Haman. There he witnesses a bitter argument about the appropriateness of continuing to celebrate this salvation in light of the events of the Holocaust. The chapter breaks off with the argument unresolved. Although Klein never completed the novel, he was soon to return to its theme of a pilgrimage to the new Jewish State, in *The Second Scroll*; and the narrator of *The Second Scroll*, in his double search for his missing uncle and for the meaning of the Holocaust, clearly owes much to Klein's conception of the detective/commentator first articulated in the character of Pimontel.

'THE GOLEM'

The final years of Klein's career, following the publication of *The Second Scroll* in 1951, were increasingly dark ones. All of the old frustrations concerning his relationship to his community resurface more powerfully than ever in the most important works of the period. These include the essays 'The Bible Manuscripts,' 'The Bible's Archetypical Poet,' and 'In Praise of the Diaspora'; the short story 'The Bells of Sobor Spasitula'; a series of bleakly powerful translations from the Hebrew poet Chaim Nachman Bialik; and, most importantly, the novel on which Klein was probably working at the time of his breakdown, 'The Golem.'

'The Golem' is Klein's last and most ambitious treatment of a legend to which he had turned several times throughout his career. The legend of the golem, a man created by magical art, is an ancient and widespread one in Jewish folklore, dating back at least to the Talmudic era.[7] However, the best-known version, and the one which forms the basis of Klein's novel, as of all modern treatments of the legend, is associated with Rabbi Judah Löw ben Bezalel (c. 1525–1609), the chief rabbi of Prague.

Rabbi Löw was a much revered figure in his day, but it was not until long after his death that he became associated with the golem legend. In early versions of the legend, Rabbi Löw created the golem merely to act as a servant, but in Yudel Rosenberg's *Niflaot Maharal im ha-Golem* (1909), the golem is created to defend the Jews against accusations of ritual murder. This is a motif which has no precedent in the original legends; its invention is Rosenberg's response to ritual murder trials in late nineteenth- and early twentieth-century Europe. Klein probably knew Rosenberg's book – Rosenberg emigrated to Canada, where he became a prominent Montreal rabbi[8] – but, in any case, Klein's treatment of the legend, like others in the twentieth century, adopts the ritual murder motif.

Klein was familiar with at least three other modern versions of the golem legend: the novels *The Golem* by Gustav Meyrink (1915) and *The Golem of Prague* by Chaim Bloch (1925), and the poetic drama *The Golem* by H. Leivick (1921). Meyrink's novel is mentioned in a note in the 'Golem' material [MS 3278], and Bloch's was a source for Klein's sonnet sequence 'Talisman in Seven Shreds' (c. 1928/1931).[9] But only Leivick's drama, which Klein refers to in an article 'Welcome to Leivick' [*Canadian Jewish Chronicle*, 28 April 1939, p. 4] and in notes for a lecture which he gave on Leivick on

6 March 1949 [MS 5649], appears to have had any influence on Klein's novel. Although in its general outlines Leivick's treatment of the legend bears little resemblance to Klein's, there are important points of similarity. The motif of the golem's love for Rabbi Löw's daughter, which Leivick seems to have been the first to introduce (Klein refers to 'making uncouth love' in his article on Leivick), is echoed by Klein; and, more importantly, Leivick's Rabbi Löw, an ambivalent figure owing something to Faust and even to Doctor Frankenstein, foreshadows Klein's own characterization of the guilt-ridden rabbi.

In all of Klein's treatments of the golem legend, the golem is portrayed unsympathetically. In 'Talisman in Seven Shreds,' the golem is an 'implacable automat[on],' an 'idiot,' a 'nit-wit,' a 'rude goth'; and its creation is 'blasphemous.' In the poem 'The Golem' (c. 1942/1942), the golem is equated with Hitler; and in an unfinished play, 'Death of the Golem,' Klein intended (according to a grant application which he submitted to the Guggenheim Foundation in October 1943) to portray the futility of 'latter-day attempts, both by scientific effort and religious incantation, to revive' the golem as a means of defeating Hitler: 'the duty of contemporary society is to destroy the golem, not to resuscitate competitors for him.'[10] In the notes for his lecture on Leivick, Klein refers to the golem as representing 'power without judgment, force without intelligence.' And in several articles in the *Canadian Jewish Chronicle*, Klein links the golem with such unsavoury topics as racist ideology, eugenics, and Communist show trials ['The Golem of Prague,' 20 January 1939, p. 4; 'The Perfect Man,' 24 December 1943, p. 4; and 'The Golems of Prague,' 28 November 1952, p. 3, reprinted in *Beyond Sambation*, pp. 423–5]. The last of these articles, dating from the period when Klein had begun or was about to begin writing 'The Golem,' contains the following characteristically critical account of

> the clod suddenly become defender of the faith; ... at length, after his many vicissitudes, and particularly at the dénouement of the tale when everything goes wrong (a golem is only a golem), one realizes that an artifact, a mere mechanical man, is no substitute for the truly human in the image of God created. A legend, it is also a parable, vibrating with multitudinous significances touching our human condition; its moral is ineluctable – the man who would fashion a human out of a clod of earth is doomed to defeat; for this creator, he is himself but earthly clod.

This passage is reminiscent of 'The Golem' in its use of the golem legend as a cautionary 'parable' about humanity's pride in its creative powers. In 'The Golem' Klein focuses on 'the creative act' [MS 3573] in the artistic and, especially, the literary sense. He assigns a central role, without precedent in other treatments of the legend, to the self-consciously literary narrator, the scribe Sinai ben Issachar, comparing the 'rules of the scribe,' by which Sinai is guided, to the procedures followed by Rabbi Löw himself in creating the golem [MS 3244]. And it is not only Rabbi Löw's 'work' which is 'parallel' [MS 3059] to Sinai's: his painful doubts about his role as an 'artist, sculptor of golem' [MS 3216][11] are echoed in Sinai's scepticism about the creative act in general, a scepticism which pervades 'The Golem' as a whole, most notably in a blasphemous account of God's creation of the universe as 'The Perfect Crime' [pp. 157–60].

Klein prepared hundreds of pages of notes for 'The Golem,' including a fairly detailed plot outline, but he managed to complete drafts only for its first two chapters. In the first of these chapters, the narrator describes Rabbi Löw's death many years after his creation of the golem, and in the second, which breaks off in mid-sentence, he tells the story of his own life in the years before he became a disciple of Rabbi Löw. In neither of these chapters does the narrator actually manage to begin the story of the golem: in fact, the real subject of these chapters is not the story of the golem at all; rather, it is the repeated, and repeatedly frustrated, attempts of the narrator to tell this story, a story about which he has profound misgivings. In Sinai ben Issachar, the storyteller who is unable to tell his story, we see Klein's final and most moving self-portrait, a portrait of the poet struggling against, but ultimately yielding to, silence.

ZP

NOTES

1 For a brief account of the contents of the Klein Papers, see Usher Caplan, 'The A.M. Klein Papers,' in *The A.M. Klein Symposium*, ed. Seymour Mayne (Ottawa: University of Ottawa Press 1975), pp. 31–6. A detailed 'finding aid' is available at the National Archives of Canada.

2 'The A.M. Klein Papers,' p. 31

3 Klein recast two episodes in 'Raw Material' as reminiscences of a convict: the bloodroot episode, which appears in the second version of 'The Inverted Tree' [pp. 39–41]; and the dialogue with the narrator's son, which appears in both the diary [pp. 7–8] and the first version of 'The Inverted Tree' [pp. 23–4]. Further evidence of Klein's intentions is a plan for incorporating passages from the first version of 'The Inverted Tree' into a prison novel [MS 7425]. The plan indicates that Klein intended to use the second half of the text [pp. 26–32], beginning with Kay's medical examination, and to combine it with a number of other texts (the short stories 'Detective Story, or A Likely Story' and 'We Who Are About

to Be Born,' and the article 'Of Lowly Things'). Although none of these items actually made its way into the completed portion of 'Stranger and Afraid,' other material from the 'Raw Material' file did (see textual notes to 'Stranger and Afraid').

4 Klein used the term 'Marginalia' to refer to three overlapping groups of texts: (1) Between 11 June 1948 and 28 January 1949 he published a series of short literary essays and aphorisms under that title in the *Canadian Jewish Chronicle*. (2) He filed manuscript versions of four of these short essays (see textual notes to 'Marginalia'), along with numerous unpublished items, in the 'Marginalia' section of his papers. (3) Finally, under the heading 'Marginalia' in his inventory of his literary manuscripts, he lists most of the texts in (1) and (2), plus a number of others, some of which appear not to have survived.

5 The year 1940 is inscribed in Klein's hand in his signed copy of the 'Oxford Bookshelf' edition of Hopkins's poems.

6 For Hopkins's influence on Klein's poetry, see Mark Finkelstein, 'The Style of A.M. Klein' (PHD diss., University of Toronto, 1988), pp. 299–307.

7 On the history of the golem legend from its beginnings to modern times, see Gershom Scholem, 'The Idea of the Golem,' in *On the Kabbalah and Its Symbolism* (New York: Schocken Books 1969), pp. 158–204; and Moshe Idel, *Golem: Jewish Magical and Mystical Traditions on the Artificial Anthropoid* (Albany: State University of New York Press 1990).

8 For an account of Rabbi Rosenberg, see Ira Robinson, ' "A Letter from the Sabbath Queen": Rabbi Yudel Rosenberg Addresses Montreal Jewry,' in *An Everyday Miracle: Yiddish Culture in Montreal*, ed. Ira Robinson, Pierre Anctil, and Mervin Butovsky (Montreal: Véhicule Press 1990), pp. 101–14.

9 See *Complete Poems*, explanatory notes, 1.387.

10 Harold Heft, 'The Lost A.M. Klein Guggenheim Application,' *Canadian Poetry* 32 (Spring/Summer 1993), 80

11 Compare Isaac Bashevis Singer, 'Foreword,' in *Golem! Danger, Deliverance and Art*, ed. Emily D. Bilski (New York: The Jewish Museum 1988), p. 7: 'The golem-maker was, essentially, an artist.' For a discussion of the creation of the golem as a metaphor for 'the creative act,' see Emily Bilski, 'The Art of the Golem,' in *Golem!*, pp. 46–7.

Editorial Procedures

CONTENTS AND PRESENTATION

All of the texts in this edition are based on unpublished manuscripts, most of which include varying degrees of revision by Klein. Whenever possible, the latest revisions have been followed.

As a rule, Klein's manuscripts are followed in accidentals as well as substantives. However, idiosyncratic abbreviations have generally been expanded, obvious inconsistencies in spelling and punctuation have been corrected, and the following categories of accidentals have been regularized in accordance with the 'house' style of University of Toronto Press: capitalization of titles; quotation marks (single, with double quotation marks for interior quotes); and ellipsis points (triple throughout). We have been very conservative in making substantive emendations. We have done so only when a passage is incoherent as it stands – generally because a word has been left out, or because a passage has been incompletely revised – and when the correct alternative is obvious. All substantive emendations are noted.

In 'translating' the handwritten text to the printed page, we were inevitably faced with choices about formatting – for example, in the treatment of subheadings, section breaks, line spacing, and indentation. While we have tried to remain as faithful as possible to Klein's apparent intentions, a certain degree of normalization has been allowed in the interest of legibility.

In most cases, the texts exist in only one version; the exception is 'Raw Material,' some passages of which recur in different contexts. We have not attempted to collate these passages and to arrive at a final version; rather, such passages are printed as they stand, as parts of the texts in which they occur.

Although most of the texts in this volume are incomplete, they are, with two exceptions, sufficiently self-contained to stand alone without editorial commentary. However, 'Raw Material' and 'The Golem' both consist of a set of texts whose chronological and thematic interrelationships are not always obvious. We have attempted to clarify the genesis of each of these groups of texts through a linking editorial commentary.

Editorial annotations in the text have been kept to a minimum:

Gaps in the text are indicated by empty brackets: for example, 'Certainly vision, but not [ ].'

Illegible words are indicated by brackets enclosing ellipsis points, each point corresponding to a single letter: for example, 'His flower is [........] with costive bijoutries.'

Uncertain readings are followed by a question mark in brackets: for example, 'disturbance in the hall[?].'

TEXTUAL NOTES

The textual notes for each text or group of texts consist of: (1) a physical description of the manuscripts; (2) the arguments for dating; and (3) a list of variations and emendations.

Physical Description

The aim of the physical description is to help clarify the stages of composition of the text, as we have come to understand it. All comments on ink, handwriting, paper, format, etc., are directed solely towards this end. More detailed description would greatly increase the bulk of the notes (especially in the case of an extremely heterogeneous collection of material such as the notes for 'The Golem'), and it would be no substitute, in any case, for a close examination of the manuscripts themselves.

Dating

This section of the textual notes presents the internal and external evidence for the dating of the texts. As precise a date of composition as possible is established for all of the manuscripts, and, where possible, the chronology of the various stages of composition is established as well.

When it is not possible to assign a precise year of composition, we indicate the likely range. In the three following cases we have been able to be relatively specific:

c. 1944 for 'Stranger and Afraid' [about 1944]
c. 1948/1949 for 'Towards a Psychoanalysis of G.M. Hopkins' [probably no earlier than 1948 and certainly no later than 1949]
c. 1942–c. 1944 for 'From the "Raw Material" File' [probably begun in 1942 and continued through 1944]

Elsewhere we indicate the likely range in more general terms: for example, 'the late forties.'

Variants and Emendations

The list of variants is not intended to record the process of revision, except in those cases where there are questions about the choice of the version printed. Such questions typically arise when it is not clear which is the latest version of a passage, or when it appears that the latest version is incomplete and does not provide a coherent reading. Klein sometimes wrote a new version of a passage in the margin or between the lines, without cancelling the old one. In such cases, the earlier version is printed.

The following formula is used to indicate revisions: — *altered to* —. No attempt has been made to describe the appearance of the page (for example, interlining, additions in the margins, overwriting, crossing-out) except in cases where such information is necessary for explaining the sequence of revisions.

Emendations are listed along with variants. Only substantive emendations are noted.

EXPLANATORY NOTES

The explanatory notes gloss obscure terms and references, and identify sources and allusions. When relevant, information about Klein's life and times is provided and parallels are drawn with his other writings.

The Jewish Encyclopedia (New York and London: Funk and Wagnalls 1906), a copy of which Klein owned and annotated, is cited in preference to the more recent *Encyclopedia Judaica*. The King James Version is cited for all biblical quotations. The edition of Shakespeare cited is *The Riverside Shakespeare*, ed. G. Blakemore Evans et al. (Boston: Houghton Mifflin 1974), and the edition of *Ulysses* cited is the Modern Library edition (New York: Random House 1934), the one Klein himself used. For *The Second Scroll*, the original edition (New York: Alfred A. Knopf 1951) is cited, and for the poetry, the *Complete Poems*, ed. Zailig Pollock (Toronto: University of Toronto Press 1990).

APPENDIX

The Appendix contains Klein's inventory of his literary manuscripts, which he compiled towards the very end of his career.

Acknowledgments

We are grateful for the help and advice of our fellow members of the A.M. Klein Research and Publication Committee: Dr Mark Finkelstein, Professor Noreen Golfman, Colman Klein, Sandor Klein, Professor Seymour Mayne, Professor Elizabeth Popham, Professor Linda Rozmovits, Professor M.W. Steinberg, and Dr Robert Taylor. Dr Taylor, in particular, was closely involved in an earlier stage of the project and had much to do with determining its final shape.

When this volume was in its planning stage, we received very useful advice from the Klein Committee's Editorial Advisory Board (Professors W.J. Keith, Robert Melançon, William H. New, J.M. Robson, Malcolm Ross, and Miriam Waddington, and the late Professors Henry Kreisel and Tom Marshall).

Others who provided assistance of various kinds are Professor Morton Berkowitz, Fred Catzman, Ron Finegold of the Jewish Public Library of Montreal, Professor Pierre Landreville, Professor Dov Noy, Professor Stuart Robson, and Roger Sarty.

The National Archives of Canada was most helpful in making available the A.M. Klein collection and in providing special use of its facilities. The Trent University Library, and, especially, its interlibrary loan department, were also most helpful.

The financial assistance provided to the A.M. Klein Research and Publication Committee by the Social Sciences and Humanities Research Council of Canada was invaluable in furthering the work of the Committee and the preparation of this edition, and is very much appreciated.

Biographical Chronology

1909
born to Kalman and Yetta Klein, orthodox Jews, in Ratno, a small town in the Ukraine, and brought to Montreal with his family probably the following year (officially claimed to have been born in Montreal, 14 February 1909).

1915–22
attended Mt Royal School. Received Jewish education from private tutors and at Talmud Torah.

1922–6
attended Baron Byng High School.

1926–30
attended McGill University, majoring in classics and political science and economics. Active in Debating Society with close friend David Lewis. Founded literary magazine, the *McGilliad*, with Lewis in 1930. Associated with 'Montreal Group' of poets and writers, including A.J.M. Smith, F.R. Scott, Leo Kennedy, and Leon Edel. Began publishing poems in the *Menorah Journal*, the *Canadian Forum*, *Poetry* (Chicago), and elsewhere.

1928–32
served as educational director of Canadian Young Judaea, a Zionist youth organization, and edited its monthly magazine, the *Judaean*, in which many of his early poems and stories appeared.

1930–3
studied law at the Université de Montréal.

1934
established law firm in partnership with Max Garmaise, and struggled to earn a living during the Depression. Served as national president of Canadian Young Judaea.

1935
married Bessie Kozlov, his high school sweetheart.

1936
active in publicity and educational work, and on speaking tours, for the Zionist Organization of Canada, and editor of its monthly, the *Canadian Zionist*.

1937
moved to Rouyn, a small mining town in northern Quebec, to join Garmaise in law practice there.
1938
returned to Montreal, and re-established law practice in association with Samuel Chait. Assumed editorship of the *Canadian Jewish Chronicle*, to which he contributed numerous editorials, essays, book reviews, poems, and stories.
1939
began his long association with Samuel Bronfman, noted distiller and philanthropist and president of the Canadian Jewish Congress, working as a speechwriter and public relations consultant.
1940
first volume of poems, *Hath Not a Jew ...*, published by Behrman's in New York.
1942–7
associated with the *Preview* group of poets – F.R. Scott, Patrick Anderson, P.K. Page, and others – and with the *First Statement* group, in particular Irving Layton.
1944
The Hitleriad published by New Directions in New York. *Poems* published by the Jewish Publication Society in Philadelphia. Nominated as CCF candidate in federal riding of Montreal-Cartier, but withdrew before the election of 1945.
1945–8
visiting lecturer in poetry at McGill University.
1946–7
wrote his first novel, an unpublished spy thriller, 'Comes the Revolution' (later retitled 'That Walks Like a Man'), based on the Igor Gouzenko affair.
1948
The Rocking Chair and Other Poems published by Ryerson in Toronto.
1949
published the first of several articles on James Joyce's *Ulysses*. Ran unsuccessfully as CCF candidate in the federal election of June 1949. Awarded the Governor-General's Medal for *The Rocking Chair*. Journeyed to Israel, Europe, and North Africa in July and August, sponsored by the Canadian Jewish Congress, and published his 'Notebook of a Journey' in the *Canadian Jewish Chronicle*.
1949–52
travelled widely in Canada and the United States, addressing Jewish audiences, principally concerning the State of Israel.
1951
The Second Scroll published by Knopf in New York.

1952–4
increasing signs of mental illness. Hospitalized for several weeks in the summer of 1954 after a thwarted suicide attempt.
1955
resigned from editorship of the *Canadian Jewish Chronicle.* Ceased writing and began to withdraw from public life.
1956
resigned from law practice and became increasingly reclusive. Awarded the Lorne Pierce Medal by the Royal Society of Canada.
1971
death of Bessie Klein, 26 February.
1972
died in his sleep, 20 August.

NOTEBOOKS: SELECTIONS FROM THE A.M. KLEIN PAPERS

From the 'Raw Material' File

A brief meditation on the 'adventures [of] the mind' establishes Klein's central aim throughout the group of texts which he filed together as 'Raw Material' – to write a spiritual autobiography which will record, not 'what happens' to him in the usual sense of the word, but what he 'think[s]' or 'imagine[s]':

Whatever I think, or imagine, is also something that happens to me. Not the least of the incidents of my life are my poems. Sentences, too, may constitute the adventures of the picaresque. The truth is, in fact, that with most people their careers are fulfilled mainly in their minds.

This, of course, is not to underestimate the influence and the impact of the purely physical even upon the most spiritual of biographies. I, indeed, should be the last one to hold such a view. A toothache, to speak of the lesser inconveniences, can alter a weltanschauung, and a world-philosophy may be disturbed by a faulty metabolism. What would Shakespeare read like, dreaming Juliet out of a belly-ache? What would Milton see were he not blind? The gut is only spatially removed from the cerebellum.

But this is only a special view of man's estate. By and large, we, in a well-ordered society, with policemen on every corner, and detectives behind every newspaper, must confine our adventures to the mind. Nor is it really a frustrate fate. Why, indeed, should a tussle with a chambermaid be a fit and proper incident for retailing, and a poem not? Why should every traveller who boards a train, or ships to foreign parts, consider the narrative of the geography he beholds and the climate he endures of interest to any third party, while the far greater peripateticism of thought is deemed dull, flat and monotone.

Of course, it depends who's travelling.

The earliest dateable text in 'Raw Material,' and the most clearly autobiographical, is a 'diary, journal of the mind,' which, although probably fictionalized (see textual notes), corresponds quite closely to what we know of Klein's life at this period. This 'diary' consists of a series of loosely connected texts of various sorts: meditations, sketches, dialogues, epigrams, poems, and vignettes of the diarist's various social relationships – as poet, family man, orator, speech-writer, lawyer, etc. – virtually all of which are variations on the theme of frustration:

September 24th

No thing happens but it is autobiographical. The irreducible residuum of all literature – the diary, journal of the mind. Ich dien its constant plumaged plot; hero, Sir Egomet Meipsum. Even those ubiquitous bards – Ibid and Anon – Blind Ibid, mute inglorious Anon – are but ego in incognito dight and doubly proud.

These are the charms against oblivion. On Andalusian cavewalls scribblings dark. Papyrus lifted – a shield – beyond this, go not, Death. Tilebook and chiselled plinth and cunniform brick – a lapidation on the head of Time. Non omnis moriar, drawls Horace, quaint and flaccid, drawing stylus from scabbard. Dogs scratching to bury an immortal bone.

O froggish belly-bursting vanity, croaking from twilit ponds bovine afflatus, windy brekekex!

*

News item: Forty Chinamen before a British court. We Wan Chu. Fail Play. About to be sworn, the accused insist on taking the oath according to the Chinese rite: Wordspoken, saucerbroken. Shiver my timbers, if I lie! The court demurred at the expensive truth. Yet, seeing an ally, would oblige. The oath of broken China.

Alternatively, Cathay demands the right to swear to the accompaniment of slit cockerel throats. I swear; – cock-a-doodle-do; so help me; slit – cock-a-doodle-done.

Denied. In rationed England, Lady Pertelote – elevated to the peerage for services to the realm – shall not be butchered to make a Chinese holysay.

I think of Li Tai Po, drunk, thinking of love.

O all the chicks of China, my dear one
Cannot overcrow the ardour of my love.
Ravage the hencoops of the provinces
Bend back all China's feathered throats; and flash
The jurative blade, it will not make an oath

Stronger than mine, no, not if the Yellow River
Run red with cockerelblood.

*

Succoth

Along the ghetto-street shuffles my unclejew, bearing palms. Palmleaf of Asia, caftan of Europe, macadam American. With every step the palmleaf sibilates above his head, whispers of the four corners of the world, of glories past and gone, of ease in Zion, lore in Babylon.

Under his arm, a nugget in a cottoned box – citron!

It is the flowerfruit of sacred memories, the paradisal apple Adam ate, nostalgic of Eden. To palmleaf sceptre a regal ball. Lemonshaped and orange-fragrant, how many hands in how many climes have held it, morningfresh, blessed it, turned it, citeron-proteron, and all day long thereafter walked clean in the ablution of its odours? Token of Israel's glories, its waxed moon, when the Lord comforted him with apples, and his savour was an ointment poured forth!

Bearing palms, my unclejew shuffles the ghettostreets.

Now, how doth the city sit solitary, that was full of people, how is she become a widow, she that was great among the nations! Flutter it north, and shake it south, stretch it east, and extend it west, the palmleaf, symbol of dispersion! To-morrow, O father's brother, you don again the torn umbrella! To-morrow, the golden citron shrivels again, a dried testicle, its power gone. Blastart Duelord!

*

What is fragrance? Does it live upon the trembling dust, or is it merely shiver of the brain? Is it bodyodour of the lilac, or magic wrought by lilac-sight? Does the rose perspire?

Perfumes there are borne on neither earth nor lotion that come heady in the brain, and stir the heart as if the blood had tides.

*

September 25

The voice of Rabinovitch, editorial, cantorial, touching the burden of Klein:

I'd like you to do me a favour.

He wants a translation – only you can English my Yiddish – an appeal to the maestro for a worthy cause – only you can make it clear to him – or legal advice. No, not that; – you're too honest.

The library is having a campaign dinner. Need a guest-speaker. You?

Speech! Speech! The bastard act – modulated wind, seduction lingual.

We are the people of the Book. When the Germans were still barbarians – as they have remained – shaking their spears in forests black, our ancestors etcetera. Spiritual resources. Am Ha-Sepher. We gave the world a ten-inch descalogue[?]. Conjure with big names. The Bible! Talmud! Maimonides! Halevi! Bialik! Argumentum ad vulgum: The great literature in Yiddish. Not a jargon, forsooth! Peretz and Mendele – fathers of Yiddish literature. (They died childless, strangers say their Kaddish.) Contemporaneity: of what avail our material struggles, if we win the world and lose our own souls? Erudition: As Emerson said, as Milton's lifeblood spoke, quoth Rabbi Yochanan ben Zakkai. Irony: The people of the bankbook, the moneytheists. (Laughter.) Not us, – disturbance in hall[?] – not any here, the assimilators, the sellers of their birthright for an officer's mess. Peroration: Our strength in our ideals. Where is the wolf Assyria? Where is Rome? Where is Carthage? (Is there a Carthaginian in the house?) They may destroy our homes, uproot our people, slaughter our children, but the truths which Israel launched upon the world, they cannot destroy. (Applause.)

No; don't accept. Give him the negative, cordial.

Much as I am tempted to avail myself of your kind invitation – nothing would please me more than to be able to address the pillars of this cultural institution, so dear to my heart – my own membership dates back to 1922 – I am regretfully compelled to forego the proffered pleasure. There are a number of reasons, but I believe that three will suffice: Imprimis: medical instruction not to tax myself with oratorical effort – save forensic, to pay the doctor's bill. Secundo: I have made a resolve not to deliver any public addresses during war-time; and tertio: there are so many more who could do the job better than I.

Unuttered the fourth reason. I will not play second fiddle! Who was he, first invited, who shall not come, that I am now called to save the day.

Rabinovitch, inquisitive: I did not know you were so sick.

He wants a medical diagnosis. Ill himself, he seeks company. Spontaneous pneumothorax – the perforated bellows. But I won't tell him.

Rabinovitch, flattering: We were thinking of getting a New York speaker, but decided we could use home talent.

Aha, a prophet with honour in his country. Honour, for a piece of himself.

Rabinovitch, personalizing: I thought you would accept for sure. After all, it's your library.

Draftdodger, why don't you enlist? Don't you know we are fighting for civilization?

I am the civilization for which you are fighting!

*

Autumn

There stands the sard-looking man with the Midas touch,
Regrating the second-hand season into Lombard gold!

Goldplate over rust;
Counterfeit dewels; and dye-mounds
Soured honeyx; immergreen emerald;
Brown hanging topaz-trees.

His flower is [........] with costive bijoutries:
Old coigns; grassware; goldleaf and bronzefoil
Chlorophilately; petalstone;
The year's opfal and warts.

He is a receiver of fallen woods, of punkrot stock,
A hordure, vexing rich.

The year is pawned in his orferrous hands.
Here is your thicket, Mister: Go, turn over a new leaf.
If you wake up in the veronal season,
You may reclaim your woods.

*

September

Father: And what did you learn in school to-day, Colman?

Son: A lot of things. Words and singing and playing. Miss Katz says we have to learn how to play.

Father: And what else?

Son: Hebrew words. Daddy, what means, shaivu, kumu?

Father: You tell me.

Son: You don't know, daddy. I know more than you. Shaivu – sit down! (Gesture sedentifactive) kumu – get up! (Gesture resurgent)

Father: That's all?

Son: Haidad – hurrah! (Indian dance, with warwhoop-haidad!)

Father: And mummy tells me something else happened. Tell me about it.

Son: Daddy, I had trouble. I told Miss Katz that I need to go to the bathroom, so she let me go. I went upstairs where the boys go, and locked the door, and made hehe. When I wanted to go out, I couldn't open the door. At first, I made noises, like for fun, somebody should hear me, but nobody heard me. Then I made myself like crying, but nobody heard me. Then I cried for real, a long time, until somebody opened the door.

Father: Why did you cry? What were you afraid of?

Son: I was afraid I would have to sleep there, and everything. I wanted to go back to the kids.

Father: Never be afraid. You know that we would never let you stay there. Mummy would call for you, anyway, like she does everyday.

Son: I know, but I was afraid I would have to sleep there.

Efface, O Lord, the memory of that hour! Let be as if it never was! Weed out its evil grass from the little garden of his brain.

Not this of childhood for remembrance! Let him not know the name of fear, nor the terror of the closed door, nor aloneness, far from friends! Let shuvu and kumu, unallied to weeping, dwell in his heart! And haidad swing through his brain, like an ever-swinging door!

*

September

Man: vegetable, animal, mineral? Aristotle notwithstanding, a rational vegetable. Regard the common garden faces: flat Slavic cabbagephiz – Kapust Kapustovitch; Danish forgetmenotsinflax; good old British turnip; Swedish carrotpoll; darknegromelon, red within; olive Italian; gold Indian maize, tufted; Brussels sprouts, and languedoïl leek; bland Mongol potato countenances; and Jew – the vegetable stew.

*

September 26

ET J'AI LU TOUS LES LIVRES

From library to library I go, –
The brothels of the mind – to seek the thrill
Exotic I shall, it seems, never know.
The condom novels, the journalonanist spill,
The cyclopedia's two score and twelve ways
Even the minette of sapphic tongue, do not
Silence the strange desires of my days
Nor still the lechery of erected thought.
Houses of fame, farewell! I go again
To walk the bookless alleys of ascetic rain.

*

9 From the 'Raw Material' File

September 28
Received letter from Peter Devries of Poetry, accepting 'Come two, like shadows.' A good poem, he says, but he wonders at the word pudendal in the last line.

Out of the yesterday, and ages gone
Come two, like shadows on a bedroom wall
To haggle for the psychic jettison.
It is a mighty wrestling, by my soul,
And which shall garner at the very last
The paltry winnings I cannot foretell
Nor which of the shadows shall give up the ghost.

Plato is one whose shadow I surmise
As one surmises the shadow behind a screen.
His words, however, phosphoric, to my eyes –
From whom, to whom, and what they nobly mean –
Love that is fleshless, passion that is dry –
Betray the spirit come to keep me clean,
Clean: tropical only in philosophy.

That other shadow has a bedside manner.
He holds my wrist; he bids me speak out *Ah*
Tell him about the dream of the crimson banner
And of the carnivorous ladies that dream saw.
– O, they are two in a surrealist void
Who haunt me: Plato and his shaven jaw,
And the pudendal face of Doctor Freud.

Refused to change the uglyduckling adjective. Held it was le mot juste, to convey both the appearance and philosophy of the learned doctor. Upon my head, the blushes.

*

September
Rejoicing and drinks – the maestro's – at the planning of the final banquet of the annual philanthropic campaign. Everybody complimented by everybody, even me, who am only the author of its slogans – the proxy of the poor – the compiler of its sob-letters. Particular backslap for an anonymous poem about the grace of charity – Ah, the charm of gilded platitude – printed on the banquet souvenir-program. Poor me! poet parsleyate to a menu. Actually the sonnet was written only to avoid writing the sickening prose called for in the

September

Rejoicing and drinks – the maestros – at the planning of the final banquet of the annual philanthropic campaign. Everybody complimented by everybody, even me, who am only the author of its slogans – the proxy of the poor – the compiler of its sob-letters. Particular backslap for an anonymous poem about the grace of charity. Oh, the charm of gilded platitudes – printed on the banquet souvenir-program. Poor me! poet parsleyate to a menu. Actually the sonnet was written only to avoid writing the sickening prose called for in the promises. But that I should write it at all. It is a humiliation only a philanthropic world makes possible.

The gloating talk – objective reached, we'll show them, etc – not a whisper about the hundred aspects of social distress, about the milk of human kindness from which this campaign sundae is dished up. All froth.

The campaign poem which was not written:

My dear plutophilanthropist
Unclench your tight white-knuckled fist,
And give, as others of the tribe
The annual philanthropic bribe:
From ancien and from nouveau-riche
The unimpeachable baksheesh.

National Archives of Canada, A.M. Klein Papers, MG30 D167, vol. 8, p. 3475 premises. But that I should write it at all. It is a humiliation only a philanthropic world makes possible.

The gloating talk – objective reached, we'll show them etc – not a whisper about the hundred aspects of social distress, about the milk of human kindness from which this campaign sundae is dished up. All froth.

The campaign poem which was not written:

My dear plutophilanthropist
Unclench your tight white-knuckled fist,
And give, as others of the tribe
The annual philanthropic bribe:
From ancien and from nouveau-riche
The unimpeachable baksheesh!
It shuts the big mouth of the poor
From seeking and from getting more,
Narcoticizing with crumb'd bread
Rebellion in the pauper-head
And it costs nothing; for returned
Is merely part the pauper earned –
The sweetest saw-off to be had:
Two cents the dollar – Is that bad? –
And even these two paltry cents
Being tax-exempt, are Government's.
For us the cake, – the poor a maka.
Great is the Hebrew ideal: zdaka!
Can better business deal be made
Than this most double-dealing trade
Which here below, preserves your own
And up above, takes to the Throne
The blessing of the synagogue:
This overlord helped underdog.
Can better profit come to you –
All this, all this, and heaven, too?

*

October twelfth
Chait all day snorting, coughing, phlegming. The dance of the houris is in the air. Pollen, says Chait, Pollen, as if he were mayor of Warsaw.

They sneak into his nostrils, as into a bed-chamber. Surely it is the evil influence of some malicious god who makes this possible. And no cure. While pollen and seed go gallivanting through the atmosphere, the lecherous dust seeking some warm flower-womb, Chait is choked for breath. Dancing and frolicking, the young flowers, released from stamen, invisible as lovers, wafted by breeze, by desire driven, seek the destined stigma, – and pollinate the nose of Chait! Roots clutch at his throat.

The burden of Pollen: For that the time was the time of love, and the pollen filled the land with their harlotries, and the seed of the flower poured forth its fornications on everyone that passed by,

And for that upon the high places whoredom was committed, yea, in the very trees, and in the covert of the grass

Until the lewdness was beyond forbearance, and the abomination beyond suffering

So saith the Lord, I would have utterly destroyed them –

Wherefore to wash away their sin, lo, there shall be one born of woman, Chait his name, a man of suffering.

With his breath shall their abominations be breathed away, and in his rheum and tears the flowers washed of sin.

*

October

The poetess to see me: crazy Slappho. Imagines herself in love with me, the grand passion, Eloise and Abie.

'I know that you talk so cruelly to me because you want to discourage me. But why be so conventional? What if I am married?'

(And at her back I always hear
The drenched diapers slapping near)

'After all, it is the breast which speaks. We were made for each other! How we could take the world by storm. I with my poetry, you with yours!'

(Aroint thee, rump-fed runion
I wouldn't touch thee with a double pentametre!)

She takes out of her purse her be-prepared notebook, her book of verses, crusted with bread-crumb, kitchen-greased. She reads some lines about her baby, and about 'beautiful Palestine.' Her voice throbs. Tears come to her eyes: she moves herself. Her bosom heaves. 'Don't you think I have something there? Don't you think it has feeling? Ever since I read those books you told me to read, I know that I'm improving.'

(Quousque tandem ...)

'I was at the Canadian Authors' Association Convention. I saw Mr. Spondee the well-known poet. He wanted me to leave him twenty poems. Twenty! Don't you think that's wonderful?'

(The Lay of the Fast Minstrel.)

'But all of this is so unimportant, compared to *us*! I know you are in a hurry, but just let me look at you a few minutes more.'

(She looks a few minutes more.)

'O, if my children were only grownup, and my husband not so jealous.'
(Blessed art thou, O Lord, who hast invented jealous husbands!)

*

Counsel for the Prince

Flattery is the utterance of compliments incredible to the flattered. It is practically impossible to achieve.

When a gentile is in misery, he is sorry he was born; when one of us is in such case, he is sorry he was born a Jew.

It is unwise to test Jewish policy by its effect on goyim. We can get better results in our own midst. Jewry has, for this purpose, even more sensitive guinea-pigs.

Every man has his price, said Walpole. And it is not a price in money. Only very cheap men are bought that way. The really expensive ones are bought – with a compliment.

To organize protest-meetings against Hitlerism is to seek to cure ulcers with a belch.

Greed is a kind of intelligence.

*

October
Attempted to re-write Keats' Ode to Nightingale. Failed. Could achieve only 'seizin of mysts,' 'close beausome frond of maturing sun.'

Read Proust – windy, garrulous bore. A la recherche du temps perdu – trying to find out how to lose time.

'Write from experience!' E.g., Joyce describing in last chapter Ulysses the oncoming pains of menstruation.

*

October
Toba seeks to have her third marriage, unconsummated yesterday, annulled to-day.

In support of her action, plaintiff declares

(1) That on the thirtieth day of September 1942, she, of the full age of majority, to wit 52 years old, was bound in holy bedlock to one Anshel Wener,

two years her senior, according to the laws of Moses and of Israel, and according to the prescriptions of the civil code of the province of Quebec.

(2) That the said ceremony of marriage was duly induced by the Reverend H. Rothblatt, who, as vicar of the Lord, and for the fee provided for by law and business acumen, gave it his blessing, bidding the turtle-doves coo.

(3) That as witnesses to the said sacrament there stood the spirit of Eli Black, her first husband, since deceased, who being presently otherwise engaged opposed not the marriage, and Ezekiel alias Haskel Cohen, her second husband, also deceased – in his lifetime a stutterer, and in his death not improved, who held his peace.

(4) That on the said nuptial night, the said Anshel Wener, in caressing's despite, was unable to follow the path of erectitude, and this although he sought carnally to know plaintiff at least a score of times, all to no avail, his gland forever prostate.

(5) That the abovedescribed circumstances caused plaintiff great humiliation, suffering, but no pain.

(6) That accordingly the said marriage was never consummated, the whole as appears from the still-sutured hymen, previously arranged for to simulate virginity, herewith produced as Exhibit P-1.

(7) That plaintiff is entitled to sue for the annulment of the said marriage for the following, among other, reasons.

(a) Impotence, apparent and manifest, potency being secret and to this day unrevealed.

(b) Error as to the person, and/or a vital member thereof.

(c) Fraud – the defendant in his courtship made violent protestations of love, leading plaintiff to believe that his virility lay elsewhere than in his tongue.

(8) That despite defendant's puff and bluster, there were no children issue of the said marriage.

Wherefore plaintiff prays that the said marriage which took place between her and Anshel Wener on the 30th day of September 1942, in the city of Montreal, before the Rev. H. Rothblatt be declared null and void, and be held as having never been entered into, à toutes fins que de droit, the whole with costs against defendant.

For plea to plaintiff's declaration, defendant avers

(1) That he prays act of the admission contained in paragraph 1 and 2 plaintiff's declaration.

(2) That paragraph 3 is ignored, defendant not being familiar with the said witnesses, either in their corporeal or spiritual state.

(3) That paragraph 4 is admitted, defendant adding that the condition complained of by plaintiff being due rather to herself than defendant, plaintiff

appearing totally different from what he had known her to be during the days of courtship, and this because on the said nuptial night she did doff one wooden leg, two rubber breasts, and two protuberant sheathes covering an equal number of non-existent buttocks, this completely altering her personality, hitherto so fraudulently enticing.

(4) That any humiliation which plaintiff suffered she did bring on herself by the above-described trickery and deception.

(5) That paragraph 6 is denied, defendant declaring that neither insertion, nor ejection of semen, nor any other physical operations were necessary to consummate the said marriage, and this because

> (a) Nuptias non concubitus sed consensus; non copula sed consensus [.......... .....] facit nuptias.
>
> (b) Marriage at the age of the parties herein is contracted for companionship and not for procreation; defendant, moreover, herewith reiterates his offer of said companionship to his said spouse, and this despite the fact that she is sans leg, sans breast, sans buttocks, and sans everything.

(6) That paragraph 7 is denied as to each and all of its paragraphs, defendant adding that his potency still exists, under proper stimulation; that all his members, and particularly the one complained of, are intact if not virgin, and that no fraud was practised upon plaintiff.

(7) That par. 8 is admitted.

Wherefore defendant prays for the dismissal of the said action; the whole with costs.

*

Neumann did a sketch of me. Most unsatisfactory. Showed me grim and mean. Which I am not always. Perhaps, since he always seeks me asking loans, that's the way he sees me. I told him that the face he did had its geography correct, but its climate was all wrong.

*

Caractère. F. is the most intellectually unscrupulous man I know. Revisionist on Mondays, quasi-liberal on Tuesdays, reactionary on Wednesdays, Communist on Thursdays, and dubitans the week-end, he lives the full life. So broadminded he entertains two contradictory notions at the same time. And all because he suffers of that great infirmity of able minds – 'he wants to get along.'

I told W. that F. was such a prostitute he went through life regretting that he had no holes in his elbows.

*

Met Sholem Asch. A vain man – and greatly over-estimated. Nine-tenths of his popularity is due to his translator, Maurice Samuel, a really talented writer though a selfish Roumanian.

The author of the Nazarene thinks he's the good earth itself; but he's only asch.

*

I become more and more impatient with merely capable poets. Second-story men, they rise above the pedestrian, but they still live in a flat, like a hundred million others. Give me the basement poet, like Villon, or the penthouse bard, like Rilke!

*

Yesterday was humbled by a dentist!

The planetary motion of the blood,
Also the peregrinations of routine,
And the bright pendulum of dialectic
    All go awry,
Lose their direction and their polarhood
    Before the keen
Weltschmerz residing in a cavity!

Sometimes, in such a dire case, this man –
He of the aloe'd pellets against pain –
Has been to my anguish – antiseptic Hero!
    But now, to-day,
I know him different, clumsy Caliban
    Narcotisized brain,
Gloating with pincers over my dismay!

The panic of the nightmare's still with me:
The ogre of the hypodermic claws,
Smelling of novocaine, and sterile mayhem,
    Knee on my chest
Still runs amok among the ivory,
    Still twists my jaws,
Still deems my groan a scientific jest!

May thirty-two curses blight that torturer!
May his gums soften! May he lose his friends,
Turning in silence from his pyorrhea!
    His tinsel wreath

Fall from his mouth, abscessed, with clotted gore
  At its forked ends!
Thirty-two caries on his thirty-two teeth!

But no! But no! May only thirty-one
Of those foul nibs slip from their gummy curves,
Leaving his food, in lumps, uncut, unmolar'd
  For belly's sake –
And may one canine, comic and alone,
  And quick with nerves
Remain – his weltschmerz and his livelong ache!

*

My world is a fountain-pen moving on its axis.

*

GIRLIE SHOW

I
What men or gods are these? What maidens loth?
What mad pursuit? What feigning to escape?
Who are these satyrs, ribald and uncouth?
What vestals, these, in pantomime of rape?
Does Pan still live? And is his rite still kept?
I thought his flutes were silenced long ago,
And he remembered only on a vase.
Hellas, I thought, all hornèd Hellas slept.
Who are these dancers, then, and these fauns, who
With beard of fingers, whistle lewd applause?

II
With quivering bubs, and ever-parted lips,
Their navels bold, and violent their loins
The dancing girlies thrill all fingertips,
As music titillates th'assembled groins.
O, in their crypts, there war the little beasts
Ready for sacrifice! The footlights blaze
Like altar-flames, where meeting comics cross,
Waving their wands: two largely-trousered priests
Doing the ritual of oblique praise
In worship of the nameless omphalos.

III
This is the temple! Here the crippled come
To throw away the crutches of their sex!
Who ails of sluggish blood, or members numb
Glows here again; who, of the dead reflex,
Stays clod at sight of the mere public parts,
Here finds his blood, goat-footed, capering.
Here, as the strip tease queen struts on the stage
To music pizzicato for g-string
Her satin'd buttocks, smooth, or quick, by starts,
The spent renew, the old forget their age.

IV
The son of Hermes lives! Not in bright glades
Nor in dark forests, seek his votaries,
But enter here through marbled colonnades
Where smile, from feathers, photo'd goddesses,
The city sanctuary of the shaggy one.
The ushers cry their aphrodisiac toys.
The flutists set their reeds. The curtains soar.
At once the legs and music are begun.
The inflamed devotees make joyful noise;
And Pan is god, as he was god of yore.

*

PAWNSHOP

I
May none be called to visit this grim house,
All cup-boards, and each cup-board skeleton'd
With ghost of gambler, spook of shiftless souse,
With rattling relicts of the over-dunned.
Disaster haunts it. Scandals once-renowned
Speak from its chattels, both their shame and woe.
The fleshless poor stalk through its rooms at night.
One should have razed it to the salted ground
O many a year ago,
And put its spectres long ago to flight!

II
Near waterfront, a stone's throw from the slums
It lifts, above its wreckage, three gold buoys

Yet to its reefage tattoo'd flotsam comes
Dropping their snared bags of exotic toys.
Also those stranded on their own dear shores
The evicted tenant, the genteel with false name
The girl in trouble, the no-good sons and heirs,
Waver, and pause before its brass-bound doors
Look right and left, in shame,
Enter, and price, and ticket their despairs.

III

Trinkets of wanhope, salvage of their plight,
Laid on the counter, sorry inventory;
The family plate hocked for a widow's mite;
The birthday gifts – those jewels of memory –
The workman's tools, the vase picked up in Crete
Old hero's medal; ring, endowing bride;
Camera, watch, lens, crushed accordion –
O votives of penultimate defeat,
Weighted, measured, counted, eyed,
By the estimating clerk, himself in pawn.

IV

This is the house built by das Kapital
It thrusts from lintel its thrice burnished bombs
Set for a time, which ticks for almost all,
Whether from fertile suburbs, or parched slums
Monument unintended, on its plaque
Decipher still the name of architect
One Adam Smith whose world of wondrous wealth
Breaks bankrupt into pawnshop bricabrac.
This is the house elect:
Shrine of the let-do liberty of stealth.

Klein made two attempts to rework parts of the preceding diary-like material into a narrative entitled 'The Inverted Tree.' Many of the themes which he develops in the two versions of the narrative are introduced in a set of twenty-five preparatory notes (misnumbered as twenty-six):

1) Expatiate on conversion of painting to music. A noir etc. and the conversion of music to mathematics via vibrations. Thus sensuality reduced to pure thought.

2) Violin – wonderful instrument – a human voice, to no human attached.
3) A scientist is one who imagines in a matter-of-fact voice.
4) Redemption of Palestine as by a mercenary people. Not with the typical legions, but with Furrier's Battalion, Capmaker's Legion.
5) No friends, no ties, no land – no lungs.
6) The radio, a little cantor at my mizrach wall.
7) The inverted tree – essay on stethoscope.
8) Par. on eroticism of illness.
9) Will-to-live, a practical joke. Like somebody trying to get off chair, but his suspenders have been tied to it. He wants to go; can't; everybody laughs.
10) Mountains get lonely. Have only each to each to speak to. Get tired, look about for others. Sometimes will speak even to hills. After all a hill is a mountain lying down.
11) Inverted tree. Locusts sitting upon it. Branches lifeless, no birds sing. Advert to Rilke poem on air.
12) Why don't you write novel. Discuss the padding, the labour.
Social significance. – Poverty only one of many ailments of human body.
Why not literature of tubercular significance or diabetic significance.
Bread for all. No great wisdom. Only first word in philosophy – not the last.
13) Write from experience – implications. As if mere fact of being born, continuing to breathe, being alive was not the greatest experience.
But language to communicate must speak in terms understandable to reader. [.....] spirit of life only to the living. Only they can grasp the referent. The others breathe by virtue of an iron lung. For them an iron lung literature, full of artificial spasms and grand gestures.
Describe small bodily blessings – Bevel in the ear etc.
14) No friends – the one political, the other social. On a desert island.
A salon, its walls full of exquisite paintings, library, civilization in the highest. A button is pushed – they are really only panels. Behind them are gratings whence roar caged beasts.
15) Convert perfume to music by air-waves.
16) First S. attempt interrupted by radio.
18) There is no ecstasy without loss.
Sum total of ecstasy of life of 70 – 6 hours. Only if it came all at once.
19) War – return of cripples, etc. Polygamous molecules.
20) Old suit – skin of myself does not die until 2 months after beggar reshapes it. Very poor buy 2nd hand clothes. Those who sell are only poor.

21) Debate on S. – Dante ref. turned into trees. = Lung.
22) Plot.
23) I did not know whether he was sane or merely feigning sanity.
24) Weather is making poetry for next week – Meteorologist is proof-reading in advance.
25) Child crying from belly of mother.
Experimentation with languages.
26) Noted her disgust – Visit to br.

The most significant of the themes introduced in the preparatory notes is 'the inverted tree,' Klein's metaphor for the lungs, conceived of as a tree with its roots in the air and its branches deep within the body. Klein uses this metaphor to symbolize the relationship between the inner world of the individual, especially the poet, and the outer world of society. In 'Raw Material,' however, the interaction between inner and outer, individual and society, has broken down; lungs are, therefore, invariably diseased, and the act of breathing increasingly difficult to sustain. The motif of diseased lungs (as well as of other bodily infirmities, such as impotence) had already occurred in the diary, where the diarist suffers from 'perforated bellows,' but it is not until the first version of 'The Inverted Tree' that Klein realizes its potential as a unifying symbol. The motif is introduced in the opening parable about a poet 'on an African veldt' who is unable to hunt with his fellow villagers because his lungs are unfit – 'when I run, one of them flaps behind my ribs, like the unlaced tongue of a shoe.' And it is developed in the story of Kay, the frustrated poet who is driven to the edge of suicide by a mysterious lung ailment:

THE INVERTED TREE [Version 1]

I feel like one who lives somewhere on an African veldt at the edge of a jungle. Now and again, a panther will stalk forth from the leafy design of the horizon, and maim or kill a child playing on the outskirts of our village. Then, my brothers, the hunters, take down their rifles and make ready for the hunt. They seek the double quarry of vengeance and security. When, finally, they bag the panther, there is great joy, the child is forgotten, and life goes on as before, a march of moons and festivals. The whole affair, with its oaths and ululations, has been but an incidental adventure. Panther-killing, it is understood, is not one of the purposes of life; it is one of its social amenities.

All about me the world is full of a terrible activity. Everywhere, my brothers, donning the raiment of the kill, go about collecting gear and tackle for the great chase. The panthers, too, having with intelligent ubiquitous eyes watched from behind their screening foliage the technique of their enemies, imitate our movements. They flex their muscles, as if on manoeuvres; they roar, as if with slogans. One would imagine that it was they who were planning a crusade for the security of the jungle.

Yet until either the guns or the beasts have ceased spitting, one cannot tell who is hunter and who is quarry. If, after the broken branches and the torn leaves have settled, the thirty centuries hang dripping from the panther's jaws, then life will have to begin all over again its wearisome ascent, stumbling over a claw, tripping over a tail. Should it be my brothers who come back shouting and dragging their prey after them, then things will be recognized as normal once more, with sowing and reaping, each in their time.

I cannot say that I remain, even from afar, untouched by this tremendous expedition. I, too, would like to be among the Nimrods. Their curdling hunting-cries stir me; their many inventions for death arouse my curiosity. I watch with envy the raising of their gay banners and would like to form part of this pageant about which other poets are already making songs. The thought of perilous paw and fatal fang only adds zest to my desire: how great must be the reward if the penalty is death. Moreover, I cannot forget that garden where the child lay with no motion save that of his slowly-gliding blood.

Unfortunately – and perhaps fortunately – I must stay behind. My lungs, say those who looked through my bones, are not fit for hunting. They say right, for when I run, one of them flaps behind my ribs, like the unlaced tongue of a shoe.

So here I am, with the womenfolk. I am like one who in meditation watches a thunderstorm, and pares his nails.

*

These are the charms against oblivion. On Andalusian cavewalls scribblings dark. Papyrus lifted, a shield: beyond this, go not, Death. Tilebook and chiselled plinth and cunneiform brick – a lapidation on the head of Time. Non omnis moriar, drawls Horace, quaint and flaccid, drawing stylus from scabbard. Dogs scratching to bury an immortal bone.

O froggish belly-bursting vanity, croaking from twilit ponds bovine afflatus, windy brekekex!

*

Along the ghetto-street shuffles my unclejew, bearing palms.

Palmleaf of Asia, caftan of Europe, macadam American.

With every step the palmleaf sibilates above his head, whispers of the four corners of the world, of glories past and gone, of ease in Zion, lore in Babylon.

Under his arm, a nugget in a cottoned box – citron!

It is the flowerfruit of sacred memories, the paradisal apple Adam ate, nostalgic of Eden. To palmleaf sceptre, a regal ball. Lemonshaped and orange-fragrant, how many hands in how many climes have held it, morningfresh, blessed it, turned it, citeron-proteron, and all day long thereafter walked clean in the ablution of its odours? Token of Israel's glories, its waxed moon, when the Lord comforted him with apples and his savour was an ointment poured forth!

Bearing palms, my unclejew shuffles the ghettostreet.

Flutter it north, and shake it south, stretch it east, and extend it west, this palmleaf, symbol of dispersion!

To-morrow, O father's brother, you don again the torn umbrella!

To-morrow, the golden citron shrivels again, a dried testicle, its power gone!

*

What is fragrance? Does it live upon the trembling dust, or is it merely shiver of the brain? Is it bodyodour of the lilac, or magic wrought by lilacsight? Does the rose perspire?

Perfumes there are that are borne on neither earth nor lotion that come heady in the brain, and stir the heart as if the blood had tides.

*

'And what did you learn in school to-day, Colman?'

'A lot of things. Words and singing and playing. Miss Katz says we have to learn how to play.'

'And what else?'

'Hebrew words. Daddy, what means *shaivu, kumu*?'

'You tell me.'

'You don't know. I know more than you. *Shaivu* – sit down! (Gesture sedentifactive) *Kumu* – get up!'

'Just two words?'

'*Haidad,* also, *haidad* – hurrah!' (Indian dance, with warwhoop-haidad)

'And mummy tells me something else happened? How did *that* happen?'

'Well, I told Miss Katz that I needed to go to the bathroom, so she let me go. I went upstairs where the boys go, and locked the door and made hehe. When I wanted to go out, I couldn't open the door. At first, I made noises, like for fun, somebody should hear me, but nobody heard me. Then I made myself like crying, but nobody heard me. Then I cried for real, a long time, until somebody opened the door.'

'Why did you cry? What were you afraid of?'

'I was afraid I would have to sleep there and everything. I wanted to go back to the kids.'

'Colman, you ought never to be afraid. You know that we would never let you stay there. Mummy would call for you, anyway, like she does every day.'

'I know, but I was afraid.'

Efface, O Lord, the memory of that hour! Let it be as if it never was! Weed out its evil grass from the garden of his brain.

Not this of childhood for remembrance! Let him not know the name of fear, nor the terror of the closed door, nor aloneness, far from friends! Let *shuvu* and *kumu*, unallied to weeping, dwell in his heart!

And *haidad* swing through his brain, like an ever-swinging door!

*

I am at my oldest sister's funeral. The day before yesterday I was called from my work to come and see her. She was very ill. Already unconscious, she was wearing the face our father wore on his death-bed. Her nose was pinched and of a waxen colour; now and again, her arms moved towards her throat seeking that which was oppressing her; her panting was like that of a runner at the last thirty yards before the tape-line. Dr. M. who arrived shortly after I did seemed to come to his conclusions by the appearance of her face and the sound of her breath; he examined her cursorily, said something about the lungs having already filled with fluid, and with his usual forthright grave-side manner, gave us to understand that soon he would pronounce her dead.

Beneath the oxygen tanks she survived for another thirty-six hours. Her bed-clothes stirred by the unseen air, and the bed itself shaken by her struggle to breathe – pathetic motion without visible cause – it was as if she was wrestling with a phantom. At six o'clock the phantom went away.

Now the oxygen tanks have been removed from her bed-room, and the bed-clothes have been quickly changed, and she is lying now, in a box, here in front of the pulpit of Applebaum's Funeral Chapel. On the mourners' bench sit her children, some red-eyed with weeping, and some pensive with thoughts of their own future. Not all of them are here; two are in far-away cities. Of the five present, three are the children of her husband's first wife; but from infancy they had been hers. Some of them remember, with that peculiar trait of recollection which knows neither the perspectives of time or of place, the grievances of former days; they are the dry-eyed ones. Myer, the son of her middle age, is at home, weeping on his pillow. Bessie, apparently, does not know how to weep. From her mother my sister she had never learned this art, for my sister was always of small religion and not much of a mourner. It is only my other sisters – may they be contrasted for long life! – who know how to weep in the traditional manner. Thus, my sister Bessie stands beside the coffin and addresses the board under which she supposes the deceased's head lies, attentive. She begs forgiveness for the offences which she, and all of us, may have committed, wittingly or unwittingly, against the honour and dignity of the departed. She begs her to greet my father in his heavenly home, and there together with him to intercede for all our family and for all of Israel here below. At these words, my brother, who suffers periodic heart-attacks, begins to sob. His whole body shakes; the blood leaves his face; his features become sharp. The pallor of his face lends an additional whiteness to his unshaven stubble. I implore him to control himself; whereupon, out of his vest pocket he takes one of his little pills, hastily swallows it, and seeks behind a handkerchief to compose himself.

As for myself, I don't weep. Tears are not for the dead. Another's pain, another's prospect of death – there is subject for sympathy, and the balm of salt-water. But not for the dead this chemical tribute.

Nonetheless, as I listen to the women moaning their great sorrow, moaning and repeating to themselves the little gracious acts of her days that are no more – some of which I recognize to be true and of my own experience – it is memory and not death that brings the tears to my eyes.

They are big tears, bubbled by restraint. The whole room is blurred and foggy, and I can no longer clearly identify any of the people about me. Even sound becomes indistinct; the cantillation of the psalms is heard as from another room. Around the coffin stand several members of the family, but I do not, any longer, perceive them in their individuality; through the haze of my tears, they have become a conglomerate family blur, a single large shadow hovering over the black-draped box.

And suddenly it is I who lie there in that box. I am the one whom all have come to mourn. My mother, clasping her fingers and breaking them backwards, weeps that her crown has fallen. My sisters' eyes can no longer be seen, they have been crying so much, and particularly my sister Dora who sobs how helpless she is now without me. She makes a scene – she was always forthright – and she shouts that there are others who should have died before me. Supported by friends, my wife, my poor wife – she has already fainted several times. And these little ones, my sons, my Colman and my Samuel – who has dared to bring them here? Did I not always want them shielded from tragedy? Probably there was no one to stay home with them; our neighbour, who would usually watch them for us, no doubt wanted to attend the funeral. Poor little Samuel – he looks so bewildered; he can't understand what is going on; he would like to play with me our old game of levitation in which I lie down on the floor, and he, like a little maestro, shouts: Rise! Rise! But something in the air dissuades him, and he clings to his mother's coat.

The rabbi mounts the pulpit to make the obituary laudation. He tells of my scholarship, of my lectures, of my articles, of my contribution to the intellectual life of my community. He speaks of my honesty, and makes a contrast between public reaction at my passing and that upon the passing of a mere rich man. He tells of how I was good to my mother, how I honoured my father, and how I brought up my children in the spirit and according to the traditions of my race. He speaks of my 'name.' Somebody must have told him about that: my mother's greatest boast – her defense-mechanism against the mothers of rich sons – was always that *her* son, without worldly possessions, without property or cars, had 'a name in the town.' At this stage, the rabbi cannot continue, for my kith and kin have abandoned their respectful and sobbing silence. They wail; they tear their hair; they faint. Strangers rush forward to still them and to console them. The rabbi finishes his speech with some biblical verses.

From behind my tears, I watch the entire ceremony, a stranger at my own funeral. Among the dead, I am beyond pain and pity, and am unmoved by the ululation which I have so unintentionally caused. But I feel a certain glow of mild satisfaction – Here, my whole biography has been recounted, but nobody mentioned the fact that I was a poet.

I have kept the secret well. Now, no one will ever know of what I died.

*

The doctor's waiting-room is full of people, and, as I come in, everybody, hitherto immersed in their own thoughts, looks up to stare at me. It is part of the waiting patients' game: to diagnose, from outward appearances, the ailment of the latest arrival. The rewards of the game are two-fold – it passes the time, and it brings company to one's own suffering. Apparently nothing sensational can be seen on me; their eyes release me, and I seek out a chair.

What, really, brought me here? I am not ill to-day, and save for an occasional twinge in my chest, haven't been for weeks. Then why am I here? The fact is that I started out to go to the public library, and it was only when I passed the doctor's sign, that I decided to go in. Why?

It was not pain. It was fear. My sister's laboured breathings had brought home to me once more the realization that the lungs of the Kays were not quite equal to their task. The Kays, it appeared, were congenitally backward in drawing their portion of air. I wanted, therefore, to take another look at how things were faring behind my ribs.

On the wall facing me there hangs, in a wooden frame, the oath of Hippocrates, written in English, but in letters that have been distorted to look like Greek typography. The oath is surrounded by an ornamental design in which the figures of ancient medicine and antique religious ritual are depicted. From where I am sitting, I can only make out the first few words: [ ], and then I give up; distance and distortion defy me.

I leave literature for life, and it is now my turn to diagnose my fellow-sitters. The traumatic cases, of course, are easy. Bandages and crutches are in themselves a diagnosis. But the others present much greater difficulty, and to me are practically inscrutable. The man opposite me with the lean face and the sallow complexion may be suffering from some grave internal disorder, or may be merely worn out with age, anxiety, or work. In fact, he looks like one of the cartoon-Jews in the comic page of one of the Yiddish dailies; they are invariably cloak-operators, and you can almost smell the odour of cloth and thread flowing from the printed representations. Alongside me is a mother and child; although it is the mother who looks sick, and the child happy, I have no doubt but that it is the other way around. Why should a woman wish to take her infant along with her on a visit to the doctor; the child is too young to serve as a chaperon safeguarding reputation. In the corner are two French-girls, one of whom reports every few minutes on the state of her health to her friend. Now she is feeling dizzy; now she thinks a tooth is aching; her headache is intolerable. There is no doubt but that her symptoms are aggravated by impatience. She has been waiting for an hour.

Finally the doctor calls her into his examining-room and she is followed by her friend. In turn, the other patients disappear from the waiting-room to submit to the doctor's ritual of interrogation, palpation, and instruction. At last my turn arrives. I know what to do; I have done this before. Stripped to the waist, I stand before the x-ray machine, its photographic mouth yawning at my shoulderblades. With a right-angled double rod, I am measured for the size of the plate; the nurse shifts the rod up and down, and its metal is very cold on the skin. There is something extremely frivolous about this operation, it is as if someone were to tickle a condemned man to cheer him up. Not being sure of the mood which is required in the circumstances, I neither laugh nor object. The room is darkened. A switch is pulled. The doctor dons his rubber apron, and heavy rubber gloves. He's going to fluoroscope me first. As he regards, like some Martian aurispex, my lungs and entrails, the light is on his face; I am watching that face so as to see his conclusions by reflections. He removes all doubt – Good, he says.

I want to ask him to let me look at my own fluoroscope, but I can't imagine how this can be acrobatically achieved. After all, the plate is in front of my chest, and I can't bend my head so far forward. I do not want to afford him amusement, so I forget about it. Some other time, perhaps.

*

Elizabeth, too, has had her x-ray taken. We promise to become one of the best photographed couples in the country. Only Elizabeth's picture, as it should be, was of her face, that face with its high cheek-bones, challenging chin, and lovely pink-and-pale pastel complexion which so took me on the very first day that I met her. Always her very presence is to me a source of health and exuberance and laughter; with her beside me, I am always living in the rose-petal-upon-milk atmosphere of the country. She is always my rustic convalescence.

And now she was sick herself. It didn't seem natural, I felt as if a universal law had been broken. Nonetheless, her left cheek did cause her terrible suffering, both because the pain was intense and because it was unreachable. There it ached, like marrow in the bone, and you couldn't do anything about it. How would the pain ever get out? Where could it escape to, so prisoned in the hollow of her cheek?

Everybody said sinus, and the house was cluttered with atomizers and a variety of odorous and non-odorous spraying fluids. It also seemed to her as if her teeth were aching. Was it cheek or was it jowl?

The doctor recommended an x-ray. To-day I dropped into his office to see it. Showing me the plate before an illuminated frame, he indicated the white spots on the left as contrasting with those on the right. Black meant air and was alright; white meant matter, and was not so good.

As the doctor continued with his explanations and his recommendations for treatment, I was no longer interested. In the first place, his discussion was purely academic inasmuch as Elizabeth's pain had stopped and I knew she would not submit to any of the murderous tools of the surgeon as long as she was not driven by agony. Moreover, I was already engrossed in the negative itself. Was this vague and shadowed skull really the head of the one I loved? Was this the true, the firm reality behind the beautiful apparition who illuminated my days? Her cheeks – those little cushions of delight, warm and of the colour of flowers – these pirate bones? That delicate sensitive nose – this black triangle? I was like one who out of curiosity approaches a finely carved cabinet, and on opening it discovers it to be an upstood coffin.

Also, I was annoyed with the doctor and the whole transaction. My annoyance was a jealousy which did not name itself. The doctor had looked on secrets of my beloved's body that I had never beheld myself.

*

I am a garden cherishing a tree.

It is an inverted tree, its doubled branches spreading in my chest, its ringed trunk rooted in the sky.

It lives on air.

It might have been so wonderful a growth, with music bursting upon every twig, my heart in its shade.

But locusts have fallen upon it, they devour its leaves, and no birds sing.

*

I fear that I am consistently losing weight. I really shouldn't weigh myself so often, for every time I discover, either on my own scales, or at a drugstore machine, that I am diurnally dwindling, the rest of the day is oppressed with the fear of ultimate extinction.

When I was a child and went to Hebrew school, the favorite theme of my bearded rabbi – a theme which constituted the text of almost every one of his frequent classroom sermons – was the contrast between the material and the spiritual. The spiritual, the *ruchniuth*, evoked his finest praises; the material, the *gashmiuth*, only curled his nose. Gross, and crass, and heavy it was, and a good Jew should strive with might and main to divest himself of it. He persuaded me, of course, although I did find it difficult to believe that all beautiful tangibles were under his anathema. Indeed, in after days, as my numbered senses flowered, they, I thought, were the five fingers to extend to God. And now I was going spiritual, spiritual by my rabbi's awesome definition.

Upon the wall before me hangs a still life – a slaughtered bird resting on a table. The artist, it seems, has made a great effort to endow this essentially gross spectacle with certain ethereal qualities, the fowl is still unplucked as if it might fly again, its neck, slit and nerveless, is concealed, the feathers have been painted with excessive care. Obviously the artist wanted the spectator to think of everything except the sorry fate of the bird, its ultimate destination. Even the table stands against a dark background, full of mysterious nuances, inducing thoughts most un-material. Yet the picture still retains the grossness of its history: something is about to move from the palpable to the edible.

Is it not possible to convert paint into music? Has not every colour an effect upon the eye kin to the effect upon the ear of its germane note? Even the juxtaposition of colours, their shades and their shadows, must have their parallel in music, its combinations and harmonies. Why then should it not be possible to convert this painted fowl into a played melody?

And having that melody – grossness, attenuated, residing in the ear only, and no longer flirting with eye or palate – would it not be but a single step to translate and represent the combined vibrations of this melody by a single mathematical formula? The fowl made pure untrammelled thought?

Under the more skilful transmutations of disease, I myself am progressing from flesh to symbol.

*

At last I had decided upon it. My mind was set, frozen into the shape of its decision. The debate, the arguments and counterarguments now belonged only to a theorizing and vacuous past. All the compelling truths which I had myself mustered against my resolve would now have to be ignored, blue-pencilled by the final imperative, nullified by my own last word. Nor would I pause to reconsider those resurrecting arguments lest at the moment of decision, I weaken again. Clean must the mind be swept, clean, with only a single instrument, in itself perhaps small, but pervading its space like a tumour which must burst.

Now, name that instrument, that deodand!

It was humiliating, humiliating that after having arrived at so god-like a determination, the great non-fiat itself, I should now, like a mere orderly, have to consider the mechanic details of its execution. There should be a providence, surely, to better arrange these things. Intention and accomplishment should be one: invisibility induced by thought alone. I resign, and vanish; I abdicate, and am no more.

Unfortunately, resignation was not enough. An act was required; the treason – was it treason? – required an overt act.

Yet it was an imperative at once distracting and dangerous, distracting – yes, humiliating – in that it made a cosmic decision dependent upon the devising of a choice between a number of fundamentally irrelevant alternatives, and dangerous in that the very act of choice breeded recapitulation, and therefore, a frustrating hesitancy.

But even death must have its committee of ways and means. The judge did not render his sentence and go home; the convict he doomed bore judge with him to doom.

Which, then, among these many panels of escape, was the true door, the door of gracious exit? What button had to be pushed to make it slide, revealing the secret passage, the long tunnel, and the discovered chamber full of light?

The knife? The knife, thrust into its wooden sheath, standing a sentinel, presenting arms?

It cries to the jugular, calls to the carotid; it sibilates to the arterial:

Come, let us make a pact, and sign it on the dotted line. It winks to the light, it smiles; it glows persuasion.

Not me does it persuade. I fear to touch it lest I feel the warmth of my wife's hand still upon its haft.

Not with this shall I make exit. I, in my final dignity, flashing a bread-knife? I, in my greatest kindness, making noisome forever to those who survive me, the sliced bread, the blade made graceless with remembered stains?

Stand, metal Levite, upon the degrees of your temple, singing the song of bread!

Animus, spirit, air, ghost, *gas*!

Circular, the gas-jets hold their breath. They would speak with me; their mouths are shaped as if they would speak with me.

Vowels lethean linger in their throats, eager to join the iron consonants.

Upon me they would breathe the sweet susurra of their secret, envelop me in the colourless carbon of their exhalations, breathe upon me as upon the skin of an apple, making it dim, the better to be shined.

But surely not for me these bellows of forgetfulness, not for these lungs of mine, so starved of the azure of oxygen, this decomposing breath.

This is a death full of retreats – throw open the window! fling open the door! turn off the gloating jets! – full of retreats, self-killing most protracted.

Protracted, too, its discovery – not sudden is it found, but after the hustle and bustle, the sniffing, the cleansing of air, surmisal and search, and then, then only, the delict corpse.

The brain evokes revolvers: the short swift thunder, blaspheming at the temple, the unsugared lozenge for the throat; into the ear the last ejaculation; the heart's explosive stethoscope.

And have the brains lie upon the floor, like bird-dung? Or the blood clotting the distorted mouth? Or the blood dyeing the penultimate clothes, staining with jig-saw red the locus of my fall?

X marks the spot – here the bullet rent his sky! Photographs from seven angles, pictures for the family-album. No.

There are who trip it from this world, dangling from rope, tarzans swinging from tree to tree – O tree of death, O tree of life – supported by the natural vine.

Hanging from clothes-peg, choked from a rafter, pendent from chandelier, the head always cocked, like a deafman's, on a side.

O how many stalactites this minute grow back to earth!

Or shall it be the sharp edge of razorblade, the rite of Nero, its votary in the lukewarm bath, filling with blood from the unsealed fountain; painless, a gradual swooning into the wine-pale water?

No, choicest of all, dissolution's loveliest prelude – the phial of veronal, inducing sleep, death with the sound of lullaby, death with the taste of the sweet half of the apple, clean to itself, and clean to its beholder.

The first version of 'The Inverted Tree' is the most complex as well as the most coherent of the texts in 'Raw Material,' bringing together a wide range of extremely varied material around its central organizing metaphor. For whatever reason, however, Klein was unable to continue it beyond the suicide episode (see MS *7425 for plans for a continuation which was never carried out). He decided, instead, to revise the text entirely. While working on some notes for the revised version, he was struck by the idea of developing the motif of the inverted tree in a poem on the subject of 'being a poet.' In the midst of his notes he sketched an outline for this poem, which would later become 'Portrait of the Poet as Landscape':*

The world diminished by the contents of my lungs – paid back.

*

Describe being a poet. Who wants him in this age, the day of gasoline and oil.

Cursed be the day I penned my first pentameter.

What prompted me. Vanity, mimesis, afflatus.

But here it is. That's what I am. I have yet in me to do something. So many things still unpraised (see Natonek) still unlabelled by my words. My inventory has not yet been taken.

Moreover I want more than discrete isolated visions. I want yet to see the world as a photographer on Mars, focusing all of the sunlit in the camera glimpse.

After sketching this outline, Klein appears to have temporarily put it aside, and to have turned his attention once more to the second version of 'The Inverted Tree,' which is very different from the first. Despite its title, the image of the lungs as an inverted tree has disappeared entirely from the text: the life-threatening illness from which Kay now suffers is angina. More generally, the second version of 'The Inverted Tree' is quite prosaic when compared to the earlier one, with almost none of its abrupt shifts of style or its complex poetic texture. Once Klein conceived of the poetic treatment of the metaphor of the inverted tree which would eventually become 'Portrait of the Poet as Landscape,' he no longer seemed interested in such an approach in 'The Inverted Tree.' It is as if he decided to drain off the poetry from it into 'Portrait of the Poet':

THE INVERTED TREE [Version 2]

I feel like one who lives somewhere on an African veldt at the edge of a jungle. Now and again, a panther stalks forth from the leafy design of the horizon to maim or kill the disobedient child playing on the outskirts of our village. Then, my brothers, the hunters, take down their rifles and make ready for the hunt. They pursue the quarry of vengeance; they seek the pelt of security. When, at last, they do bag the panther, there is great joy in the village, the mauled child is all but forgotten, and life goes on as before, a march of moons and festivals. The whole affair, with its oaths and ululations, has been but an incidental adventure. Panther-killing, it is understood, is not one of the purposes of life; it is merely one of its social amenities.

All about me the world is full of a terrible activity. Everywhere, my brothers donning the raiment of the kill, go about collecting gear and tackle for the great chase. The panthers, too, have with intelligent ubiquitous eyes watched from behind their screening foliage the techniques of their enemies. They imitate our movements; they flex their muscles, as if on manoeuvres; they roar, as with slogans. One would imagine it was they who were planning a crusade, that it was their jungle which was in danger.

Yet, until either the guns or the beasts have ceased spitting, one cannot tell who is hunter and who is quarry. If, after the broken branches and the torn leaves have settled, the thirty centuries are seen dripping from the panther's jaws, then all over again life will have to begin its wearisome ascent, stumbling, as is the custom of its progress, over a claw, tripping over a tail. Should it be – as may it be – my brothers who come back, shouting, joyful, dragging their prey after them, then things will be recognized as normal once more, with sowing and reaping, each in their time.

I cannot say that I remain, even from afar, untouched by these tremendous expeditions. I, too, would like to be of the Nimrods. Their curdling hunting-cries stir me; their many lethal inventions arouse my curiosity. I watch with envy the raising of their gay banners and would like to form part of this pageant about which others, less sensitive than I, are already making songs. The thought of fatal fang and perilous paw only adds zest to my desire: how great must be the reward of such effort if the penalty for its failure is death.

Moreover, I cannot forget that garden where the child lay with no motion, save that of its slowly-gliding blood.

Unfortunately – and perhaps fortunately – I must stay behind. The medicine-men have added an insulting initial to my name; and I am not fit for hunting.

So here I am, with the womenfolk. I am like one who in meditation watches a thunderstorm, and pares his nails.

*

Yet physically – I ignore for the moment the mental anguish of ill-health – I have never felt better in my life. I feel no pain, I do not even feel discomfort. My appearance, too, is normal; perhaps a little haggard, somewhat kohled under the eyes, a little too poetically pale, but nothing to set people conjecturing as to whether it is syphilis or tuberculosis or cancer which is laying me low. Nobody, in fact, could ever surmise, merely by looking at me, that I was a marked man, an intruder upon their scene, out from the graveyard on a ticket-of-leave. And, of course, this is just as well. I would not want to have my good neighbours shake their heads over me as I walked down the street, whispering across balcony-space the guessed-at number of my days, already commiserating with my poor wife and bitter orphans, already twittering obituary comment. I would not want – in such a case I would die a thousand deaths before my designated one – I would not want to enter into the midst of my friends only to sense an immediate change in their behaviour, a sudden fall of temperature as if a cold wind had broken into the room, and they, its stiff and motionless occupants, sat frozen and unconcerned, too polite to shudder. It is good that they do not know, the diagnosis is secret, I am grateful, pity is more unendurable than disease.

It is bad enough when at home, engrossed in a book, my mind valet to some statesman, or poet, or buccaneer of bygone days, I suddenly raise my head and catch my mother, presumably knitting, in the act of watching me. The doleful expression on her never particularly happy face – tears upon parchment – at once saddens and enrages me. I know what that expression means: it is as if I was dead already and she were mourning me, so young and already among the departed, so full of promise and look what happened to him.

No doubt if I was rosy with health, bursting with blood, fleshful and colourbright, she would still have that melancholy pall upon her face. For my mother has a talent for sadness, a native and indoctrinated gift for misery. The happiest days in the calendar are for her the fast-days, the routine non-eating Mondays and Thursdays, the anniversary penitences in memory of some long-forgotten and since-nullified salvation of Jewry, the self-mortifications retroactively grateful for martyrdoms recorded only in encyclopedias. That, as they say, is her meat. And as for the Sabbath before the Blessing of the New Moon, when, alone by the window in her room, her siddur and her handkerchief on her knees, she sits reading, weeping the old-fashioned Yiddish of seventeenth-century prayerbooks, addressing herself to God for that He should preserve her children and her children's children that they come not unto the sons of men for favours, that they be not shamed of men, but that they live decent and honourable 'because of Thy lovingkindness, Rebono shel Olam' – that is a real orgy from which she rises, red-eyed, but confident and relieved, gaped-at by my little sons who do not yet know the meaning of idle tears. Some people go for picnics in the country, but my mother visits the Jewish cemetery where our discarded family bones lie buried, including those of my dear father; she tears up clumps of grass and puts them on the tombstones, she talks to the granite, she seeks to storm the Heavenly Throne through a side-entrance. Of course these activities wring her heart, she returns pale and tired, afterwards she will rest in her low chair pensive for hours; but I know that secretly she is filled with a sense of great worth, the elation of piety. Not she like the other Sabbath-breaking perruqueless apostates who emigrated to Canada, but beloved of her God is she, the God of her hometown Ratno and of other parts celestial.

Nor are these her self-abnegations confined to activities sacred and ritual; even from a family-party she will return full of pride at what she didn't eat there. 'It was a wonderful spread,' she will say, 'as from the generous hand of the Czar. Whatever in the world is good to eat, that was set on plate and dish. Others there were of course who grabbed, devoured and guzzled as if they just came off the boat from hungry Europe. Mrs. Cohen kept eating on both jaws, and Mrs. Grossman kept cramming her little kaddish from both sides. But me I put nothing to my lips, I did not touch as much as the size of an olive. A cup of tea I had. Do I lack food at home?' This for pride. 'Am I sure that the dishes are kosher?' This for piety. 'I don't need their food, thank God. As for the tea, after all, you can't spit in a person's face ...'

That's my ascetic mother, a little dressful of bones, a face wrinkled and runnelled, like a topographical map, and hands bony, the veins transparent through the very sheer skin. I should call her Mummy. When she looks at me, therefore, in that pained and surprised way of hers, as if she found it difficult to recognize me in winding-sheets, she is wholly in character. But I don't like it just the same, I hate pity, even from my mother.

'Look,' she says to Elizabeth, 'look at my stalwart son! How thin he is, bones and skin. He eats, and it eats him! As if for the grave! A fine portrait of a man!'

I am accustomed to these Jewish compliments. Of course, I don't like them because they hurt my vanity. Elizabeth does not like them either because she suspects in them some lurking criticism of the way she is looking after me. But I know that this is merely my mother's uncouth way of goading me into fatness, taunting me into handsomeness. She has no notion of how much her picturesque and innocent locutions pain me; no doubt she was spoken to in that fashion by her mother, and feels that the tradition belongs to the family. No doubt, too, she has an eye on the demons and spirits which come into houses to destroy them; if they, eavesdropping, will hear from her what kind of a miserable prize they have in me, thinks my mother, they will go away, abandoning their bargain to the natural ravages of time.

Nor can I argue with my mother. After all, she knows what's the matter, she may not know accurately and scientifically the full horror of the diagnosis, we have kept from her as much as we could, but that I am not going to win a prize as Montreal's healthiest child, age thirty, that she knows.

Strangers, however, are not aware of what is ailing me. I have never told them, I don't care for their sympathy, nor do I wish to furnish them with satisfying gossip for the dinner-table. It's my affliction, and I'm not supplying the groaners or the gloaters with material.

'You have lost weight lately,' they say, as if beginning a paragraph that I am to finish.

'Yes.'

They are not satisfied with the confirmation of the obvious. 'Not getting enough?' they suggest. 'Or is it too much?'

'Neither,' I say, unamused. 'Just working too hard. Providing for the old age of my bosses. Writing copy for the shoddy we advertise is no cinch. Commodities blown up by literary afflatus. Even Falstaff would grow lean on that. The materialistic interpretation of the immaterial, you know.'

I don't know what this last means, but it sounds wise and epigrammatic, and serves to change the mood and trend of the conversation. So my comforters leave their subject, convinced now that I must be rolling in dough. What began as pity, tentative, ends as envy, established. That is good.

*

I recall how it first happened. Suddenly I couldn't catch my breath. Every inhalation, wilfully delayed until it was no longer resistible, was accompanied by a great, a malevolent pain, as if a secret hand were clutching my heart, a sponge of agony. The cold dew of panic beaded on my forehead, and my lips, as I looked in the office-mirror, seemed to turn blue. The cyanide grimace.

I called for a taxi; if I was going to die – the sense of impending importunate death was the most constant symptom of these seizures – if I was going to die, it was at home that I wanted it to happen, on my own bed, with my wife and children beside me. Not for me the glory of the boots-on! Barefoot as for a pilgrimage, not shod as for a forced march!

The taxi-driver, who could tell by my breathing that he had a sick passenger, escorted me upstairs to my address. His bill was a dollar, which I had, but I did not have the dime for his tip. I longed for my bed, the soft, the white, the reclinable, while Elizabeth, at my request, hunted for her purse, found it, hunted in her purse, didn't find it, found it, the dime of respectability. How careful the poor are of their commercial reputations!

'What's wrong, dear? What happened? What shall I do?' Elizabeth was bewildered, panic-stricken, her mind a pandemonium of conjecture and contingency, as it always is when she encounters the suddenly unpleasant. I found it difficult to speak; I gestured, I pointed to my left lapel, I pointed to our bedroom, I pointed to the phone. 'Lomza,' I said. It must have been very comical, now that I record it in tranquillity, myself in the role of courier in a melodrama bringing to the rescuing garrison a message of breathless and mystical syllables.

Elizabeth phoned Dr. Lomza. As I lay down, prepared to meet my Unmaker, I could hear her. 'He isn't in?' she repeated, in the tone of one who is informed that the appeal has been dismissed. 'He's expected any minute' – to the music of Reprieve granted. She came back to the bedroom. The pain was barely endurable, I was certain that my minutes were numbered, and I was filled with a great self-pity. It trembled, full and round, in the corners of my eyes, it quivered on my lips.

'We have so much to live for,' I said, 'so much to do, and this, this is – it!' Because it sounded phony, because I thought it uncannily apt, I could not bring myself to say 'the end.'

'Don't talk like that,' Elizabeth said, 'I can't stand it! You mustn't talk like that.'

Her lower lip curled and quivered, heraldic of tears. But she didn't want me to see her crying, lest her weeping be taken as a confirmation of my diagnosis. She ran to the telephone again, and I could hear her hurriedly, franticly, not with her own voice, explaining to the doctor what had happened.

'He's coming right away,' she said, and stood beside me, holding my hand as if we were watching a movie, speaking little, not knowing how to fill the eternity that yawned before the doctor's arrival.

The pain had decreased somewhat, and now I was sorry for Elizabeth. 'You'll be a rich widow,' I said, 'a rich and beautiful widow. In the right hand drawer of my desk you'll find my insurance policies, – you're the beneficiary – and I'm worth more dead than alive.'

Some joke that was! She burst into tears, her wifely and nursing restraints all shattered, her true terror revealed, her face marked with the salt minims of misery. And that was good, too, because now she was the invalid and I the consoler.

And then he came, announced by the messianic ring of the door-bell, the wonderful Dr. Lomza, beautiful Dr. Lomza, the lady's man who personally made me an enema, Lomza, the sympathetic, the garrulous, the good-natured, who never timed his visits, prescribing balms, dispensing gossip lethean, Lomza with his little kit of miracles, his big nicotined thumb over your pulse, his husky body protective, Lomza specialist in nothing, good reconnoitering scout coping with the sudden, holding your life in his large palms until he handed it carefully to the consultants! He eased my pain; he made the stiletto'd air endurable once more!

For seeing my great pain, and unable to say definitely what was ailing me, he administered morphine. The spittle of angels, dripping from transparent fang. Through vein and vessel, the potent droplets raced, king's messengers skeltering through corridors and chambers of the palace, hushing the quarrel of the blood, silencing the duel of the clanging corpuscles. The eyes are made smaller, narrowing the ingress of the unfriendly world, and twilight settles on the castle wall. Peace, and the blood moving again, ceaseless, untroubled, without eddy or downfall, like a murmuring river in a darkening land. No doubt the enmities in chamber and corridor still persist, but they are silent, the king has spoken. Perhaps the castle is besieged, the hosts of the foe clambering up the cliff. Who knows? Within the palace there may already be defection, dissension, silent, with the silence of treason. Majesty is undisturbed.

Rush on, you serried redmen, over the drawbridge, across the moated veins, lift battering ram against the studded heart! Conspire your conspiracies, you eaters of my bread! Blow hot, blow cold, my gusty chamberlains! I fear neither your cabals, nor yet the assaults of the stranger. For I sit in the highest tower, crowned with horizon, robed in landscape, the wind my flattering chancellor, the clouds my courtiers ermined! I am at peace. I am at peace, and these bones these walls, these casements these orifices, this flesh this tapestry, are the least of my chattels and kingdom!

And thus, royally, I fell asleep.

On the following day, Dr. Lomza came again. He couldn't understand it, he said, he couldn't for the life of him understand it. The symptoms were undeniably those of an acute angina; but he had never heard, either in his practise or in the books, of a case of angina in a person of my age. The disease, he said, was a Jewish disease, an intellectual disease, graciously I nodded, but not a young man's disease. He recommended, definitely, the taking of an electrocardiogram.

And so within a week I bore Israel's constricted heart up the hill towards Sherbrooke Street to the Aesculapian hive. The bees were busy gathering money, and I had to wait my turn. I was thankful for the pause, for the climb to the Medical Arts Building had put me all out of breath and I feared, no doubt in an ignorant untutored way, that that would have an effect upon the heart's graph. At last the doctor came out of his office, peered in the diary he held in his hand, said, 'Kay,' and seeing me rise, beckoned to me with a repeated crooking of his forefinger. It was as if his forefinger was endowed with a private personality, and did speak. The doctor was a tall Englishman, red-faced, his jowls shaved purple, immaculate, odorous as if he soaped himself every fifteen minutes. This to me was incongruous, inasmuch as he was a heart-specialist, and that organ was reputedly clean, when encased.

Hovering over me with his bulk and his aroma, he sat me on a table and asked me to roll up my trouserleg and my sleeve. Then he interrupted himself to inquire about my symptoms, my curriculum vitae, all pertinent autobiography, details of which he jotted down on what was presumably my card. A case, it appeared, was about to be born. Then, as he put straps and thongs upon my exposed limbs, I noticed for the first time the heart-measuring machine. The whole procedure shuddered me, reminiscent as it was of those tabloid photographs of the rites of Sing Sing. All that was missing was the plate of pheasant and dish of strawberries that the prisoner should have had. Smiling professionally, the doctor threw the switch; the machine, whence emerged the tubes, wires, and straps attached to my arm and leg, like so many bodies ophidian, began to rattle its rattlesnake noise. Electricity probing my heart-beats, voltage eavesdropping upon the dialogue of systole and diastole, the imprisoned blood pounding upon its walls, *I have a confession to make*, and the whole taken down in stenographic spurts by the impersonal machine.

All the time the doctor was accompanying his executioner's operations with cheery laconic jokes – English ones. I did not laugh, and he must have thought me a glum humourless churl, most unappreciative of the subtler joys of life. But I was interested only in the inhuman oracle, the black box that stood there like a coffin attached by tentacles to my body, the cardiac Urim and Thummim that would soon make clear their sibylline verdict. The sputtering ended, and there was no smell of charred flesh. The doctor set to reading his mystic little diagonals, their rise and fall, their summits and valleys, their frequency, their regularity. He looked like a teacher marking one of those exercises we used to do in copybooks when we first learned the slanting of script. Belshazzar and the writing on the wall.

'OK, my boy,' he said, 'there's absolutely nothing wrong with your heart. As strong as a horse. Perfect. Not a murmur. You've wasted your money.' *This* time I laughed, laughed uproariously, laughed with relief, beyond the meed of the witticism, laughed so as to prevent myself from weeping, or being demonstrative, or singing, or performing other antics unEnglish.

With pneumatic limbs, with torso billowed, on resilient feet, I tripped down the hill again to Ste. Catherine Street to take the No. 97 that would bring the news to Elizabeth. I had not told her of my appointment, I did not want to give her those hours of concentrated anxiety, and now I would bring her the surprise. Angina, is there anything finer?

*

That's how it happened the first time; then it came again, once every ten or eleven months, each time with murderous impetuosity, – the end, the end. Now the doctors had finally tracked down its name, and here I am, looking out upon the month of April, and wondering whether May shall also be granted me. 'With this condition,' the doctor had said, 'you may live until you are eighty, or you may die next week.' 'But that applies to you, too, doctor, without this condition,' I had answered. I knew nonetheless that there was a difference, a mathematical difference which the actuaries, to whom I have since applied for insurance, calculated in dollars and cents. They're putting their money on the doctor, not on me.

The first instalment of Spring is about to be made. Already as I pass Fletcher's Field and sloping Mount Royal – my own parcel of imported Nature – I can smell the earth giving off the odour of rebirth, the cleansed musk of last year's autumn, whose snow-soaked leafage now feeds the delicate white teeth of April. The snow has melted quite away, look to the clouds if you would see it! Even the dust and dirt and soot of the chimney-puffing and sand-strewing months which until yesterday smudged the cool linens of the year – the stableboy's bootprints on the princess's bed – have disappeared, gone down, to nourish roots and to support grasses. As yet the fields look brown and squishy with last year's sloshed stubble; one singing night of rain, one day of pin-prick showers, and the chlorophyll will rush to its face again the green and comely blush; people will come out of their houses housing winter into a new, a just-delivered season. April with her long hair freshly washed, and her clothes smelling of Sabbath.

It is Sunday, there is no school, and Colman is bored.

'You promised to show me the flowers on the mountains, daddy,' he says, 'Let's go to-day.'

'But I don't think the flowers are out yet. Next week perhaps. If it will be nice outside.'

'It's nice outside to-day and maybe there are flowers. I saw a kid carrying flowers on Park Ave. A whole bunch of them.'

'They must have been bought in a flower-shop. The flowers on the mountains are of a different kind.'

'Free?'

'Free, when they are there.'

Colman, disappointed, looks to his mother.

'Why don't you take him out sometimes,' she says, 'like other fathers do?' She says this privately, with gestures, whispers, so that Colman should not hear his father invidiously compared. Aloud, and freely, 'It's such a nice day, dear, and you promised him a long time ago – the time you were supposed to take him to see the skiers – that you would show him how flowers grow. It's only a couple of blocks away.'

'Yes, daddy, you promised; and we'll bring the flowers home for Mummy.'

I was getting the business all right. Touched, 'Life upon his little head,' said Elizabeth, lapsing into benedictive Yiddish. 'The little gentleman, the sweet lover. Come, let him go out with his daddy for a change.'

'For a change? Didn't I take him to the Y.M.H.A. last Sunday for a coke?'

'Yes, last Sunday you took him to the Y.M.H.A. for a coke. Big doings.'

'And didn't you enjoy it, Colman, watching the swimming pool, the gym, the basket-ball game, the library, the goldfish?'

'But I would like the flowers better. I want to get some of those flowers that the Indians used to use to paint themselves, like you told me.'

'You told him about it, too,' – Elizabeth [ ]. 'First you make it attractive with Indians, and warpaint, and adventure, and then you back out.'

Colman was beginning to get that sunrise glow around his eyes, his lips pouted at the world's injustice and plighted troth not kept.

'There,' said Elizabeth.

'All right, all right,' I said, 'I'll make like a father.'

We entered the woods through the Mount Royal Avenue gate, always open, sunk in the soil, which leads to the cemetery. It is hot, the trees are bare, and the sun, unhindered, comes pouring down upon the grassless earth, in many places still wet with soggy leaves and little mirrors of water in the hollows. Colman is wearing his rubber boots, and enjoying the mud into which he can now slip with impunity, so receptive it feels, so intimate it sounds. He has picked up a fallen branch and is using it, with exhilarated bravado, as a weapon against unseen foes, Indians and such-like, and against shrubs, bushes, vines, exposed roots. Victorious, his mind moves on to new fields of conquest. 'Where are the flowers?' he asks.

'These are wild-flowers we are looking for, special flowers that grow only in the woods. You have to know the snooks, we will soon come on one.'

True enough, I soon descried a piece of white peering above a brown burden of dead leaves. Blood-root! 'Come, Colman.' We climbed the knoll, he going first so that the released twigs should not lash him in the face, and at last he saw the blossom too. He plucked it. The plant gave way before his careful ritual grasp, coming up with its bleeding roots, its clinging soil, its delicate thin rootlets. 'Is this really blood?' He looked at me as if he had perhaps done something wrong, guilt and elation in his face, thrilled and shuddered. Reassured, he was like a bird, an excited bony bird, hopping from hill to hill, pecking at white here, jumping at yellow there, sometimes duped by brown, gulled by green, disappointment flooded by quest, his constant talk a bird's bubbling.

A lovely morning we had, full of discovery, discovering the three-leaved and three-petalled trillium, the robin, its red bib, its tuxedo stance, and the mound, hit by sunlight, quivering with the yellow adder's tongues, vibrating in the small breeze on their fragile stems, between their long-leaved brown-speckled sheathes. And the crackle of dry branches under our feet, and the smack of the juicy soil. Poking at leaves, surmising the rot of maple, the punk of tree-trunk, skeleton elmleaf, the thick preserved mummy-leaf of oak. In the air, spangles of sun, dart of sparrows, and bird-whistles vaguely identified. And whenever we wanted him, our third companion, Echo.

Homeward bound, Colman proudly entered our street, flanked by his envious friends, his fingers stained, his rubbers muddied, his little trousers linted by contact with sharp shrubbery, his legs scratched, but bearing bouquets for his mummy who stood on the balcony, smiling us all the way up to our doorsteps.

Hurriedly he mounted the stairs – the anaemic petals of the blood-root were already limp, and the cluster was falling away in his hands – 'From daddy and me to Mummy and Baba and Samuel,' he said. Baba glowed; Mummy melted, and Shmulikl wanted to touch, to hold, to smell, to appropriate. Some flowers – and over Elizabeth's protests – some blood-roots for Samuel, the rest placed in two vases and one glass of water.

These flowers have no odour, but my house was full of fragrance.

Not to mention, of course, muddy footprints, dried burrs, and crumbs of root-earth.

*

Messrs. Duncan and Hodges, *Advertising, Merchandising, Commercial*

Research, are over the period of their doldrums. The office is brighter now than it has been for months; Hodges calls Duncan Duke because that is his name, and Duncan calls Hodges Marquis, because his name is Mark; the periodic formality of reciprocated misters – always the sign of a quarrel or disagreement – is over; they smile benignly at each other, they wink; they are engaged in a continual routine of mutual congratulation. Duncan is forever caressing his shiny glabrcus dome, the globe of the world he loves so well, and Hodges is either adjusting his florid tie or fixing demure triangles on his pocket-handkerchief. Everything, as they say, is hunky-dory, as merry as the klaxon of a bright-hued springtime roadster.

The head-shakings, the ruminative monologues, the murmured conferences behind glass-doors, the gloom and the testy tempers are things of the past. The danger which Messrs. Duncan & Hodges thought lowered over them is gone, the Duke had seen it and had ingeniously circumvented it. Again the slogan was business as usual, and again the partners flitted in and out of the office, running from public luncheon to private party, from cocktail session to stag affair, from set appointment to casual meeting, and always, always returning with the bacon.

And were it not for the Duke – that at least is the fiction which it is necessary for discretion's sake to maintain – it might have turned out otherwise. But a few months after the outbreak of the war, and we copywriters and art-men, the scribes and pharisees, were already wondering about our jobs. Stan, in fact, had already sent in his application to one of the government bureaux at Ottawa; he strutted about the office as if he had a secret nest-egg, ransom for the hour of his need, while the rest of us moved amidst a barrage of dismal metaphors about the writing on the wall, the falling axe, the sword of Damocles. In their scheming cubicle, the Duke and the Marquis were engaged in earnest conversation. (Credit line to Miss Woods whose desk is located right by the sanctum.)

'We weren't so smart as we thought we were,' says the Duke, 'everybody sitting pretty, with accumulated stock in their hands, demand rising by leaps and bounds; and we, merchandisers and commercial researchers, left holding the bag. Mr. Hodges, we are the war's first casualty. Take Consolidated Tobacco, for example. Advertising, they say, Don't make them laugh. Invite the public to buy, and then not be able to furnish the goods? Don't be ridiculous. "Go see our customers," he says, "let *them* advertise."' The Marquis was in gloom, his mind a bankrupt blank. As usual, he contributed recrimination.

'But I told you a year ago that we ought to go into some side-line, some production business. Hell, with our experience, our insight' – the Duke winced – 'it would have been a cinch. To-day any damn fool with an article on his hands is a merchant, with two articles, a purveyor to His Majesty the King.

And with my connections. But no, you were against it. What this country needs is vision!'

Mr. Hodges was quoting Mr. Duncan's most powerful sales-line.

'Certainly vision, but not [ ]. Everybody was caught with their pants down, not only us. Fortunately for the tycoons, they could reconvert and pull them up again. But what can we pull up – the clan sporran?'

'Cut the staff, perhaps reduce wages, take smaller premises, stop for a while putting on the dog!'

'That's no good at all. Chicken-feed. You know as well as I do that we must have turnover. Turnover.'

Here Miss Woods had to answer the telephone, or powder her nose, or something.

And then there came the inspiration. Later we discovered that the Duke had read it in some American trade journal, but when he first sprang it on the office and on his partner it came like the revelation of a secret weapon. He was full of enthusiasm, a veritable Churchill; he wrapped himself in the flag, he gestured like a paratrooper, he opened commercial beachheads, he made the world safe for advertising. With a straight face, he hurled at us who knew him all the clichés of democracy, patriotism, *our* way of life.

The plan was simplicity itself. The advertiser was not interested in creating an undue demand for his merchandise. Good. That was patriotic, it curbed inflation. But certainly the advertiser did not want to lose during the years of the war – and it was going to be a long war – the goodwill which he had created for his trade name throughout decades of plodding self-sacrificing public service. That goodwill represented an investment of millions. If a vacuum of no advertising now ensued, that investment would be lost. The advertiser must advertise now to protect his advertising of last year, and the year before, and five years ago. But what is he to advertise? That is the question. Yet the answer was simple, indeed, he was surprised that some enterprising member of his staff had not come forth with the suggestion. But nobody had. Yet anybody who read a newspaper, anybody who was at all moved by the great struggle of our generation should have known the answer: Advertising must harness itself in the service of the war. This was a total war, no one was exempt, least of all the advertising office whose duty it was at all times to serve the public weal. Morale must be kept always at a high point; there was no better morale-building medium than advertising-copy. If, at the same time, the interests of our accounts were advanced, their name kept before the public, their record of war-contributions made known, so much the better; that was but another instance of how under our system of free enterprise enlightened self-interest and national altruism might go hand in hand.

Already he had sold the idea to a number of our most forward-looking customers; it remained only to convince the more stubborn accounts. The office, therefore, would devote itself in the coming weeks to going through our accounts and preparing copy and layout suitable for each, and all in accordance with the new policy. Find the war-angle! And play it up!

Our office now looks like the headquarters of the High Command. We invent strategies, we issue communiqués. V's for victory are plastered on all our walls; the members of the staff salute each other with spread fingers, accompanied by ribald greetings. At our desks, we work furiously at the two standard techniques of intimidation, now serving the crusade for civilization: we conjure the pink-brush phobia, the tattle-tale menace; we appeal to the reader's vanity and self-esteem: *This Means You*. Every time an international statesman makes an important speech we comb it frantically for the picturesque phrase, the usable quotation. Prime Ministers work for us, without pay. Our work has been converted into a macabre charade, a grim crossword-puzzle. We are also heroes at fifteen per cent, and immortal – far from fire.

While Rome burns, the fiddlers fiddle. Our tobacco ads now show men in uniform puffing contentedly between victories. Their uniforms are always clean; that builds morale. Rising from the smoke of Singapore, the hell of Dunkirk, the sand of Libya, our soldiers clamour for a world-renowned soft-drink. A shoe-manufacturer contradicts Napoleon – an army does not march on its belly – it advances on Buckland's Boots. Our soap account asks, challengingly: Do working wives still wish to keep their hands enchanting? *Secret Service* announces our matrimonial agency. We are certainly making a job of it; before we are through, this war will be won, not by the armed forces, but by the butcher, the baker, the candle-stick maker.

I am thoroughly ashamed of my work, as a matter of fact, so is everybody else. We protect ourselves against our humiliation only by an assumed cynicism, it's a living, somebody's got to do it, and it might as well be us, who can do it well. Most of my fellow-scribes, moreover, indulge in a form of penance, or sublimation. Either one is active in The Reserve Army or one is writing The Great Canadian Novel. Prostitutes who adopt children.

But I don't fool myself, I am simply Kay, kindler of copy, delving at desk, sheepskin for show, hung over hilding, swinking in slogans for mongers and martmen, writing their warwhoops, heiling their heroes tobacco triumphant victorious vests, skop of the sales-force, bard of their booty with zest for zippers, for gussets gusto, shrilling the shoddy, hawking at hest; Kay, kinsman and con man, homey with housewifes, chaffering chattels, pally with paters, buttering buyers, frighting with fable the yokels unyielding, fighting the foeman – in safety – for silver.

*

An echo from the past. *Current Jewish Affairs* has just reviewed [ ] published four years ago. I had almost forgotten the book existed; when it first appeared, it received a few notices in the Anglo-Jewish press, and then was lost, like a letter-bearing bottle on the ocean wave. The liberal English periodicals had seen it, sniffed it, smelled gabardine and ghetto, citron and Zion; and had turned away. It was the decade of an all-embracing glutinous internationalism; poems particular to a single tribe, to one twelfth of a nation, were too narrow in scope for the cosmopolitan taste of the critics. Only one distinguished writer had written favourably of it, speaking of great verse left to a little clan; but he himself had fallen upon evil days because of his obsession – that was the word that was used – his obsession with his kith and kin. For the most part the reaction to the book was motivated not by its style or manner, its technical achievement, or passionate sincerity, but by its theme; thus Jewish periodicals who recognized in its pages the spectre of their own plight or the image of their own hopes hailed it with hyperbole, at last a poet writing in English who spoke the authentic voice of his biblic ancestors, at last, the Semite naturalized into Saxondom, etc. etc. while the English journals saw only what they suspected was a narrow chauvinism, a retrogressive nostalgia for outmoded traditions, a too-zealous remembrance of things past. They ignored the volume.

Now the letter-bearing bottle, jettison of my literary course, has in the form of a peevish little note in *Current Jewish Affairs* floated to shore again. I had expected it; some time ago I had written a facetious paragraph about this pontifical bi-monthly, had praised the high scientific standard of its contents, its fine literary style, the regularity of its appearance (for an Anglo-Jewish magazine, a high and satisfying compliment), but had commented upon the dullness of its articles and the monotony of its format. Both were justifiable criticisms; the articles, in large measure translated from the lucubrations of German-Jewish refugees, were characterized by a stodgy Teutonism, wingless and unimaginative but meticulous to the point of frustration. Even the translation was phlegmy with German ch's. As for the format, it suited the contents. I said so. Subsequently, the ubiquitous and gossipy Earl had told me that he had been in New York, had met the editor of *C.J.A.* and that the latter, a Mr. Allen Little, had read my comment and was laughing, as the Yiddish phrase has it, with hemorrhoids.

I opened the magazine to read the review with some misgivings. They were soon dissipated; the fellow unquestionably was a mean little prig, a proper son of a bitch. Pairing me with a poet whom incidentally I admire very much, he praised that other only for the purpose of accentuating his denigration of me. He found that I used the term 'little Jew' too often. Earl had told me that Little was only about five foot two, but how was I to know that my book would fall into the hands of a sensitive dwarf, aptly named? He objected to me describing junkmen as 'mottling' the city lanes, and he found that the term 'yclept,' obviously inserted in my poem as parody, was archaic! He didn't think much of my volume.

If he had come to that conclusion after reading it, or after expounding his reasons honestly I would not have minded. After four years I hardly felt as if the thing was my own. But the gallant manner of my dismissal enraged me. Also infuriating was the fact that it was the *C.J.A.* which was publishing the only derogatory comment coming from a Jewish periodical. From the goyim I knew what to expect, but this from my compatriots? And the circumstances. And the time of the review. And the knowledge that Little was himself a climbing assimilationist who didn't know the difference between an aleph and a swastika – they both looked so much alike.

I had, therefore, to write a letter, write a letter or burst a blood-vessel. But what kind of a letter should it be? A plea for fairness? Absurd; the reviewer knew he was being unfair. A disquisition on literary standards? There was no scope for such a discussion, the reviewer had not invoked standards, he had merely confined himself to stating that he did not like me, Dr. Fell. Then, perhaps, an insulting and libellous epistle, as unreasoned in its animosity as the paragraphs which provoked it, an epistle addressed to a stercoraceous coprophage, a helminthic merdivore? Beneath me; and too honorific for the target. No, the situation called for arrogance and oratio obliqua, a feigned megalomania, a talking through the corner of one's mouth.

My dear Nachtigal

I am not accustomed to writing letters to the editor, but I do address myself to you as the contributing editor of *Current Jewish Affairs* to tell you what I think of the feeble and malicious squib that appears in this month's issue of that journal. I do not, of course, hold you responsible for it, but I do think that for old lang syne (we had met many years ago, and had watched each other's writings) you would probably want to know what I think of literature with which you are related, if not by blood, then by alliance.

As a matter of fact, I had known that my book was to be reviewed some time ago. I expected from the tone of my 'reliable source' that the review would be a thunder-blast. It turns out that it is only an ill-mannered belch. I say the review is malicious because I knew from the abovementioned source that your assistant editor was somewhat annoyed at an article written by myself in which I had chaffed *C.J.A.* for its sombre format and pedantic content. As a matter of fact, after my article, the format was changed. It probably was pure coincidence; I cannot find it in me to grant your editor the capacity to learn from his betters.

I must interpret the review therefore as nothing more than an attempt at reprisal. The fact that a journal which calls itself current reviews the book of an author who had punctured its dignity *four years* after publication strengthens my conviction that I am dealing here not with a 'literary critic,' but with a spiteful nobody, an afflated ego constricted within his own shrivelled little torso.

But what a flop Mr. Little is even at the infantile business of vengeance. Me, I have no respect for incompetence even when I profit thereby. In seeking to achieve the purpose which Little had in mind, he failed dismally. For after taking three quotations (and good ones at that) with which to reveal to a wondering world his obtuseness, feigned or real – he concludes by quoting the highly laudatory remarks made about your humble servant by no less a critic than Mr. Wilson. Surely, that is not the way to do it, surely the end he had in mind called for ignoring the comments of Mr. Wilson, even as he ignored all but three lines of the one hundred and fifty pages of the book.

Had I not known that you were associated with this magazine, I would of course have greeted the review with that olympian aloofness which the antics of the little breeds invariably evoke from me. As it is, I complain, if at all, only for the sake of the reputation of the journal whose masthead bears your name. From the *C.J.A.* one expects a higher type of criticism than that Kay's Jews are not six-footers, as if Kay were King Frederick of Prussia, or that Kay's junkmen – the greasy compatriots of Allen yclept of yore in old Judaea Abie – 'mottle' the city lanes.

Anyway, I don't mean to make you feel bad. The book has received so many favourable reviews from literate persons that an analphabetic stutter adds a note not entirely unwelcome. It is good for my immortal soul. Bad it is only for the stutterer. Its base intention leaves me unmoved; I know that when the *C.J.A.* reviews will be archives, it is I who will still be current.

As for Mr. Little, extend him my forgiveness; he knows not what he does, nor how to do it. Assure him that I will keep the manner of his disgrace as secret as it presently is within the pages of the *C.J.A.*; and for the rest, wish him for me a ripe old age, during which he may sit at his fire, and tell his wife's children how once, when he was young and the weather hot, he snapped at my heels.

With kindest personal regards

Kay.

P.S. I need hardly add that this letter is not to form part of your contributions as contributing editor, unless paid for at the rate of one dollar per syllable, payable to myself, in U.S. funds.

By the final section of the second version of 'The Inverted Tree,' the letter to Nachtigal, Klein seems to have abandoned altogether the idea of imaginatively transforming the 'raw material' of autobiography into fiction: the letter is an almost verbatim transcription of an actual document, a letter which Klein had written to Abraham Duker, editor of the Contemporary Jewish Record *(see explanatory notes). This movement from fiction to document is carried even further in 'A Documentary, with Commentary,' in which Klein's life and work are summarized and tabulated so as to illustrate 'the frustration of all elements.' With this final, 'rawest' entry in Klein's 'journal of the mind,' the 'Raw Material' file comes to an end:*

A DOCUMENTARY, WITH COMMENTARY

Exhibits

1. Newspaper clipping. Report of death. Suspicious circumstances. Coroner's Inquest to-morrow.
2. Rejection slip. (Subsequently gay letter re rejections. See essay written re rejections.)
3. Letters – Re veldt – to someone overseas. a Carbon Copy.
4. Essay – to one of the vanguard publications on burden of being a poet.
5. Letter to wife. (a) [......].
(b) Re x-rays.
7. Poem on stethoscope.
8. Dr. Brown's report.
9. To reconstructionist – on not being an Angel.
10. Poem on Suicide.
11. Story of we who are about to be born.
12. Story of utopia.
13. Ghetto poem.
14. Notebook. Projects – Lyrics.
Detective Story.
New styles.
New language.
15. Birth Certificate.
16. Letters addressed to us – Re consolation on father's death.
17. Montreal poem – Show it to Professor S. Maybe there's something in it.
18. Photographs – Me & Marian[?].
Me & Talmud.
Me, she & tree.
College picture.
Me, She & two sons.
19. Marriage Contract.
20. Bundle of love-letters.
21. Poem on old age.

22. Poem on bread.
27. Inverted Tree.
28. Section on Lomza.
29. Editorial re Jewish situation.
30. Letter to Nachtigal.
31. Last Will & Testament.
32. Copy of application to McGill professorship.
33. Radio Script?
34. Bible with notations, and underlined.
35. Political pamphlet.
36. Doctor's bill & report.
37. Playlet re Colman.
38. Script for wedding describing all the members of family.
39. Book Review – Contemporary poets? – in clippings of book reviews for [.....].
40. Poem on contraceptives.
50. Poem on poisons.
51. Analects.
52. Ashkenazate Anthology.
53. A diatribe in latinized English.
54. A pantomime?
55. Epitaph for Shakespeare.
56. Poem on father, check – father died of arteriosclerosis.
57. Surrealist Scenario.
58. Cryptogram.
59. Fingerprint.
60. Confession under Narcosis.
61. Stenographic Report of Conversation or Deposition.
62. X-Ray.
63. M-card.
64. Depositions of witnesses – Impression he made on contemporaries.

*

a) Apparently written by someone in Coroner's or D.A.'s office – presents documents, and every document followed by his own remarks.
b) Arrange so that the frustration of all elements *develops*, one by one. Look up *Roget*.

*

Personal	Social	Jew	Poet	Angel
Veldt	Pictures	Return to Ghetto	Account	Senses
Father	Bread	Firing from Adv.	Article re [.......]	utopia
Bank Account	Advertising	Autobiographical	Enamort	On not being an angel
Stethoscope	Sermon	Telegram	Reviews	We who are about to be
Colman	Wedding Badchan	Ghetto of Warsaw (Editorial)	letter to Little	old age
Correspondence W.	Correspondence W.	Correspondence W.	Correspondence W.	Correspondence W.
Dentist	Montreal		On fame	
Doctor's Bill	Latin Diatribe	Ashkenazate Anthology	Last Will & Testament	always after
Poisons	Average man	Rejection University	Rejections I have known	Visting Card
Notebook	Notebook	Notebook	Notebook	Notebook
Lomza			Suicide	
Deposition	Deposition	Deposition	Deposition	Deposition

'Stranger and Afraid'

(Any resemblance between characters portrayed in this book and persons living or dead is purely accidental. It was not intended; if it has occurred, it is an act of God.)

At last I have been granted the privilege of a pencil.

It did not come without fasting.

On the fourth day of hunger, when I was already beginning to regret my devotion to letters, the guards took me to the warden.

Don't you approve of our menu? he said.

He was a witty warden.

I did not reply. I thought I recognized the kind of question that's bait; in any event it was not on that premise that I had built our conversation. He, however, pointedly waited for his answer. For him life was a catechism between warden and convict.

You know very well the reason for my hunger. It's a strike, I said.

Really?

And I insist upon my rights. Deprivation of writing-material is not part of my sentence.

Quite right, convict no. [ ]; but in addition to laws outside this jail, he said, there are, as you know, rules inside it. To grant your request would be most improper, most. Imagine my embarrassment if you tried to kill yourself!

With a pencil?

It has been done. With a pencil. You need not feign stupidity. All the articles of which we so considerately deprived you – shoe-laces, suspenders, comb – all of these things may be, and, at some time or other, have been, converted into instruments of suicide. I'm not taking that chance. If you, a cherished ward entrusted to my care, should suddenly be prompted to do away with yourself – and who can foretell the actions of genius? – why, I should have a first-rate scandal on my hands. I should be mortified.

He was also a very humane warden.

Would it be preferable, I asked, would it be less scandalous if, enjoying your hospitality, I perish from hunger? After all, my objective, as you are flattering enough to assume, is immortality: is it by self-destruction that I will achieve it?

He was silent. His silence seemed to say: You know the answer.

O, I said, do be good to me, Sir. It is not much that I ask, only a pencil, the stub of a pencil, if that's less dangerous, anything, anything that can write. For I must write it down. So much at my trial has been left unsaid, so much before my trial is not explained. I must explain myself. The decision of the court I can't change, I know that, but it's necessary for my sake, my peace, my future, that I explain myself. I must, Sir, I must –

Upon the warden's lips there now curled the curved triumph. I knew, then, that my request would be granted. Obviously what this custodian of keys wanted was my self-abasement; not every day did he have tenants such as I; a life of political frustration finally topped by appointment to a sinecure ought to be accompanied also by its spiritual compensations; and these could be afforded, not by the easy tribute wrung from the usual riffraff sent to him, but by the much more reluctant obeisance won from spirits hardier and more cultivated. At first I had not realized this; overcome by hunger, my skin fevered, my lower eyelids puttied to their sockets, and my mouth, like a noisome flue, stinking in my own nostrils, it was through a sort of haze of disintegration that I had been brought to the warden's office. Gropingly, more through instinct than through reason, I had assumed – to hide the fact of my impending surrender, already secretly contemplated – an air of bravado, an attitude which with an elastic audacity was designed to let the warden know that I considered myself no inferior, that I was aware of my rights, and that I meant to insist on them. But the warden, very apparently, had had earlier experience with the antics of defiance, and recognized – and showed that he recognized – in my performance a poor, ineffectual and stumbling technique.

It was then that some *souffleur* within me prompted a change of tactic. Acknowledge yourself, it said, as about to be philanthropized. Genuflect. Bubble with gerundive gratitude. Cry *Master, Master.* Blow up the balloon of his ego. This counsel I accepted. Subtly, not in words but by insinuation, I admitted the warden's omnipotence. I sirred him; into his face, sleek, unparched, and not like mine, I looked imploring. And this did please him. With my *curriculum vitae*, of course, he was familiar; he had, therefore, triumphed over no ordinary convict. It was something for the memoirs.

And how about paper, he said, we don't exactly run a stationery store, you know. But I forgot, we have already supplied you with paper – not the best bond; admitted; but it has its uses.

He was, as I have said, a witty warden.

It is so good to eat; and so humiliating. That I, the last perfected – presumably perfected – link of a long chain of generation should still find it imperative, at given intervals, which know neither my intention or convenience, to surrender to the insistence of a gut, to abandon ratiocinations the most cherished for the purpose of concentrating entirely, expectantly, with rendezvous impatience, upon the imminent consumption of the ugly satisfying prison-stew; to find myself reacting only with a stomach; to use the prison-meals as subdued metaphors for imagined banquetting; to listen to my blood-cells, literally to listen to them whispering in the veins' narrow corridors and only about food; to see myself, despite all the hansards of philosophy, still on the same level as the beasts of the field, still subject to a common set of table-manners – this nauseates me.

But it is only a nausea of the mind. The belly knows no sophistries.

O, if only air were nutritious! – how like gods we would be, immune to these procedures penultimate to defecation! How olympic, how free from the pull, the gravitational pull of hunger! Every exhalation would then proclaim man's sovereignty, and to breathe, truly, would be to live. Then could all energy, now wasted in the gathering of crumbs, and in the quarreling over their division, be better used to some high purpose, a purpose our food-fettered existence does not permit us even to imagine.

And if, at the same time, sleep could be abolished –

But even then also, I fear, the warden would have his function. Always there would be found the shrewd promoter, the calculating careerist; and all too soon would he discover an ideal in whose name he could ration my breathings. Already do I see him in his role: with double-entry book-keeping he keeps record of my inhalations and my exhalations – lest I upset the equilibrium of the social atmosphere. Even the instrument of coercion he finds ready at hand – the vacuum.

Have I an obsession with bread? Certainly I find it a constant reason for the denigration of God's work that the *mere* absence of food should so upset in a man his loftiest concepts, his most bold imaginings. Time is an instance. Never does the hungry man permit his thought to dwell upon it, for thought of time past, full as it is of the cornucopia of former ingestion, only accentuates his present longing, and thought of things future has meaning only as of something possibly nutrimental to be snatched toward the jaws of the moment. It is the hollow present that holds his centuries. All time, thus, is concentrated in the unhappy pass of his hunger, and even eternity, after a manner of speaking, is poised upon the plate he craves.

It is only now, after having eaten, that the planetary system for me again begins it revolutions, and only now that I can descry things past from things to come. But four days ago, and I walked, from the accused's waiting-room, into the court, still technically a free man. The scene was not new to me; the furniture and the faces of that room I had beheld before. For two years I had come every week-day morning to this Hall of Justice – Room No. 1 –, had taken my seat at one of the side-tables, listened professionally to the proceedings, and snatching from the mass of charges one that had what Seton-Coughlin called 'human interest,' had repaired to my desk at *The Montreal Courier*, there to write down – so that all its readers might be both amused by the antics of distress, and by the contrast between their plight and that of the actors of whom they read, fortified in the esteem of their own virtue – write down the record of other people's infelicity.

It was a column which was widely read. The doings in chancelleries and the goings-on at stadia, it seemed, held but a secondary interest to these occurrences which, as everyone realized, were such as might happen to all. A little touch of crime, it makes the whole world kin. But this kinship, Mr. Seton-Coughlin had always insisted, must not be too greatly stressed. These petty tragedies were not to be described, he smiled, so as to purge with pity and with terror – *The Montreal Courier* was, above all, not a journal which catered to morbidity – a spirit of humour, a progress of sprightliness was to gambol through my paragraphs so that the reader might know that although these events might possibly happen to him, in all probability they would not. By these narratives the subscriber ought to be made to laugh; perhaps, if he was sensitive, even to sigh, but on no account ought the writing to be such that the lump would rise in his throat, or the tear fog his vision. After the long day in factory or shop, the newspaper-reader wanted to come home to his winter-parlour or summer-balcony for relaxation and amusement; and since our society provided neither arena nor gladiators, it was the function of Room No. 1 and its visitants to add, vicariously, the nightly circus to the daily bread. Until the week I left this employment – Seton-Coughlin's criticism of my work having reached the impossible, and my continuance at my desk the improbable – I had, indeed, faithfully fulfilled my instructions to make all culprits clowns.

As I looked about the courtroom – at first, despite familiarity, a bewildering sight, like a large canvas suddenly thrust within an inch of one's face – I sought the reporters' bench to discover who was going to make human interest out of me. All the old hacks, companions of my former drudgeries, were there, all the French reporters, including Turcotte who noted for his paper only those cases in which Jews were the accused, and Martin for *The Gazette*, and for *The Courier* my former desk-mate, McAllan. I had read some of his columns; he was obviously continuing the tradition of whimsicality amidst misfortune. Nonetheless I was gratified that it was he who sat there, and not some sycophant of the hyphen, one who would immediately run to his master to tell him how right, how perfectly right he had always been.

Mac, I knew, would definitely not choose my case for his daily theme; true, he might catch hell – in British understatements, of course, – from our Seton-Coughlin when that one would discover that I had been spared the publicity, but Mac, I was certain, would risk the chance. Not that his relation to me was that of friendship – by way of simple exposition and without self-pity I must state it: I've never known a friend, – no doubt the fault is mine – but there did exist between us some kind of indefinable bond. Mac considered himself, I believe, my patron, not in the sense that out of his paltry salary he lavished money on me, or that he honoured my works with his approval, but that always he arrogated to himself the joint role of my business-agent, and custodian of my immortality. The things I published in magazines he clipped and filed away in a scrap-book, and then, when he happened to show them to me, he would say – so as to take the sugar out of his admiration – that he was, of course, motivated only by a desire to make, in the fulness of time, money out of literary rarities. Whenever I was prompted to go quixotic in the public prints against some undeservedly esteemed windmill whose eminence annoyed and insulted me – this, however, was not often, I was soon reconciled to the accidents of reputation, – it was he who argued the wisdom of silence and the profits of discretion. He printed letterheads on which he described himself as a literary agent; and I was his sole client. He urged me to apply for prizes, to petition scholarships, to seek out patrons. He wanted, he would say, and that earnest Indian face of his, with its skin of pock-marked bronze, its sensitive aquiline nose – it *really* was like an eagle's – and its thatch of hair, so black and silky it looked like some recently invented textile – that face would remain set, as if in a peroration, he wanted to ransom me from my job. Leisure was what I needed, he said, and freedom to exercise my talents. If the doing of things friendly makes a friend, he was, of course, my friend. Unfortunately he only admired and liked me, he walked beside me, I could almost say he held my hand, but he really was not going my way. He thought that I hungered for fame – and I did have an appetite for it – but what most moved me, well, – he did not even suspect that it was there. It was – I mean neither to insult him nor flatter myself – it was beyond his horizon.

But the horizon which loomed before me now, stretching out of Room No. 1, 'the leisure and the freedom to exercise my talent,' that, I was sure, he saw. And my plight, I know, affected him not a little. I suspected, in fact, that he suffered a personal, and not merely a sympathetic, pain; after all, to put it in a way that does injustice to my appreciation of him, he was losing his sole literary client. No, he would not take me for the hero of to-morrow's column. I was immensely relieved. If Seton-Coughlin was to have the news, he would have it when it was stale.

As for the other heads that globulated that room, vegetables that only now and again crystallized into outlined recognition, I did not mind them much. The interpreters, the lawyers of my acquaintance, the clerk of the court with his booming and continually-amused voice – I was never very pally with them, and was even farther away from them now. Their gaze was as little embarrassing to me as if they had been, in fact, vegetable, and not animal. Even when I used to walk the court-corridors with them, waiting the judge's leisurely arrival, I had not failed to observe that these people had developed what could be nothing but a vocational disease: a psychological incapacity to consider their clients as of their own kind. They just couldn't see in an accused anything more than an accused. He might as well have been a costume. Even in the argot which served as the medium both for their table-talk and their formal pleadings, the names of individuals figured rather as numbers in a catalogue than as disclosures of personality. The case of *Watkins vs. Pearce*: neither Watkins nor Pearce were, in their utterance, evoked as mothers' sons – they were merely the pro and con of an impersonal argument. When they looked at me, therefore, it was not difficult to read the thoughts that teletyped in their eyes: First, *Rex vs. Drizen*; then, *Seem to know him*; then, *Ah, yes, the reporter*; then, *Gave me publicity in his column*, or *didn't*; and finally, *Somebody else's case*. As for the reason for my presence in the dock, that would no doubt trouble – not them, their curiosity – when they got home.

All this time I was aware that in the room there was a face – like the word *Jew* on a page of unread print – which brushed but had not yet settled on my consciousness. Now I defined it – in a distant corner of the courtroom, huddled behind spectators and witnesses, the shawled head of my little mother. Why had she come? She knew that she could do nothing for me, she knew that I hated this kind of moral support, that in fact it demoralized me: Why had she come? She couldn't find her way to the court herself, she had had to have my sister bring her; but she had to come. I resented it. And it was so like her.

Always she held me to be an object of pity. Lately, before the unhappy happening, when I would sit in my red rep chair, engrossed in a book, valet to some statesman, or poet, or buccaneer, I would suddenly raise my head, and surprise her, presumably in the act of knitting, watching me. The doleful expression on her never particularly joyful face – tears upon parchment – at once saddened and enraged me. I knew what that expression meant – it was criticism: once he was so full of promise and of hope, and now, look at him, blighted, ambitionless, a reader of books. Like the rest of them he might have been, only more successful, a buyer of fur-coats for his mother, a car-owner, a proprietor – instead, distorted values had steered him away from what was rightfully his. She was, of course, occasionally proud of my unpragmatic achievements, achievements she did not understand but read only in reflection in other people's compliments – she wasn't unpleased; my son, she would say, *has a name*; but it wasn't a real pride, only a consoling substitute, a sort of defensive honour.

Everything about me seemed to call forth her pity, – my frustrations, my not being wealthy, even the complexion I had inherited from her. No doubt if I was rosy with health, fleshful and colourbright, she would still have worn that melancholy pall upon her. For she has a talent for sadness, my mother, a gift for misery, both native and indoctrinated. For her the happiest days in the calendar are the fast-days, the non-eating Mondays and Thursdays, and the anniversary penances in gratitude for some long-forgotten and since-nullified salvation of Jewry. And as for the Sabbath before the Blessing of the New Moon when, alone by the window in her room, her *siddur* and her handkerchief on her knees, she sits weeping the old-fashioned Yiddish of seventeenth-century prayerbooks, addressing herself to God for that he should preserve her children and her children's children that they come not unto the sons of men for favours, that they be not shamed of men, but that they live, decent and honourable, because of thy lovingkindness, O *Rebono shel Olam* – I remembered them from my earliest childhood as events which at first made me sorry for her, and then angered me with their servility. God, I felt sure even then, did not ask for such weeping and ululation.

Later I realized that these prayers were their own reward. They answered my mother's needs, first for drama, because they placed her on the centre of the stage, then for snobbery, because they established relations of intimacy with God Himself, and finally for self-pity, because that was the major theme of this liturgy. The same attitude showed itself in the other activities of my mother's pious routines. Some people go to the country for picnics, but my mother visits the Jewish cemetery where lie buried our discarded family bones, including those of my dear father. There she takes her position at his tombstone, and weeping, tears up clumps of grass and places them – an old rite – upon the granite; and she talks to the granite, as if through a side-entrance she would seek to storm the Heavenly Court. These activities, of course, wring her heart; she returns home, pale and tired, to rest in her low chair, pensive for hours. Secretly she is filled, I know, with a sense of great worth, the elation of piety. Not she like the other Sabbath-breaking and perruqueless apostates who emigrated to Canada, but beloved of her God, the God of her hometown Ratno, than which no other place, except Jerusalem the Holy, is saintlier.

Nor are these self-abnegations confined to doings sacred and ritual; even from a family party she will return, full of pride at what she didn't eat there. 'It was a wonderful spread,' she would say, 'as from the generous hand of the Czar. Whatever in the world is good to eat, that was on plate and dish. Others there were who grabbed, devoured, guzzled, as if they had just come off the boat from hungry Europe. Mrs. Cohen – the one who is president of the

Ladies Auxiliary, kept eating on both jaws, and you should have seen Mrs. Grossman, she crammed her fat little *kaddish* I thought he would burst. Me? I put nothing to my lips, I did not touch as much as the size of an olive. A cup of tea, that I had. Do I, then, lack for food at home? (This, for pride.) Am I sure that the dishes are kosher? (This for piety.) I don't need their food, thank God. And as for the tea, well, I drank it, of course, you can't, after all, spit in a person's face.'

And now, a little dressful of bones, a face wrinkled and runnelled like a topographical map, she sat in her corner, watching the proceedings, wondering what was going to happen to me, 'her crown,' as she named me in her lachrymose Sabbath monologues. Now, too, she was red-eyed; she must have been at the Lord plenty of late. So many strange faces, so many important-looking people. Who was the head, the one to whom she could appeal in her son's behalf?

I had no doubt but that despite my warnings and my pleas she had already visited the Jewish social services, imploring that they intercede for me. I had told her that I wanted no part of it; for I hated these pious people who lived on the world's trouble, who rose every morning and wondered whether there would be enough misery that day to engage their benevolence and justify their pay. How self-righteous these people were, with nice scientific words to describe every unfortunate plight, and checkable budgets for all heart-aches, and a regimen to re-orientate every lost soul into the good society. Techniques they had, to discover malingering; they knew experiments to test the gradations of felicity, and in all their experiments and techniques there was not a spark of fellow-feeling. Just like the lawyers, only the lawyers were more honest; there was no pretence about them. These salaried saints, however, were storing up credits in heaven, at the very moment when they were having themselves a good time comparing their own lot with that of their beneficiaries, and deriving, through a quiet and polite sadism, the last throb of pleasure out of 'the case.' I had told my mother, therefore, that if she went to any of them, I would never forgive her; I had endured enough, without suffering also the soft hygienic hand of the social worker, palpating my wound.

But, I was sure, she had gone to see them anyway. Among the busybodies floating around the clerk's nether table, I recognized one of the employees of The Jewish Community Agencies, whose annual campaign-slogan was: We look after our own! He had all the earnestness of one who was doing precisely that.

Frankly, I didn't care whether he would succeed or not. It didn't really matter. I had been refused bail at my first appearance, and during the week that I had remained in custody, I had had plenty of time to think about all the pros and cons, and I had decided to plead guilty. I didn't want to go through the ordeal of a hearing, with questions that were irrelevant, and answers that only partially made sense, with objections and counter-objections making a bobbing pantomime as the two mercenaries battled over my fate. I had, in fact, refused the services of a lawyer; for this, strangely enough, I had a good practical reason. I had been caught red-handed, and not all the talents of the entire Bar Association could alter, as they would say, the flagrancy of my delict.

Suddenly the jig-saw conversations in the courtroom ceased, and everybody stood up. I turned, by imitation, in the direction of a side-door leading onto the bench. The Judge had arrived. He was a little man, his hair was neatly plastered down on his head and his shrivelled face received its final twist in his pursed lips, as who should say: I shall not be fooled, I was a lawyer myself once, but now I am determined to hand out Justice. I had known His Lordship before when he had seemed not at all lacking in the attributes of humanity; indeed, my write-ups of his pre-penal sermons had elicited from him appreciation all too human. But now, as he looked in my direction towards the dock where I sat, in a common impatience with the other collarless and unbailed individuals, he showed no sign of recognition. Had my appearance really changed so much in one week, or was this the usual amnesia of impartiality?

The clerk handed the Judge his role. The Judge placed his elbows on the table, and his jaw in the cup made by the two uprights of his hands. He was waiting. It was for the people below to make the first move; he was Society, and could afford to maintain the *status quo*. The clerk barked: Motions. A number of lawyers began to shoulder each other about the table in front of the bench, and finally one got himself in position to raise his voice. My Lord, he said, the case of Butler, fifth on the role. The Judge looked for the case of Butler.

Behind the rail which divided off the spectators and witnesses from the lawyers and court officials stood a young man. I recognized Butler – the short, wiry, dynamic little debater of my college days. His name really wasn't Butler, but Bettelman; he adopted the English name, as we used to say, the better to smile at you, my child. The last I had heard of him was that he was a labour-leader. I'd never liked him – he was another one of those who was too full of goodness for me. At McGill he was always running for office, and always running against his will, the group he represented, he said, insisted on it; he was always espousing the under-dog – and somehow that way always emerged top dog himself. Throughout the four years that I knew him, he never had the same set of friends for more than a semester; his ambitions changed that often. His most remarkable talent was his mastery of language, – no one that I knew could use the benign words – like justice, freedom, equality, brotherhood, – with a stronger blare of sincerity. When he announced, as he did in one memorable peroration, that he loved, yes loved, mankind, there wasn't the slightest flush of embarrassment on his face. The special trick which placed him above the ordinary love-monger was the subtle way in which he advocated the practise of altruism as something crafty – thus, his listeners, who otherwise might have taken him for an evangelist, simple though pure, attributed to him all the mental rigour of a *real-politiker*. In this they were not wrong; for Butler early realized that professions of love were themselves instruments of power. Moreover, and here Butler was superior to his audiences, these professions of love cost him nothing. They involved only his syntax.

I wondered, without emotion, what he was charged with. His lawyer was talking: An important witness, he was saying, had been called out of town, and he would like a postponement until next week. The Crown, he affirmed, had no objection. The Judge looked inquiringly to the Crown, a pale moustached French lawyer; he nodded corroboration. Granted.

Butler walked out behind his lawyer, smiling to some friends. I didn't think he had noticed me.

There were some other motions, and then the clerk gathered together and squared up the pile of dossiers. Mine was on top. He read the charge, with his usual bored inarticulateness, so that the offense remained a secret between him and the accused. How do you plead? He raised his head from his reading. Guilty or not guilty?

I had stood up at the call of my name. My hand sweated on the brass rail of the dock. Guilty or not guilty. I had, as I have said, made up my mind not to present a defense, but this curt alternative almost jerked me to regret. How simple everything was for the safe, the untroubled, the innocent! Guilty or not guilty. All the categories were neatly divided for them. There were only two directions – right and left – only two altitudes, up and down, only two colours, black and white, and only two states – guilty or not guilty. The narrowness of the choice was bad enough, but the pistol suddenness of its presentation was worse; its implication seemed to be that anybody should be able to recognize one from the other, and that at a moment's notice.

What did he mean: Was I guilty or not guilty? Did he want me to take into consideration only the facts, or was I also to consider the motives? Did he seek a relative answer, or an absolute one? Was the standard of determination a purely personal one, or was I being called upon to view my behaviour *sub specie aeternitatis*? Was it my intention which gave the character to my plea, or did the deed alone suffice? Was I guilty because my act was culpable in the particular circumstances in which it took place or would it have been equally heinous in any context?

The clerk, apparently, was not concerned with these distinctions. If I had energy enough, and discrimination, to be a culprit, I could muster the same qualities to be a judge. He saw nothing wrong in making out of the plight of an accused and the function of a judge a single role. He was expediting his dossiers. He repeated: Guilty or not guilty?

The Judge looked on, as if from ambush.

My voice choked for a moment, and then released: Guilty.

The Judge extended his arm over the table to reach down for the dossier which the clerk raised up to him. He studied it. The little Jewish social worker sneaked up on the side steps leading to the bench, and whispered earnest secrets into the Judge's ear. The Judge pursed his lips.

I stared at the crucifix which hung on the wall. It had always annoyed me as constituting a theocratic intrusion into an essentially secular environment. But now, as I realized that the Judge had his back to it, I saw that it was no intrusion.

Setting himself up on his throne, and placing his hands on the table, he adjusted a judicial face. It was as if he was taking a picture. Drizen, he was saying, you have pleaded guilty, and despite the numerous intercessions which have been made on your behalf, particularly those of your aged mother – he was saying this on purpose, I felt sure, to bring the lump to my throat – I have no alternative but to pass sentence upon you.

It was all so smooth, so logical, so inevitable. Effect followed cause, and itself became a cause for further effect; and he, the Judge, was merely an impersonal instrument for the execution of the laws of God and of Nature. What he actually said I did not, at the time, really hear; all I was conscious of was a crucifix before me, and faces looking at me from all directions, and one face, that of the Judge, looming out over the rest of the room; and it was talking. Only now do I recall, out of the syllogistic paragraphs which he so neatly set up into a reasoned pile, some of the things he said. That I ought to have known better, seeing that I had been given all the advantages of a good education and a good home – my mother's sob I distinctly remember – that this really was not my first offense, that I had done the same things before, but that apparently no charge was pressed, or I was not discovered; that the ideas which I entertained were dangerous to society, and that if all did as I did, where would we be? That if I wanted to live dangerously there were other activities in which I could engage, constructive endeavour, honest effort, as for example, in the ranks of my country's fighting forces. That to consider the error of my ways I ought to be given time for contemplation, repentance, and reform; that such, indeed, was the purpose of the penal code, which crystallized the good sense, nay the wisdom of the ages, and that therefore I was to be confined to Bordeaux Jail.

As I said, I didn't fully grasp what he was saying. All I knew was that I was being transformed from a free human being into a convict. I felt like the hero in one of those movie shockers – one of those werewolf pictures – as he undergoes the mystic transformation, and his human aspect falls from him, and in the haze and speed of the film he begins to grow hair all over, and his teeth go jagged, and his face is bestialized, and he stands up – a thing that stalks.

But I was grateful for at least one favour. Whether it was through forgetfulness, he so excited by his routine sermon, or through sensitivity, the Judge had spoken about my crime in the most general terms; he hadn't even repeated the details of the charge, and the eavesdroppers in the courtroom knew only that I was a criminal, but how much of one or what kind they did not know.

The guard took me by the arm to lead me back to the cells. Dixit; the Judge had spoken; repartee was not part of the ritual of these proceedings. I looked back, and my mother was waiting for my look, she was leaning on my sister, and was sobbing quietly. I don't know with what efforts she controlled herself, but she didn't make a scene. I was grateful. My good dear mother, who for my sake clenched her heart.

I can imagine, however, what goings-on there will be at the prayers this Sabbath.

As I was marched upstairs to the cells, it struck me that Elizabeth had not come to court. Was it because she wanted to spare me the humiliation, or because she didn't care? Or did she, like the Judge, also have her special reasons for feeling insulted at what I had done?

It was a van that brought me here, a large coffin-like vehicle, with seats running along both sides of its length, and, just beneath the roof, a number of screened apertures, – air-holes rather than windows. In charge of this van were two guards; one acted chauffeur, and the other sat near the door of exit, a gun on his lap. Between them, there was no doubt of it, we were bound to keep on the right path.

About a dozen prisoners sat there in the twilight darkness with me; outside, as we knew from the cube of light through which we walked into this tomb, it was bright noon. Like smudges on an old photograph, they sat there in the various attitudes of depression. Some even feigned an exaltation which, it was easy to see, was only a cover for their true feelings, a sort of dynamic depression. Some showed no emotion at all; recognizably, these were derelicts to whom this routine was as familiar as the procedures of a seasonal cure; immobile, almost like potato-sacks, they awaited the destination where at last they could spill out into comfort. Two, not at all embarrassed by the presence of the guard, were arguing loudly; apparently one of them had answered the judge's questions with insufficient foresight, and thereby both had been discovered and condemned; *you should have said this, you should have said that* – like a volleyball, it flew through their altercation.

In a corner a young boy was silently weeping, and the occasional ray of sun that sometimes flashed through the screen from time to time pearled the tears that stood in his eyes.

We were moving, but I couldn't make out the route the guard was following. The city which I loved – that is, the impersonal city which I loved – was now rubbed out for me, boarded and screened against my sight, a noonday eclipse. As in a moving tunnel, I sat in darkness, and the trip would not be over, I knew, the blindfold not unsealed until we had rolled the nine miles – how dantesque a number! – which stretched from the court house a few blocks away from the St. Lawrence to its annex a stone's throw from the Back River. It was an ingenious paradox of imprisonment, I thought, this *moving* across the whole length of the Island, and yet continuously in durance bound; it was a fitting preliminary.

Since I could not have the sights of the city which had so often infatuated and tortured me, I sought at least to catch its vagrant sounds. Now, I said, we are travelling over one of the older streets, the cobbles gabble with antiquity. Now we have approached an intersection – the brakes have screeched, and the van has hunched and slowed down. At this some prisoners jump up, thinking they have arrived, so lost have they been in thought, which distorts time; but the van again begins to move. We are on a tram-route now, and the round rumble of steel growling announces a streetcar travelling by. Now we are travelling upon asphalt, the sound is the sound of the purring intimacy of rubber and macadam. The voices of children: *Les Prisonniers, Les Prisonniers.* This must be the East End, and our passing a daily interruption of the children's play. They must wait for it, as for the iceman's waggon, the baker's horse. And then a quiet street, and the voices of women as across a clothesline. An intersection again; the honk of a horn, and a truckdriver's curse. A long stretch, and not smooth riding; I can hear the crunch of clods of ice, thrown on the road to melt.

It is all riddlesome and labyrinthine. I can't name the streets; we have made so many turns, I cannot even surmise the direction. All I know – I have given up this eavesdropping on the outer world – is that I am moving, moving through darkness and bewilderment in a world which is already constricted, in a transporting cell, in an earthworm passage. And yet I am possessed by none of the feelings which my plight, if I had considered it in anticipation, would have certainly evoked in me. The weeping boy's despair is not mine; shame I do not feel, not in this company anyway; and I am not even driven into apathy. It is, as a matter of fact, with adventure gusto that in my slow sunless shell I travel through my city. A king who must not be looked upon? A monk assuming vows? A parcel with a time-clock in it? A conspirator in a sealed train? The roles flash through my mind and are dismissed, like the lights and shadows sifted through the screens. Anyway, I am getting accustomed to the dark.

Arrived, as the travellers say, at the jail, I was stripped of my possessions. The phrase is, to tell the truth, not very precise; there was not, as the word might seem to imply, any violence in the stripping, and possessions is perhaps too grand a name for the things to which I refer. Too grand; and yet not grand enough, for in reality I am divested of all the indicia of civilization.

Outside the shower-room I am told to undress, and one by one the articles which until that moment I had still controlled, are taken off, and taken away. My fountain pen goes, and with it, insofar as my personality is concerned, the ages that invented writing. Out of the guard's impulse of kindness, I am permitted to retain my double package of Turrets, but my match-pad is taken away. My wrist watch and my snake-ring, – made out of the five-rouble gold piece which my father brought to Canada, his complete estate – are included in the inventory. Thus am I left without the invention of fire, without the recorder of time, and without the sumptuosity of adornment. I am relieved also of the note-book which I carry in my bosom-pocket, and in which I write down addresses, appointments, poems in germination – my culture is now minus geography, history, literature. My identification card, too, is taken from me; but that is not a new loss, only the emphasis of a loss I suffered in the courtroom. I feel as if the accumulated culture which the past has left me as legacy is being, at least symbolically, liquidated, that the props which succeeding generations had built up at last to maintain me are being knocked from under me, and that I myself am now slipping, slipping past my grandfather, quickly past my remotest ancestors into a possessionless and naked primitivism. I am, in fact, naked; my clothes, my neatly tailored suit, my shirt, my shoes, my socks – so bright and caducean – are all parcelled away. Narrow-shouldered, bony, and terribly conscious of the dark leaf and lighter fruit of my sex, which seems to draw away all the whiteness of my body, I stand with my package of cigarettes in my hand. I also hold, strangely enough, some money which I have been permitted to keep. That part of my civilized impedimenta is apparently forgiven.

This is where it happened, here came the first echo of the outside world. Even here, in the drab equality, and behind the stone that shut out my past, I wasn't safe from it. I really should not have been surprised; for precisely here where everything is reduced to the primary emotional colours – no mauves, no purples, – here, I should have known, it was most likely to happen.

We were all standing beneath the showers, – I and the thiefs and the vagabonds and the brawlers, all equal, all suffering, I supposed, the purgatory which must be a necessary preliminary to punishment. There was noise, and shouting, and loud comment – voices competing with the loud hiss and sprinkle of water, voices uttering statements of approach to this essential performance. There were ejaculations of pleasure, as for something long desired; finicky mincing phrases, as touching some luxury enjoyed only by snobs; the sudden reactions to temperature; playfulness; and of course the obscenity which such a place, such a condition, and such an array of masculinity had to inspire.

I felt shy, I was ashamed to go through this public ordeal. The touch of the male body revolts me, and some of the prisoners, in going in and out of their booths could not but brush past me, and my skin seemed to curl up at the spot of contact. Also I felt fledgling; despite the common sex of our undress, I felt myself stripped of manliness, reduced to the boyhood of a gymnasium, the adolescence of a swimming pool, the age when the master stands by to see that all behave. I resented it; and when I considered the company I was in, an ineradicable – as yet ineradicable – snobbery filled me with a great pity for myself.

I sought to turn my thoughts away from these subjects. I listened to the talk that went on all about me, I even managed to extract some amusement out of the bandied ribaldries. Was it that the job of reducing me to a basic primitiveness was already succeeding, or was it that these people displayed so acrobatic an imagination on a subject eternally and ubiquitously fascinating?

I had finished the procedures of my shower, and I felt refreshed. The soap I had been given was a very coarse soap, but the needles of water had been sharp and clean, almost glassy, like the transparent bristles of some self-renewing brush, and I felt good. It was then that the youth whom I had noticed crying in the van came up to me, and, as if striking up an acquaintance, asked me:

Of what nationality are you, chum?

I was so taken by his use of the word chum – not because it was a gesture of friendliness – already, without analyzing it, I sensed something unfriendly – but because it afforded an illustration in actual use of a philological phenomenon I had earlier observed – the Anglicization of the French language – *chummer* used as a verb – that I did not realize that the question, in the answering position in which all of us found ourselves, was really stupid, if not impertinent. I was about to answer, in his own idiom, Je suis Juif, moi – when I caught the challenge.

Je suis Canadien, I said.

Not Juif Canadien. Canadien. That is the word that French Canadians apply only to themselves. No hyphen, just Canadien. The rest are English, or Jews, or Polaks. I was, therefore, as challenging in my reply as he was in his question. At the same time, as soon as I had said it, I was ashamed: Was I denying my ancestry? But he accepted the challenge.

Hey, gang, he said, come and see un Canadien. *Un vrai Canadien.* He really says he is un Canadien.

And as the prisoners issued from their booths, he danced about me, pointing at my pudenda. They did really feel pudendal. I was tempted to put my hand over the place, but didn't; that would have made me look ridiculous; these people wouldn't fail to catch the virginal comicality of such an attitude.

They were all looking at me, but at one place, like so many converging telescopes; and they were grinning. I could see by the expression on the youth's face that he was debating with himself whether to make a pass at me, lift up the cynosure of all eyes, and hold it in view – see, un vrai Canadien. But I was bigger. Instead, he put his hand on his own uncircumcised pride, and pranced about, barefooted on the wet floor, shouting Je suis un Canadien. As laughter greeted his witty cavortings, he became even more enthusiastic. He placed, – *pour l'emphase, messieurs,* he said – his other hand on his nose. Je suis un Canadien. Fired by further applause, he now went into a fan dance – waving his hands in the air, he revealed for a moment both nose and phallus. Voyez, he said, Je suis un Juif! – and then, concealing – presto, je suis un Canadien!

The guard stood at the end of the corridor, smiling.

O, how I would have liked to strangle him, strangle him, strangle him, one hand on his throat, and the other, vicious about his filthy scrotum! How he would dance, then, inwardly and without motion! The impossibility of fulfilling my desire agonized me. It brought tears to my eyes. But I couldn't start anything, this was a strange place, I was a stranger here, – and the guard was smiling, and all of them were his fellow-Christians. They were laughing. There was no one to appeal to, I was helpless. I could, of course, make a gesture – and take a beating, but would it end there? Authority would step in, and to the indignity inflicted by men would be added the penalties imposed by Justice.

It was as if my heart, all revengeful tentacles, would burst. My head swam – I had taken off my glasses before entering the shower-booth, and I could not see distinctly, I could only see a haze and caricature of the scene, like the horrifying aura of a bad dream. It must have shown on my face, I must have looked pitiable and broken, for suddenly a voice interposed – I turned my head in its direction, it was one of the prisoners, an older man, a tall husky man; he radiated authority, though naked.

C'est assez-là, he said. That's enough now. We here are all in the same soup you know. Besides, c'n'est pas sa faute.

It wasn't my fault I was a Jew. The prisoners walked out, still laughing. I stayed behind to let them go first. The youth strutted out in front of me; then, stopping in his tracks, he turned around, and legs far apart, rolled his belly – J'ne suis pas – he said – and then, like a burlesque queen, made his bump – un Juif!

We are given our new clothes, denim trousers, jackets of the same material, and pea caps. They are shabby, of course, unpressed; they have no stiffness about them, they look laundered. But that is not their distinction. The distinction is that the suiting is made up of pieces of cloth of different colour; thus half my jacket is pale blue, and the other half a deep dark colour. The legs of my trousers, too, are of different colours. I am altogether pied, dressed in motley. The prison authorities are actually playing up to the popular theory – we are arrayed like clowns.

I am led to my cell; I am to occupy it together with Slickey, another convict who came up in the van with us. He is a man of about thirty, but baby-faced, innocent-looking; a pickpocket, he is already showing me tricks with his fingers. We get cell No. 11 on the first tier; it has two bunks, an upper and a lower, a little window facing onto the jail-yard, a table, and a washbowl. He tries out his bunk; I read the list of typewritten rules pasted onto one of the walls.

[ ]

I am reliving, only now that its motion is slowed, more intensely reliving, the humiliation in the shower-room. Jew. My head is dinned with the sudden monosyllable whose snarl in so many accents I have so often heard. It translates itself in my mind into its score of variations. Jew! Juif! Zhid! Jude! I hear it as identification, as taunt, as obscenity. Turds lifted and flung. Everywhere it is pronounced with the same malevolent gusto – a watery expectoration, salivated and aimed. And to the hiss and breath of the accursed name are added, like the excited chitterings of pigmy apes, the ugly yammers of its vernacular, yammering *youpin,* sounding *sheeny,* cackling *kike.* The entire atmospheric layer of the earth, it seems, is full of air-pockets; they wait only the approach of the unlucky element to harden into the word: Jew. Wherever he goes the unlucky one evokes it, like a leper the nausea of his bell. It is a relationship which has almost the inevitability of a law of physics. I ask myself with the stupidity that comes of despair, I ask myself – as if I was the one responsible – why should this be so?

And why should I, who might have discovered an alternative, an escape, a plausible alias which would have sundered me from the strangling Jewish umbilical cords, persist in this torturous allegiance? And why should I, why *do* I, against the obscenities and yammerings, heard to-day, heard yesterday, heard almost since memory began to pick them up, the prickly things, continue to accept the ejaculated J as if it were my expected portion? After all, that circumcision of mine which bled so sympathetically from the youth's brain was not – how shall I say it? – of the essence. It might be said that it was merely the stigmatum of an early operation. In any event, not that, the *ding an sich,* was the object of the boy's burlesque. He was scoffing rather at my category among people, my place-name card at the world's table whereon he seemed to find some ironical comment privately conveyed to me by an inhospitable host. In fact he was doing honour – it is true, in an exaggerated fashion – to a recognized convention of society. Witness the easy comprehension which his antics received; that man from Mars would not have understood them; nor laughed. Perhaps, there wasn't even any malice in his performance, just an effervescence of feeling brought on by the shock, as it were, of recognition in the flesh. But there he was, acting out a viewpoint which also the judges who sent him here could understand and appreciate. It was not to be denied; the word, and its special enunciation, was of universal currency. Why did I wilfully remain a target unmoving?

The convention, moreover, was one that only a fool or a professional prophet could hope to abolish. Too many talents had been devoted to its inculcation, and upon its continuance too many interests were staked. At least for the time being, short of millenium, this convention, it appeared to me, would continue to thrive. Why, then, did I leave myself its ready victim? Was there no way to defeat it? To shuffle the cards, and get lost in the pack? To so arrange it that one day as the taunter stood eager with his taunt, he suddenly discovered, prostrated and speechless, that the target had disappeared and was now, indeed, lost among the taunters?

It is true that, here in my native city, I have not suffered much from this Jew-baiting. Certainly not from its violent forms, its forest-ferocities. Only a pin-prick of prejudice here, a rub of racialism there. But nothing that required medical attention, not unless one wanted to go pamper the psyche. Trivialities, things that never, or only seldom got reported in the papers. Nothings.

I am returning from school with my friend. To-day we have been taught the meaning of unity, for to-day our teacher told us the fable about the sticks that could be broken, one by one, but could not be broken if held in a handful altogether. She said that the sticks meant the people of Canada. On our way home, we have to pass the streets where the Frenchies live. At the corner a group of boys, somewhat older than ourselves, stands scrutinizing us. Suddenly, as if in a pre-arranged chorus, they burst out in sing-song: Meestah with da wheeskahs! Meestah with the wheeskahs! We hurry on, afraid; we are two, and they are many. Safely away from them, on the other side of the ghetto boundary, we turn back, and yell: Pea-soup! Pea-soup! French pea-soup!

I am in the courtroom, at the press-table, my notebook before me. The judge is rendering his judgment. He has summarized the evidence, and now is enunciating principles of law. Witnesses, he says, should be weighed, not counted. The testimony of Mr. Herscovitch, he continues – and he adds up his sums. The fat Jewish Herscovitch did not weigh much.

The streetcar is rumbling along. I hang on a strap, listening to the talk of the overalled labourers, their tin-cans on their laps. They have worked hard. The car stops, and an old Jew, bearded and sweaty, puffs up the steps. He is hauling two huge bolts of cloth. The conductor gives him an argument, he is taking up too much room, he says, for his seven cents; he should have used a taxi. The Jew smiles ingratiatingly: 'What you care?' he says, 'Is it, then, your car? It's the company's car. The black year won't take them.' Nonetheless he tries to constrict himself into a corner, and he and his bolts become one. The labourers, amused, have watched the argument. They have stopped talking about their hard lot. 'Did you hear,' says one to the other, loudly, so that the whole streetcar may listen, 'the story of Ikie and the fingerbowl? Oi,' he mimics, 'is that a story!' Then they oi it right and they oi it left. Everybody titters, particularly the women. Even their bosoms seem to part and grin. Disguised by my clean shave and my nondescript appearance – I have been taken for both a Russian and a French Canadian, depending upon the recency of my haircut – I swing on the strap, reading the ads, swallowing hard.

An incident; nothing; harmless fun.

The dean is a very cultured gentleman. He writes books on philosophy, proving that Bishop Berkeley was right, that everything exists only in the mind. Nonetheless, he is scrutinizing my papers, the records of my entrance qualifications. The marks are very high and he can find no fault. I will have to be admitted. He makes a note of my name, Alvin Drizen, and then with a benign smile, as if sharing a secret with me: 'Abraham? I mean in Hebrew, is it Abraham?' I play his game, I exchange linguistics. 'In Hebrew,' I say, 'it is Avrohom.' Drizen, of course, requires no comment; whatever he is, the dean is not unsubtle.

At the corner of St. Denis and Ste. Catherine, I have just bought, at the French bookstore, *Les Fleurs du Mal.* I am waiting for the streetcar home, and in the meantime I read the large type on the newspapers suspended outside the corner kiosk. Whether because annoyed that I am nibbling his headlines without buying a paper, or whether out of a desire to share important intelligence, the newspaper vendor draws my attention to a new hebdomad, *Le Chameau.* On its cover there is displayed an ugly cartoon – a frightened female, scrolled Quebec, and a leering Jew hovering over her, all nose and lechery. *La verité,* he says, *pour cinq sous.* I give him his nickel for the truth. I will read this before the poetry.

I am walking with my father to the synagogue. My faith in the efficacy of prayer has long since been lost, but I do honour my father upon earth, so I accompany him. Moreover, I like the cantor's singing. We arrive and find that the door of the synagogue is scribbled over with all kinds of symbols and graffiti. In the centre is a double triangle, a swastika superimposed upon it, as if to cancel it out. Nor can one erase it; it is the Sabbath. I want to pause at the door to decipher the lewd and insulting inscriptions. But my father hurries me along: Let the heathen rage, he says. We, we enter to the service of our Creator. You see now where I get this this-is-nothing stuff. My father, however, he can afford it; he knows his reward in heaven.

It is election time, and the orators are out. I have a free evening, and I decide to go to the Salaberry School where a meeting is to be addressed by Camillien Houde. He is a brilliant speaker, colourful, witty, histrionic, a character, and I love to hear him talk. But Camillien has not yet arrived. A lesser worthy is called upon to mark time until his arrival. He speaks from a working man's point of view, he says. He is also a wag. He makes jokes, not pertinent, but laughable in their own right. And he also has his serious side, – a theory. The theory is that all of the world's ills are caused by international finance, and that all Jews are international financiers. I do not know whether to laugh or to spit. Unconsciously, I feel for the several coins in my pocket. I leave the hall, Camillien unheard.

They pass through my mind, like the flashes of a newsreel, one scene fading into the other, all leaving the disturbing shimmer of a mental montage. But truly they are nothing. – Or the signs on the summer resorts, *Restricted Clientele*, at which I inwardly sneer, telling myself that I don't care to go anyway, and childishly content myself by calling down upon their owners the detailed imprecations of Deuteronomy. Or my friend the poet and the radical who tells me that he is scrupulously careful about the race-question. Why should he feel that he has to be scrupulously careful? Or the Marxist who is of the opinion that important party resolutions should not be moved by Jews – bad publicity. But really these things are nothing; they can be endured; they sting, but they do not devastate. Trivialities. Things to be ignored.

But no matter how much I try to ignore them, I cannot, I cannot ignore them – these nothings. I shut my eyes to them, I please myself into believing that these things are merely signs of an absence of breeding, vestiges of old prejudice, frivolities, not really important. I make myself the statuary monkey: I won't see, I won't hear, I won't even mention what I haven't seen or heard. It has happened, it is gone, it has passed through consciousness as through a sieve. I am, I assure myself, living in a country that is free and civilized. These things are anomalies, and ought not to bother me. And then, as I pause to consider my Self, myself, the focus taken from off my environment, I am amazed to discover that these things have never passed through my consciousness, as through a sieve, at all, at all. They cling to my mind, and at the most unwelcome moments reveal themselves in the strangest forms. I meet a casual acquaintance on the street, engage in conversation, and am soon embarrassingly aware that he is talking too loud, his thoughtways, his inflections are objectionably Jewish. Objectionable to whom? I shudder at the revelation: objectionable to me. I consider the behaviour of my fellow-Jews, and find myself passing judgment upon them, not according to the general social code, but according to some unwritten laws which I apply to Jews only. It is I who am now passing discriminatory legislation. I come to a gathering to which the general public has been invited, and soon realize that I am counting the number of Jewish faces present – it is I who am proceeding according to a *numerus clausus*. I walk into a room, and unintentionally and unknowing gravitate towards my own – it is I who make the ghetto bench. A horrible dialectics has taken place. The hater has converted the hated.

But even this is tolerable – it is, after all, a conversion with reservations, and I do know what is happening to me. At any moment the mind will snap back to scorn its obsequious role. This is discomfort and embarrassment, not agony; and, as my Hebrew teacher used to say, making philosophy out of necessity, what a small price this is to pay for belonging to an ancient race, a Chosen People. Big words, the defense-mechanisms of Jewry, the clichés of an impotent chauvinism. We are the sons of peddlers, but we are the grandsons of prophets ... All western civilization moves according to our lights ... When the English were still painting their bodies with woad on the banks of the Thames, our forefathers had already erected Temples for the worship of the Living God ... And more, and more. Big words, but they have never, except perhaps for a moment when the Judaeophobic foam disappeared for a while, lathered itself out, and the whole subject became comfortably pale and academic, never impressed nor consoled me. The grandsons of the prophets – but hereditary title discountenanced, and the prophets themselves reviled. Western civilization – are we really so eager to assume responsibility for it? Muse and metaphor, words, words, words, the assuring monologue of the suave doctor in the psychiatric ward.

For though my own experience has been marked only by thrusts and needles, there are those, I know, who are being subjected to a much more business-like treatment. And it is only an accident that our positions are not transposed. Shall they, too, rejoice that they are of the seed of Abraham, and that Moses their ancestor lit ten lamps by which the world still sees? That the saintly Hillel was of the blood, and Maimonides kin? O, of what use is the pedigree, lineal or spiritual, when the last heirs live like mongrels and die like dogs!

Even from far, I have smelled the blood, and caught the fear. Only about a month ago – a week before I 'committed my crime' there was revealed to the world the exact details of the policy which had been adopted against – against people who walked the streets I might have walked. That was that terrible week when every room in which I slept – franticly I changed my sleeping place from night to night – seemed wallpapered with nightmares. There wasn't a night – my mind had dwelled so long upon the theme – inhuman cruelty visited upon those whom I could not but regard as my substitutes – there wasn't a night of calm untroubled sleep. Once it was a man who looked like my father, beard, humility, and all, – I did somehow realize that my father was dead, and this unrealized subconscious of the subconscious did console me a little – who was being slapped and spat upon, and then from a rail hung by his feet, and his head dipped and raised, dipped and raised, a little lower each time, into a barrel of human dung. I was standing by, and my turn was next. Now and again, the men who viciously held my arms, looked into my face, without comment, searching the effect. Then, at one point, as the inverted face spluttered and retched, I could stand it no longer, and began to struggle and shout, seeking escape or justice – and found myself flailing my bedclothes and pillow.

There were also the cold spectatorial nightmares – those in which I seemed to have lost all capacity for emotion – I was merely a pair of eyes, a pair of eyes watching, not the monsters who peopled my dreams, but the geometry they made, the designs that their actions construed. The act of sliding a body into an oven, like a baker a plank of loaves – left only the impression of horizontals and verticals. The act of injecting children with air-bubbles, until they went convulsive – a cauchemar of concentric and eccentric circles. The simple act of flogging – segments, arcs, semi-circles meeting, slowly or quickly, their diameters. These designs mesmerized me, and it was only upon waking, when the full realization of what I had seen came upon me, that I was seized with a sweating and heaviness that made it impossible for me to fall asleep again. I was frightened at the passive role I seemed to have played in the dream. To horror, there was added a sense of guilt.

Those dreams, I knew well enough, sprang from the unearthly items which now and again made their way into the newspapers, and which, with such a mixture of eagerness and hatred I read. Tidings to be broken with one's bread. The facts seeped in during the day, at night they sprouted their monstrous blossoms. Daily the Jewish press had reports of new thousands bubbled to death, new thousands heated to ash. Even in the scientific journals the phenomenon was being noted. Already there appeared in the ethnographic magazines long and authenticated essays in which professional statisticians, eyes clear both of prejudice and of tears, surmised in round numbers – golgotha sums – the tempo and incidence of death. They were so calm, so objective, these essayists, as if they were discussing the ravages of some long-forgotten plague, or the strange disappearance of some tribe alluded to in classical writings.

I know, I well know that this happens only in other countries, countries that everybody agrees to call barbaric. It happens, moreover, to people I have never seen, and whom probably I would not like. It does not, it would seem, really concern me. Thus do I find myself reproducing, – not wholeheartedly, only tentatively, and only to pacify my troubled spirit – that very attitude which in others is, in the final analysis, the true cause of my humiliation and alarm. For I cannot forget the horror with which I watched in others the indifference which – if even only as rhetoric – seems now to persuade me. For years those who proudly counted themselves non-barbaric, the preachment-makers, the church-goers, the principle-enunciators, looked with a passive unconcern upon the doings, a plane's throw from their shores, which insulted their professed creed, and which should have evoked, at least, a syllable of disapproval. They were silent. They regretted, perhaps, that on the face of the earth and in the most civilized century of the world's age, these things should be; they no doubt found them distasteful, unpleasant to read about, embarrassing. But they did nothing. They did not interfere. They turned their heads away and talked about Western civilization. They continued, as vigorously as ever, to impress upon their children the charm of the copybook virtues. They hailed the outstanding act of kindness. They grew angry at the sight of cruelty in their streets and wrote letters to editors complaining about the occasional maltreatment suffered by horses. They petted cats, they loved dogs. But to the dirty evil that raged unchecked beyond their frontiers – well, it was beyond their frontiers, wasn't it? The impertinence of Cain: Am I my brother's keeper?

And yet, civilization, it can mean nothing unless it is accompanied by a realization that there is something more wicked in passivity to the occurrence of evil than in actual participation in it. The perpetrator of an atrocity is, after all, somewhat deranged by the afflatus of his own act, it excites him; it distorts his view; he is at the centre of an emotional vortex, and of course cannot see himself, in his full malignity, from the outside. He is no longer passing a judgment, he is already engaged in an ecstasy. But the witness, the passive witness, for his calm cruel spectatorial indifference, he has no such defense. He does not participate in the atrocity (although he is still a part of it), his faculties are not unhinged by hybris; he has no excuse. In a lynching scene, where stand the criminals? Yes, frenzied with faggots, rapt with rope, the minor characters stand beneath the tree, but it is in that circle of heads, that wicked watching circumference that the arch-criminals show their impassive faces.

This is a realization which cannot long withhold the inevitable question: How far is it from the act of watching to the act of participation? In a sense, watching *is* participation. The question is really technical: At a lynching-tree, what does it take to make the spectator, presumably only mildly curious about the civic rites of his municipality – a lyncher himself? Only a shout. A neighbourly shove. And then, he too staggers beneath the intoxication. Does that, then, exonerate him, seeing that now he, too, may plead afflatus? As much as it exonerates the original lyncher. The point is that there is no distinction between them.

Everywhere about me, therefore, I sense the possibility of that neighbourly shove, the imminence of that inciting shout. It is a possibility which is an actual terror, the imminence is a chill against my spine.

Let me consider it in its true light: how far indeed have I fallen? I am not pleading now for privilege or even equality; I am arguing for the right to live! It was not an accident that when I had collected my first volume of verses, and was looking about for a title, it suggested itself that I use some mnemonic words out of Shylock's famous speech about the common anatomical constitution of the Jew, and his routine reactions to environmental stimuli. Upon such a plane was I exercising my apologia! The Jew, like others, was an animal, and cruelty to animals was a vice! Here were no lofty concepts of high morality, no egalitarian slogans, no highfalutin palaver about the essential dignity of man! If I had, in this day, invoked such arguments, people would have thought me crazy, or Rip van Winkle. The essential dignity of man! It was the essential pity for animals that, like Shylock, I did plead. Moreover, no one noticed the incongruity, no one realized that I was invoking arguments which should have passed out with the spacious days of Queen Elizabeth. They were – and is not this the bitterness? – found quite pertinent to our age.

I interrupt myself here, or rather, I make a large pause to gather up the interruptions that I have suffered throughout this writing by my cell-mate who seems troubled and distracted. He is staying in his cell to-day, – unlike the first four days when I was fasting my fast, he has to-day not volunteered to work in the fields – and although he doesn't bother me with conversation, for he sees me engaged in an activity he seems to respect, namely writing – his frequent jumpings from off of the bunk, and his visits to the bowl have considerably annoyed me.

Not feeling well? I ask.

No, not so good, he says.

Must have been the food.

Hell, no, never is enough of that. Besides, I hardly touched the mush. Turns my stomach. He was moody, he was debating with himself whether to tell me or not.

Can't understand it, he said. She looked clean. Young, rosy cheeks and a nice white skin. And she smelled good, too.

Yea, I said, So?

So I laid her, what do you think? I had picked her up the night I pulled the job, picked her up in a nightclub, and then took her to a room around the corner. She didn't want to go – after all this was only the first time I had met her, she said. I should have known she was a goddam whore. Talk about an easy pick-up, why, no sooner had I flashed the roll, tipping the waiter, and she was crawling all over my pants.

They are like that, I said.

But she did smell good. What kind of perfume have you got on? I asked. You like it, dear, she said. Swell, I said. It's Nuit de Paris, she said. It was Nuit de Paris alright. And now I got it.

What do you mean?

I got it, that's what I mean. Been running all day. The bitch. At first I couldn't believe it, but it's the thing alright. A bloody clap.

You better do something about it, big boy, I said. And if you don't mind, you can stay away from me, and my things. I don't even get a good smell out of it.

He laughed.

Yea, he said, I'm laughing.

Why, then, do I not seek the road to escape? Why don't I change it, my name that seems a pornography? Why do I persist in my identity, flaunt it, boast about it? From what actual depths of humiliation does it spring, this weak faltering I'm-proud-to-be-a-Jew bravado, as if the thing was the result of an exercise of choice, and not a mere reconciliation with one's fate?

Is it the religion of my fathers that so ravishes me that I will suffer all these revilements? For the true faith? But that is absurd. To me the thirteen credos of Maimonides are mere literature, and the six hundred and thirteen injunctions of Holy Writ historic curiosities. I have lost my father's faith. I am not of the stuff with which one kindles auto-da-fés. Nor are my fellow 'co-religionists.' They, in fact, are not even curious about the six hundred and thirteen, and to them Maimonides is not even literature. That can't be the bond.

Then, perhaps, it is race, the cohesion of the chromosomes? Perhaps; the universal envies and the ubiquitous hatreds certainly do bestow upon us a distinctive identity. But that is a distinction which comes from without; it is not inherent. Moreover, I cannot entertain a loyalty based upon the assumption of race; it would belie all my human convictions. Besides, I cannot but ask: Am I really of the race? Would it not be a grand joke, an irony of the subtlest refinement if, searching my genealogy, I discovered that somewhere in the dark backward of time, my ancestors, through war or through passion, mingled their bloods with strangers? Would not there ensue the classic pay-off – the man persecuted, convicted, condemned – and it's all a case of mistaken identity!

Perhaps, then, it is mere indoctrination, the comfort of habit, which holds me to those I am accustomed to call my own, and to their traditions. That there is much due to it, I have no doubt. They are forever part of me, the ceremonials of my childhood. The seasons do not roll around but each one brings me symbols of the customs of my father's house; I cannot smell the winds of April but that I sense also the gust of air that flew into our banqueting house when the door was opened for Elijah to drink from his cup, nor can I hear sad music – music of the minor keys – without remembering the intonations of the synagogue. Good Canadian October, florid with leaves, still brings me the rites of the Feast of Tabernacles, and the memory of the branch-covered Succah my father built on the back-gallery, and the delicious fragrance of citron, redolent from the benedictive hand. And Purim, and the penny for the mask; and the Fifteenth of Shvat, New Year of the Trees. The calendar conspires for my soul. Nor have the days of my childhood really passed; I am still that child who with patriarchs and prophets peopled St. Lawrence Boulevard, and City Hall Avenue; the big tree on the corner was the Oak of Mamre to me, and any day I expected an Angel to stop at my door, to leave some happy message for my father, away at work. Over the street where I played my childhood games, hiding under the legs of staircases when it rained, it was Noah's Rainbow which shone for me, like the wrapper of some new chocolate bar. And O the days when I bore the heavy folio of the Talmud through the streets. I walked with Tannaim, my head full of the subtleties of its most clever rabbis, and of the romance of Resh Lakish, gladiator turned scholar, and of Rabbi Akiva, poor, and sitting on the window-sill of the academy, hearkening Torah, and Rabbi bar bar Hunah. Time, and the advent of worthies from other spheres, speaking other accents, has not banished them. They still escort me, like good wishes, on my way.

Yet surely that which is indoctrinated can be exdoctrinated? Is it because – because I read a book – that I am forever bound not only to all its readers, but also to the non-readers who only heard of the reviews? I have read other books; yet I am not one with its circulation. That, surely, cannot be the motive.

Shall I then be eclectic, and say that it is a combination of all of these factors – race, education, religion, – that keeps me self-willed among the chosen? But the whole cannot be made up of deficient parts. What, then, is it, this secret force of the magnet?

I am beginning to think that it cannot be anything but honour. A sense of honour. Ignoble and base is he who forsakes the weak in whose midst he finds himself to go over, and for that reason alone, to the camp of the strong. It is treachery. It is a coward's choice. It is a despicable desertion. Its perpetrator ceases to be not only Jew, but also man. It is the endorsation of iniquity – a kissing, a sneaking up to the other end of the whip. Who does this abjures his integrity. He is the man in the country of hunchbacks who wills to walk with a stoop – mean, wretched, and with no honour.

And is this not a good one, one for the raconteurs – me, writing of honour, in a jail!

We have been brought our meal, bread, and some indecipherable stew ladled out through the door into tin dishes. I taste the stew, it is saltless, gooey, impossible. I content myself with bread, which I follow up with a luxurious cigarette which the guard has been good enough to light for me.

Slickey, however, has eaten – he must have been very hungry – and he is vomiting all over the place. The smell is terrible, soon I almost join him. It is the cigarette smoke which saves me. Attracted by Slickey's oaths, the guard has come back to the cell. He tells us to clean it up. He waits a while, and he does.

We talk. Because I am older than him, he seems to look up to me. But not on questions of vocational guidance; in this, he is his own authority.

The trouble with picking pockets, he says, is that if you are caught, there is no alibi. They've just got you. With the pants down.

That the way you were caught?

No, he said, that happened to me only once – and then I got away. The old goof was yelling that I had his wallet, and sure enough I had, and he was calling police, and the crowd was surrounding me, and a couple of guys – you find them everywhere, won't mind their own business, were making for me to grab me. This was in the tramway terminus, on Craig Street. So I turned towards the ticket-wicket, threw a ticket in, and the crowd couldn't get after me. They had to stall to find their tickets. Once on the other side, of course, I ran up a side street. By the way the guy had been yelling, you'd have thought there was a fortune in that there billfold. Five bucks, five lousy bucks, and a lot of pictures of naked girls. He'd a looked nice identifying his pin-up girls – the nice respectable bastard.

The pictures were worth something to you, weren't they?

Not my type. All fat ones. I don't like them skinny, but not fat like that, either. Practically a complete loss. Certainly not worth the risk.

Sure not. Hope you made more on this one, the one they got you for?

But when I was arrested, it was all spent, all except a ten-dollar bill that had some mark on it that the guy was able to say was his. But that wasn't it. I was spotted as I was doing my act, and then a description was given to the police. Not hard to describe, baby-face they said, and they got a picture. To top the cake[?], I was wearing one of those flashy ties, hand-painted. The funny thing was that when I was arrested I had changed the tie, but – you got to think of everything in this racket – afraid it was also flashy. Anyway, my face I couldn't change.

Should have worked with disguises, I say.

Brother, this profession is enough of a strain without having to worry about a mustache falling off. But maybe I'll have to try it one of these days. Unless I decide to go to work. Say, what are *you* in here for?

Oh, just a scrap. Got into a scrap with a guy. He started it, too. Wasn't my fault.

Framed?

Yeah, framed.

Sitting on my bunk, I feel as if the cell were full of time, a granary full of it, and that it is the condemnation of my sentence to pick off the grains one by one, like in the story. It looks like a hopeless task. When will I ever finish it? Will I ever finish it?

One complaint about the furnishings of this cell, I cannot have. There is no clock.

I had made up my mind that, seeing that my sentence carried no hard labour with it, I would use my time to write. To write – the fatuous vocation. I knock on the steel door to get the attention of the guard. I ask for pencil and paper. Against the rules, he says. I argue, I beg him to be a sport, I offer him cigarettes. Against the rules. OK, I say. I'll write just the same. You'll see.

I was determined to make an incident. I wanted to be reported to the warden so that I can get my request before him. So I took my tin spoon and began scrawling upon the wall, scratching out my text. Slickey stood at the door, covered what I was doing. Finished, I yelled. 'Say, guard, I have something for you!'

The guard looked in through the door.

See, I said, I've written.

The guard didn't say a word, but just gave me a meaningful look. He went away, and returned with another of his kind. They opened the cell, to examine what I had done.

See, I said, a message to Garcia. Something for all future tenants to read. A mural, that's what it is, a mural. Do you know what a mural is?

Using my finger as a pointer, I read: These are the charms against oblivion. (Get that?) On Andalusian cavewalls scribblings dark. (See what I mean, pithecanthropus?) Papyrus lifted, a shield: beyond this, go not, Death. Tilebook and chiselled plinth and cunneiform brick – a lapidation on the head of Time. *Non omnis moriar*, (and Latin, too) drawls Horace, quaint and flaccid, drawing stylus from scabbard.

Dogs scratching to bury the enduring bone. (No offense meant.)

O froggish belly-bursting vanity, croaking from twilit ponds bovine afflatus, windy brekekex! (What do you think? Class, eh?)

The guards looked at each other.

The guy's nuts, said the one who had been called. Come on, buddy, come with us.

The warden is very firm. He tells me what he could have done to me for my breach of discipline, but he won't, seeing I am the nervous type. I can't have pen and paper; it's against the rules. This is a prison and must be run on a system, and there could be no exceptions. I could write a letter if I wanted, but I couldn't sit in my cell and write and write. He wasn't running a school. And if what I did happened again, he would, he warned me, bring me to mark. This was my first day, so he was being lenient. Anyway, I was to be taken back to my cell, and I was to clean up the wall. I was to wash it down, and scrape it, and rub it, until not a letter appeared. Did I understand?

It wasn't an easy job, and when I finished, I was good and tired. I didn't mind that; I welcomed it. Slickey was already in his bunk, – he had the upper one – and was staring at the ceiling, thinking. About disguises? I lay down in mine; my fatigue, and the dim 20-watt lamp, increased my drowsiness. Yet I could not fall asleep. The events of the day, and their protracted prelude, kept revolving in my mind, but my thoughts were not sequential; interrupted by the tread of the guard who marched up and down the corridor, they hopped from subject to subject. The lights went out, and still I could not fall asleep. Yet my thoughts all have this in common – they all centre upon the varied aspects of my plight. Me – and in jail.

Long ago, during those summer Sundays when I used to motor, guest of a more affluent friend, up to the Laurentian Mountains, there to spend the companionable day, it was this jail, rising in all its ugly geometry against an idyllic landscape of furrowed field, and rustic road, and river flowing by, this jail that stood out as the last landmark of the city. There it stood, with its six wings radiating from beneath a central dome, like some huge and carapaced monster, motionless in the sun. A high thick wall surrounded it; behind, the prison proper, in several stories, rose; and above, the ponderous dome, like a heavy leaden weight, like the cupped hand of some giant, the arm invisible, held the whole structure down. All was solidity and weight, as if some eccentric architect had thought to design the model dwelling-place for the force of gravity. Prison walls, pierced only by the regularly placed slits, seem black as if of some metal, all else implacable blankness; the dome, the dome again, it suffocated thought; and then the outer walls, thick, impenetrable, not to be climbed, a cement negation. The intrusion upon our view, sudden, and in these bucolic surroundings so unexpected, of this bastille oppressed us; its stone, its steel, its cement, dungeoned our spirits; we felt as if in the midst of density itself, encased in the very heart of some irrefragable tremendous solidity. We sped on, across the bridge of the Back River onto the highway; in a few moments we abandoned even the jocular clichés which the sight of the prison had suggested, and gave ourselves over to a full enjoyment of the more splendid and less terrifying dome which extended all above us.

And now, now that I am in fact within this solid block interred, it is not at all its heaviness which is my burden. On the contrary, it is the systematic and designed transparency of this place – yes, transparency – which afflicts me. I realize now that the dome was no dome, but a bell-jar under which might be viewed, as by a passionless scientist, the insects that lie beneath it, and vainly crawl up its walls. Indeed, in the very hub from which the six spokes of the prison extend, there sits a turnkey; there he is placed, so that he may at will have look-out upon all the sides of his hexagonal domain. This point of vantage is called a panoptikon, an all-seeing Eye; like God's. No one can pass along or across any one of these extending corridors without being spied by this watchful overseer. He sees everything. His agents and subordinates, moreover, stroll along these self-same corridors, and peer, as the inclination prompts them, into our cells. They are made of stone and steel, for exit; for entrance, for inspection, they are all lucidity. One is isolated, but one is never alone; always a pair of eyes is on its way to catch you in seclusion's occupations, shameful or innocent. If that is not enough, your very thoughts are subjected to close censorious scrutiny, and, when they think necessary, deleted. So they look at you from on top, and they look at you from the side – this is not a mortared tomb, but a glass case.

I am a smear on a slide of a microscope.

And yet when I would help them see – see from the inside – they tie my hands. Again I am full of self-pity, and it is against tears that my eyes shut in sleep.

Out of their names I make a ballad, such as was sung in the old French times. First it is their names which suggest themselves, and then it is a perfume which associates itself with each name, and at the end my mind is a pleasant confusion, a garden trembling with scents, a bell ringing with names.

At first this naming, this trembling roll-call is quite impersonal, like the evocation of an alphabet. Upon the black of the brain, they flash in bright white but only for a very little while, soon the afterglow of the names brings back the sensations – muffled, of course – of first acquaintance. Names, but they are not mere Clarissas and Chloes, all petticoats and plastics, but real bodies, emanating a private warmth, as of blood at the human temperature, and skin not cold. Miss Martin, Mrs. Mosco, Catherine, Sylvia, The Lady Watson-Porter, Yvette, the almost anonymous ones, the girl with the limp. And then, in a category all by herself, Elizabeth. To whom I was to be joined in wedded bliss, ineffable and eternal.

Elizabeth's image, however, soon fades as image from my mind. She arrays herself into syllogisms, arguments, recriminations, practicalities, and general unidentifiable regrets. Why did she say this? Why did I do that? She becomes a debate, a situation, not a person.

But the other ones. They bring into my cell the easy humour of retrospective experience, and some of the tantalizing memories of desire not entirely exhausted. Not without aftertaste I recall the incidents in which we were involved – and all the incidents are of one kind – this one's excited moans, that one's body-odour, the shyness of this one, the brazenness of the other, the failures, the frank enjoyments – and no incident is complete but it merges with the next, dallies there, returns, and again, by imperceptible transition, is transferred to other beds. But the incidents are still recognizable, they bear names – Yvette, Catherine, The Lady – it is a kind of meditation.

Suddenly, however, it all becomes anonymous, not meditation any longer, but craving, an endless yawn of the heart. Not for a person, not for a name, but for that thing of comfort, that nook of cosiness, the sweet recess. The cell smells female, the darkness is pubic, and the flesh is crazy with search. To pull down the walls of the cell, to make the stone soft and warm, to be enclosed therein – these are desires that shear the heart to shreds, the shreds to tentacles.

The entire prison, I am sure, is now full of such aspiration. Upon the many cots they lie, voyeurs. Their mind has lost its Latin, they think only in the words fourlettered. At the same time, the very thought, while thinking itself, knows itself frustrated. If only the mind had a fiat!

Conceive a great machine, huge enough to fill an entire hangar, fitted with wheels, and belts, and pistons, suddenly set in motion, its pistons moving mightily up and down – and producing nothing, nothing at all. It's merely a try-out! These iron limbs are only showing their muscles! Such is the population of a jail, the hour before it falls asleep.

And the guards, come from their wives, still dewed with semen, titter, and turn no locks.

It must have been a dream. Wanting return back to the womb, the original safe place, over cluttered time I must have wandered in that general direction. Only I didn't arrive. I found myself instead – nearer the goal, of course, but not quite in it – in a corner of my private childhood. My nonage playground! My first world! The beautiful ghetto!

A million million watts of sun shone down upon the street, and in the distance padded my Hebrew teacher, bearing his curled umbrella. On the corner, in the windows of the big cafeteria, philosophers sat stirring the livelong tea. At the door, old man Ungar, as usual took up his stance, his tzitzith dangling from his fly, in his outstretched hand pamphlets – the miracles of the Baal Shem Tov, the Jewish Calendar in a twelve-page book. Across the street, a dog was leashed by a bitch's tail.

My friends played in the street the game of frogs, the game of running sheep, the game of ball and mitt. The staircases stretched their legs down from the buildings, so good, so warm.

A water waggon passed with its crystal broom of water, and the asphalt changed colour, and the air changed odour. But the sun was still shining, licking the barber's candy-pole, warming the hot-house garden in the grocery window. And I, on a stoop watching the players, watching a horse nuzzling his oats from a bag, and the lady on the balcony who didn't wear any pants, and the passers-by, and the standing baby-carriages. I was munching on an unpeeled cucumber, salting it with salt from a paper, and making it last with bites from a heel of bread. The little cucumber-seeds were good, the smell was fresh and watering, and I was thinking of the always bitter taste of the last cucumber-bite. Would I bite that bite, or would I have the strength to forego it?

Suddenly someone shouted *Look out!* and I got the feeling that a ball had maliciously been aimed at me, either because I was standing there, innocent and smaller, or because I looked happy eating my cucumber, or because I seemed to be engrossed in myself and in my doings and the ball would shock me out of my daze. I turned my head in time, and dropping my food – I wouldn't have the last bitter bite, after all – caught the ball in my hand. I flung it up the street. They would have to run for it. It might even roll into a drain.

Hey, whadaya tink yer doin'? The ball-thrower was running up towards me, all fight and indignation. It was Simki, whose mother kept going to the Juvenile Court to plead for him.

Whadaya mean throwing a ball at me?

Balls on you! – Everybody laughed – It was an accident, and anyway, you caught it, din't ya?

The ball – nobody had run after it, all the kids had crowded around us to see what was going to happen – came to a dead stop, near a still steaming pile of turds.

Gawon! he said, Gawon and get't! His hand was extended, like that of the picture in school showing Columbus pointing to America.

Yah, the gang chimed in, you threw it, you get it.

You threw it first, I said, and you threw it at me, you get it.

Simki turned to his henchmen, with a look which said Leave this to me, boys.

We'll see who'll get it, he said. He heaved his body against mine. I staggered and almost fell.

I regained my balance. I made myself look bold and brave.

Who d'ya think you're pushing? I said.

Nobody, he said, nobody at all. Just a little runt. C'mon, get a move on.

The cucumber lay trodden on the sidewalk. Simki bent down, picked it up, and dipped it in the dirt of the gutter. 'Good salt,' he said.

Now, he said, a master of the situation, will you get the ball? Or shall we drag you there? Or does mamma's little baby, that's so hungry, want to be fed?

You fucken bastard! That gave me status. Take this! And I knocked the cucumber out of his hand.

A fight! A fight!

I flailed into him with both my hands, and we were at it, for a long tiring time, fists and elbows, puffings and bumpings, clinches and withdrawals.

An uppercut, the kids were shouting. Hit him in the muscles! Hit him in the kishkas! Simki landed a blow plop on my nose. It began to bleed.

Blood, the boys shouted.

I was frantic, and full of pity for myself. I wanted to cry, but held back my tears. I wanted to shout, to insult him, to fling out asides, but I was afraid my voice would give me away. As we clinched again, I felt my upper lip. There was blood. We drew apart again, adopting stances, like in boxing photographs. Then he rushed me again. My arms whirled, my heart pounded, my head bobbed up and down, and my legs were very tired. I lost count of the blows I was receiving. Only now and again I would be startled out of my windmill frenzy by a flattening of my nose – pain, and a sense of imminent sneezing – or by a sparking from my eyes.

Cheese it – someone said – his old man!

It was so good to hear that. They scattered. Simki looked around and saw that it wasn't his old man. He took to his heels. Someone went for the ball.

And there coming up the street was my father, walking quickly toward me.

Even on Sunday I can't rest, he said. What happened? Why did they do this?

Now I could weep.

They started up, I said. They threw a ball to hit me, and then wanted me to go and get it!

And if you had gotten it for them what would have been? You would have lost something?

Sure, they would have called me coward.

So they'd call you coward. Fighting is for goyim. A big thing – to show a fist!

But I gave him good, too. I'm sure he's going to have a bump on his forehead.

Alright, come in the house. How many times have I told you not to go near those bums and tramps. They're not your equals. Truckdrivers, that's what they're going to be, truckdrivers and icemen. America! Only fighting! Heathen! Jewish heathen!

I walked meekly beside him. It was so good to be near him, he so protective, and knowing all about the true things in life, and what God really esteemed. Moreover, he never made any great fusses. Everything, he felt, would pass. Nothing that happened to him or his was unbearably tragical. But not so my mother.

Woe is me! she cried, a calamity, a misfortune! She wiped my nose with the hem of her apron. My fighter! she ironized. Look who stands up to maintain his dignity. A word goes, remain the blows! But look, his eye is swelling! O, all the evil dreams that I dreamed yesterday, and the day before yesterday, on *their* life and limbs may they settle! The bandits!

We were only fighting, I said, hoping to jolly her. I went into a bit of shadow-boxing. We were only fighting –

Say, buddy, what's up? Having a good time? Slickey, in the upper bunk, was prodding me with the heel of his foot.

Was just dreaming, brother. Something I didn't eat. Goodnight.

I am not quite sure that that which comes in at morning through the bars of a prison window can be called dawn. The word to me has always been a wide one, something to print upon an horizon, a synonym for expansive vistas of illumination. Such a thing couldn't get through a prison window. It would be more accurate to say that it hung outside my cell, like the cardboard sign of some impecunious mechanic.

Anyway, it was morning; and I was relieved that the night had at last ended. My sleep had been tossed with dreams, dreams induced by the hardness of the cot, the nature of the food I had eaten, and the general strangeness of my situation. I would fall asleep, a temporary and sweaty submersion, only to wake in the midst of some confusing action, not quite a nightmare, but a general hallucination in which things most incongruous – incident, milieu, and stage properties – stood combined by some sophistical and not quite convincing logic whose fallacies I could not unravel. Then I would sink again, only to rise anew upon some different scene and some equally unreasonable performance. It had been a bad night.

The guard who now peered into my cell quite apparently had rested well. He was bright, cheery, eager for a good day's work.

Do you want to come out, you? he asked through the barred door, his keys dangling from his right-angled arm.

Could it be I was being liberated? His face didn't look tricky. And it really was too early in the morning for practical jokes. But there was no reason or even possible accident which could have brought about such a sudden liberation. Was I again in the midst of one of my dreams?

Come out where? Cautious, to avoid discomfiture.

Come out to work, of course. It's good for you. In the fields.

In the fields. It sounded particularly ominous. Things usually happened 'in the fields.' That was where victims got buried. *It's good for you,* too, didn't sound reassuring. I did not know whether the guard was solicitously expressing a concern for my health and welfare, it will be good for me, or whether he was subtly informing me that I richly deserved my fate: it's good for you: and the fate which awaited me in the fields.

Nothing doing, I said. No hard labour for me. His Lordship didn't say so, and whatever he says, goes.

And whoever he doesn't say, doesn't go, eh? Everybody in this jail was witty.

As you wish, you'll change your mind, I'm sure.

The sound of his bootsteps [ ] down the corridor.

Why would I change my mind? Was there some reason – some good reason, it's good for you, – why I should prefer labour in the fields to leisure in my cell. Or were there even worse fates in store for those who resisted the prison's invitation to the farm. But certainly if the punishment for my crime had involved hard labour, I would have been sentenced to it. That little judge was not one to overlook such a detail. I had rights, even if they were only negative ones. I would insist on them. But I was puzzled, and not a little afraid.

The situation was also very funny. Not to laugh at, but for the mind to be amused by: what was I afraid of? That work would kill me?

But soon I understood the guard's assurance. He knew, he knew with what he had left me in that cell, he knew that neither he nor his master had to do anything at all to make me come crying and begging to be taken out into the fields, anywhere, as long as it was out of that cell. Laissez-faire, that's what it was that would work the revolution in me.

He was not wrong. A cellful of time, – and what to do with it?

I let my mind wander into the alleys of the past, to hurry there, and linger here, but invariably it returned to the knowledge that my wandering was on a leash.

I played games with my mind. I tried to remember things in alphabetical or chronological order. I took at random a subject and divided it into its categories and the categories into subcategories, and into divisions, and subdivisions, and time did pass, but always I returned to the headpiece of the paradigm: my cell.

I evoked the recollection of all of the people I knew, I sought out and gave them sobriquets, I invented sobriquets and sought out names that would fit them, I made a dictionary of communal biography, and some more time passed. But how many people did one know?

I dwelt consciously upon the cell itself, I measured, with footsteps, its length and its breadth, I took inventory, I contemplated the materials of their construction, I pondered upon the raw goods which went into them, their extraction, their processing, their transportation; it was now later in the day; and I had built myself – a cell.

Time. The cell was full of it; and by some glutinous quality inherent in it, it did not flow out between the bars and netting of the cell-door. It remained to suffocate, drown, collapse, overwhelm me. And if, now and again, I got the feeling that some of it – was it liquid, solid, gaseous? – had indeed escaped out of the cell, that feeling was accompanied by the knowledge that more of it, tons, gallons, clouds of it, were seeping in, were pressing down upon me, crushed and embedded beneath their weight and ubiquity.

What was it, this Time, this secret sharer of my cell, this obstreperous and greedy companion who at once wanted all space for himself, and yet would not let me go? He it was, certainly, who was the conspirator planted in my cell who would, in due time, with the expansion of his personality, see to it that I would clamor for exit, release, hard labour. The stoolpigeon in my cote. My invisible opponent, the expert gladiator, a cruel wrestler, master of many holds and tortures.

Thus I thought of him when I wanted to *underestimate* his prowess. To think of time as gladiator, conspirator, wrestler, was after all to personalize him, to endow him with human characteristics, to believe him an entity through which one might hope to pierce. The truth, I knew, was otherwise. Time was impersonal, not a he, certainly not a she, but a macabre *It*.

How to define It? Invisible yet ubiquitous, intangible but potent, shapeless yet extant. It couldn't be conceived; it struck the mind, yes, but left no impression upon it beyond that of a blow, indescribable, a series of blows received. It had tentacles which choked, feelers which caressed with some maddening system, fists that knocked you down, and wings that fanned you back to dismal consciousness again. What was this creature left in my cell with me, like some unimagined monster suddenly encountered in a cave?

Somewhere I had read that Time could never be understood save in regard to something else. It was neither its own revealer nor its own measure. Thus it could be understood if one posited it within space, the *distance* covered by a pendulum in sixty swingings was an hour! The distance covered by the revolving globe in one sun's tour was – a day! Yet even if things remained stationary, time proceeded. How to measure it? And here in this cell where nothing moved, where I had nothing to measure it by, where all was deadness and motionlessness, I could hear Time moving, slowly, quickly, with a rustling, with a rush, and could almost sense it, the invisible monster grinning because it was not known.

And suddenly I felt the cell full of a myriad of clocks, like a corps of policemen arrived to see what was happening. All manner of clocks, every policeman with his own expertise. Invisible, but not soundless, in every corner of the cell, I could hear them stalking their prey. An interminable shuffling of feet, tick, tock, tick, tock, like the gait of automata that could not move except by jerks and jolts. Tabetic. Springs coiled and from their eccentricity unloosed, like lassoos, to bring down a steer. Cogs stuttering. A loosening of sand, grain by grain, dropped from the ceiling, dropped from the bed, dropped from the walls, the whole cell becoming a mound, a gurgle, a whorl, a Time glass sucking Time. Little doors snapped open, and insane birds crying Cuckoo at *irregular* intervals. And the battering ram, the pendulum, striking first this temple, and then that, *if it won't come out here, it'll come out there, it'll come out there, or come out here*. And my brains like ticker tape, trailing contradictory news.

And, of course, no report. The furious sand, the rattling serpent springs, the swinging clubs – the clocks! the clocks! showed nowhere any clockfaces at all. No information, nothing to say. We are still investigating. We expect the case to break soon. We have a clew.

And then, at first refreshing, for sound of water always is refreshing, the triturations globulating time, refreshing at first, and then – the Chinese torture. On the forehead. Drop by drop. On the forehead; and behind it, still ignorance, and the first curds of lunacy.

Sudden silence. Time, as usual, silent; and the clocks – in conference? – silent. But I hear the dial. I hear the shadow graze itself against the dial. Stealth. The shadow, too, would steal up upon *It*, throw over its own black cloak, muffle, suffocate, lay it low.

They are at it again. The clocks, the clocks. The mad chorus of waterdrop and sandgrain and shadowsneak and drumstick and falseteeth rattled like [ ]. Their incantation is for Time. Or me. Or me, and Time. Or Time, or me. Tick-tock, tick, tock.

Nothing to do. Nothing to think about except time, teeming time entombing. Not a thing.

I see now what he meant, my Mr. Guard. On the cot, off the cot; up the wall, down the wall. One, two, three, four; four, three, two, one; up and down and turn about and down and up again.

I play the game of superimposition. Given the area of the cell as the size of the map I superimpose thereon the cartographic outlines of the Island of Montreal. It fits – nine miles wide, twenty-seven miles long. Here is the Back River, as indeed, there it is; here the city of Westmount – self-contained houses, flower-beds, cellar-garages; and here Sherbrooke Street full of nurse-maids wheeling perambulators and gentlemen walking canes. A quiltwork, patched and parallelogrammed, with the city's wards: Laurier, Ste. Cunegonde, Ahuntsic, Mercier, Montcalm, Villeray, St. Jean Baptiste, Notre Dame de Grace, Papineau, Cremazie. My world, my cosmos. The quadrature of the globe. All time and space within my cubits four.

Northwest by north – the cemetery of the Chevra Thillim Linath Hatzedek. The synagogue of the two dark duties: the saying of the psalms for the souls of the moribund; the night vigil beside the floor-stretched niftar, exonerated corpse. In the sixth row, second plot from the gravelled path, at an angle of thirty degrees from the bricked and tallow-smelling tomb of Rabbi

Simcha Garber, four feet underground my father lies. He lies in darkness, diminishing with the seasons. The black hail – clod on clod on clod – has melted on his coffin-boards. His blood has turned to water. Even the worms that excavated him like an ancient city have slid away; the parasites are gone; he lies there now, in dark Mizraim a white palace of bone. He is freed of the rigour of labour and of the bitterness with which his life was embittered. It is over, the pagan dance before the cat-eye gas-lights of the press-machine, *holy, holy, holy,* in the sweatshop tailorshop of the old deaf Farovitch. At ease and rested, he dwells now, beneath rameses headstone upon pithom-plinth, builded by his sons for a memorial for all time, the work of Tomarkin, stuttering mason.

And here the Shrine of brother André, also with a dome. And the streetcar running smooth down onto Ste. Catherine Road, past the hanging gardens, the terraces mown with a corded mower, the high homes of the gentlemen rentiers of Outremont, and onto Laurier, and down Park Avenue, and past Fletcher's field, – in Fletcher's field we sat down, and hung our coats upon a crabapple tree, and ate our sandwiches, and snoozed in grass, and dreamed the foreman came back from his weekend needled and stitched and sewn, – and through medical Bleury, and down into St. Peter's alley, leaning on Craig. The secondhand paradise.

No, here. The blanket fold. A pleat. The Art Gallery. Technicon of eocene glyptics and plastics agamic. Discoboloi non-ithyphallic; nymphs only partially ecdysiast. The temple that apopemptic Butler apotheosized: O Basilicoria!

Upon its walls, lost in lethean space, the eremite anaphrodisiac chromes, the ikons on their pedestals, hymned by no glossators. An aulic megacenotaph. Only at etesian symposia come the ethnarchs, in tuxedo chitons dressed, in company of their psittaceous hetarae. It is Maia's month, and in the baluster'd agora, the olympiad is on. How they do chatter and lalagate, the barbaroi, enchiridion in hand, wandering the hypostyle, paeanizing the ioxantholeucomelachlorose ikons and images. A pantomime, a mimesis. The nostalgia of marsupial midas adoring the hieratic.

O georgic, bucolic, architectonic, this patria is no country for art. Pragma & Gasteropragma – this the bride Kalla, that the sister Agatha. Numismatic is the true hedonic. Along galactic marble they walk – the patrons – through hyaline corridors, accomplishing a rite. Gemmadactylate towards glucosity; to callipyginous marmor [ ]. Their rhetoric is of the morphology Kanadian: hyperborean landscape with dryads anemonate; zeugmic hippos at hespertime; halcyon biograph; the oneiratic West; Lake Superior brontapoplect; portrait of the archon of the Kappa Pi Rho.

They admire; but anaesthetes, psilaformal is their panegyric. Not this their sarcocarp; unpragmatic. The dolytrichose – for them these ikons and chromes. For them the hoi phalloi, the proctoscopists – these gluteal petrifactions, alpha and omega, genesis and eschatology. But not for heroes and athletes [ ]

Diary (1944)

April 2

Was supposed to meet Dave at W. Circle at 10 A.M. Hence arrived early but he was not there. Morning cold, and hall chilly. Finally Dave appeared. Had been at meeting where he was guest-speaker and was called upon to speak at 1 A.M. The local kibbudim had to be disposed of first; accordingly Dave spoke only to a head-table.

Everything in readiness for convention – whole thing cut & dried. All the trouble expected from the conspirators – the implacable Bundists and the intransigent Poalei Zionists – did not materialize.

Rubinstein in chair. Announced purpose of meeting, and called upon Albert Eaton, joint-chairman. Eaton spoke incoherently, psychologically handicapped by fact that he did not wish to reveal the fact that candidate had already been chosen. He did reveal it, just the same. Speech summarized itself into a statement that we do not want to have again the apple-selling decade of the thirties. He could have said that even in Eden all our trouble came from an apple; but his knowledge of history apparently goes back only unto the thirties.

Nominations called for. Dave, Mike, Jacques Casgrain, myself. Casgrain takes it as a joke; which it was. Imagine the Jews of Cartier voting for a Casgrain. Dave makes address refusing nomination in my favour. It must have been ordeal to him; he almost admitted as much. The cicatrice of his defeat last August not yet healed. Recalls our common youth, the which memories touched me almost to tears. Regretted our differences of opinion of last summer.

Mike launches into biographical sketch of myself. A masochistic effort inasmuch as he had hoped for nomination. Recalls my father's membership in Union and his refusal to work on Sabbath during period of two years unemployment. Quotes Shakespeare Hath not a Jew, and attributes authorship to me. (The cultural niveau is very high.) Withdraws in my favour.

Am visibly affected as I rise to accept. It is already 1:30, and inasmuch as it is the purpose of the C.C.F. to diminish the hunger in the land, I make my remarks brief. I call for unity on fundamental factors. I distinguish between politeness and tact by quoting tale of bell-boy who breaks in on woman half-undressed. 'Excuse me, sir,' he says. The excuse me is politeness; the sir is tact. I will not recognize the sex differences of the varying ideologies in our own ranks.

I repudiate the too great emphasis upon my poetic career. Intend that my opponents should never suspect that I am a poet, either from dreaminess or delicacy of my utterance. At the same time it is fitting that a poet go forth to pluck a rose.

Nomination unanimous. 100 delegates, 26 organizations.

Walked home with Dave. He was sad. Did not know where he was going to run himself.

Lewis Sr. congratulated me. Said to him I did not know why I was doing it – 'going with a healthy head into a sick bed.' He doubted, smilingly, whether the head was healthy. Mentally recalled his reported remark after his son's defeat – 'I wish he had lost his legs and arms, before he decided to run here!'

In the afternoon received phone call from Hirshhorn[?] that Eagle had cut report of convention. Medres, Russian wolf-hound in Eagle office, evoked[?] question; Wolofsky phoned and he consented to synopsis.

April 3

Saw Wolofsky. Was cordial with him, the old knave. Unashamed he was in his declaration that he was sold to Liberals. Feigned worry about Chronicle editorship; but knew he would do nothing since he feared my reaction. Assured me he would not attack – fact is, he wishes to play both horses.

Nothing in Star, though Star reporter at convention. Felt like a lunatic; here I'm running but nobody looks!

Phone call from Gerhardt of Gazette at 6 P.M. Wanted biographical note to append to C.P. release from headquarters about my nomination. Was very helpful. Reflected how true it was that one cast one's bread upon the waters etc. Had helped Gerhardt several weeks ago at Ludwig dinner, and apparently he felt grateful.

At night radio announcement – maliciously phrased. A.M. Klein distinguished lawyer, etc. He has written a number of poems.

April 4

Star finally publishes announcement, as radio announced it.

Met the little lawyers in court. Amusing experiment. Many congratulate but their words choke them. Envy – for what – stares from their eyes. Can size up their different characters by words they use in felicitation.

Emily Postish – I hope you win.
Concerned, & hopeful – You're gonna have a tough fight.
Secretly gloating with small consolation – So you've written a number of poems.
Argumentative – Since when are you a C.C.F.er?
Probing for an Achilles heel – What will B. say?
Facetious – So you're handing out cigarettes already.
Neumanesque – What can you do for me? I promised him the murals of the House of Commons.
Maternal – May those be paralysed who will run against you!

April 5

Phone calls, congratulations, offers of help.

Derive a sadist pleasure out of watching Tynkoff, Fogul, Herzl Shapiro and others offering congratulations, and inwardly wishing that I be smitten with double pneumonia.

April 6

Ruddick tells me Pegi says I can easily be unmasked – a Bronfman man. 'But don't we all work for capitalists?' says R. Doesn't Patrick, too; he educates the Bronfman children at Selwyn House. Isn't that what the fight is about?

Told him that I would place L.P.'s in dilemma. They praise Wilson of B. of M., Jones of American Mfgrs. Ass., Wall St. etc. – but not Bronfman. Are in favour of collaboration with capitalists; but not Jewish capitalists. And they prate about Antisemitism.

Besides, I doubt whether they will raise B. issue. B. has supported Russian aid, greeted Michoels & Feffer, closed his eyes to their infiltration into Congress.

B. himself does not know whether to be joyful or otherwise at my decision. I think he is glad about it – although has not said so. Hypocritically expressed fear lest his Liberal associations be marred by my running C.C.F. Assured him that I still would prefer professorship at McGill to House of Commons seat.

Landlord fixed lavatory bowl. A seat for the future M.P.

April 7

Good Friday. Met J.F. – polite but begrudging. Told him that thus far I had done better than Willkie – I had made the primaries. Ben Caplan there, unusually pleasant; we ate at Café 400. But I refused to have snapshot taken in front of it. Klein & the 400? A nice set-up. Instead, we posed in front of the Navy House, H.M.C.S. Donnacona, right beneath its flag, – or 'ensign' as a female marine corrected Joe.

Met A. Levine. Really happy at my nomination, although he did not approve my party.

Phone calls from Nat Gaisin (looking for printing), Rosenstein (looking for kudos about his articles on cartels) and [......], honestly happy. Harold Freeman can't make up his mind about parties. That's why he's a bachelor at 42.

Anderson, editorial director of C.P., lives where he lives because he loves anonymity. He loves anonymity because he hates the draft-board. Nonetheless he insists on a second front!

Pomerance's wife works as sec. for Fred Rose.

April 8

Batshaw is moving heaven & earth for Liberal nomination. Promises to read me back my speech for [.....] (at a time when I disagreed with C.C.F. policy on war). Intend to get copy of photograph showing him & R.B. Bennett. Also statistics of property owned by Batshaws & Tarshises.

A little rabbit was found in a frigidaire.

What are you doing here?
What is this?
A Westinghouse frigidaire.
I'm only westing here.

B. will be only westing in Cartier, what with his Temple & his Shaar Hashomayim & his Reform Club.

April 9

Am full of misgivings. Wonder why I a poet should allow myself to be contaminated by this political struggle. Here are so many mean motives, so many ignoble drives; in poetry, only cleanliness, starched words, and the smell of air.

Sophie phoned. She, too, trembles lest I am elected.

April 10

'Man's heart is full of deceit and very weak; who can know it?'

Bauman[?] was in. Wanted to congratulate me: 'Anything I can do not to help you, I will.' Restrained myself from telling him that his remark revealed his impotence. The fact is that he has no children.

Am told that Erlich[?] with the big ears – and now the big mouth – goes about telling people I write all of B.'s reactionary speeches. He knows it to be false, he who came in that office snivelling for a job in Federation. O, the victims of frustration worshipping their zero!

My ears should tingle all day, so ubiquitous is evil talk.

My son, Colman, wants to know if two people can be elected. His poor little heart is ready for compromises.

And why am I running? I am not driven by ambitions in that direction; and I surely have too much humour to have a mission.

It must be – for the exercise.

Proofread the Hitleriad to-day; read my poems in Preview.

Diary (1945)

May 4, 1945

Had lunch with Dr. James at the University Club. A club right out of a cartoon in Punch, deep leather seats, trophies on the wall, lackey at the desk, heads in newspapers, and frigidity pervasive everywhere. One fogy seldom looks at the other, if he does, it is with fish-eyes, and as if he were seeing the man through water. Waited for the Dr. who arrived – a punctual man – at the first tick of one. So good to see you, he said, have you washed up? I had, so he went himself to the rear of the club to doff his clothes; I could hear the mumblings of the old dodderers in the lavatory.

We went upstairs, up a carpeted staircase that seemed to say – Come, curl yourself upstairs in me. He ordered two martinis. I had accepted just to be sociable; the damn stuff is too heady for me; I find it a handicap in [.......] conversation. (I shall never suffer from gout.) Discussed the war, Germany was capitulating by instalments. Holland and Denmark were gone, and in the rest of the Third German (lesser) Reich the pockets of soldiers were emptying themselves. Very good. The Dr. wondered what would happen to Germany. He disapproved of their enslavement – unsound economics. I agreed, if slave labourers were introduced into France, also Frenchmen would be enslaved. Convict labour competing on the open market.

What will the Jews do, he asked. I said Jews were in a dilemma. Five million had been murdered, and those who survived would very likely not want to return to the scene of their martyrdom. Palestine, I told him, was the principal subject of discussion in regard to the Jews of Europe.

A difficult problem. I agreed. I showed him that I knew the English viewpoint, nonetheless, all we wanted was 8800 square miles. Ibn Saud could hide that in his flowing robes.

A great man, Ibn Saud. I met him when I went to see my brother who was a councillor at his court. Very primitive. Justice Solomonic. My brother tells me of the time a woman came to Saud, and demanded the death of the man who had fallen from a date-tree upon her husband and killed him. But surely it was not intentional? It was, she said. Anyway, she demanded her rights, blood for blood. Good, said Saud, I can't do anything about that – that is your right, and I must grant you justice. But I still am at liberty to prescribe the manner of his death. He is to die like your husband. He will lie down beneath that unfortunate date-tree, which you will mount, and from which you will fall, so as to kill him.

I could gather from the Dr. that he was in love with primitive things. The bloody picturesqueness of the Arabs is our most difficult obstacle in appealing to the English. They prefer natives. They are colourful, and easier to deal with. But the goddam Jews, they're always quoting from the same books as you read, unpleasant occidentals.

The doctor did not say that, but that was the wind that blew from his remarks.

We proceeded to lunch. He looked for subject of conversation. Do you do any gardening, he asked. No, I said, I don't, neither I, nor my ancestors for two thousand years. Just haven't had the chance.

How do they manage in Palestine?

That precisely is the miracle of our generation. Lawyers, doctors, university graduates, all took to the farm. Blackest of labour, and made a success of it.

The Dr. was still thinking about the primitive. He quoted from the Golden Bough. A great book, as important in its way, as Marx's Das Kapital.

That, too, was a sort of Golden Bough: Cited the cases of Akhnaton, and Tutankhamen. I felt uncomfortable; the general tenor of his remarks, I felt, deprived my race of the distinction of the discovery of the one-ness of God. The Babylonians and the Egyptians, it appeared, suspected that unity long before Abraham.

I apologized for my ignorance of the subject. My parents insulated me against such doctrine, I said.

Still on the primitive, I thought the manner of Mussolini's death was abominable. I was revolted by the desecration of his body. That, after all, was the only thing we had in common, our human likeness, our corporeal similitude. In Effigo Dei. I admitted, however, that I might not have felt the same way if it was Hitler who was hanging in that fashion – side of beef, strung upside-down from a hook.

He didn't. He would feel the same way, if it was Hitler. I thought, Naturally. To you he was only a belligerent. To me, he was a blood-enemy.

I'm afraid, I said, that's the primitive in me. After all, this is a great day for me. I never thought I would live to see it. In the early years of the war – Dunkirk, Tobruk, Singapore – when all came crashing, it still was, for everybody, just another war. But for Jews, it was the beginning of an end. We could not survive in a world where Hitler was victorious. I could feel the man reaching out for me, personally, across the ocean.

Our coffee we had downstairs. The Dr. – I can see the secret of his personal success – a great considerateness – wanted to have it served there, because he probably remembered that I liked to have my cigarette with my coffee, and in the dining room smoking was prohibited. Last time, the dessert was an ordeal to me, without nicotine.

Finally he got down to the subject. I was to get a Visiting Lectureship in Poetry at McGill. For three years. It was an experimental thing. He had to tell me frankly that Dr. MacMillan was dubious about the experiment – I hadn't a Ph.D., I was away too long from the University, and Mac didn't much fancy my poetry.

But, added the Dr. – probably he thought he saw a pained expression on my face, it was really scorn, not pain – he thinks the same about all living authors.

How much time would it take? I asked.

Nine to twelve hours per week.

Are you happy?

I don't know yet. What is the compensation? The reason I ask is because I want to know whether it is a full or part-time job.

O full time. Salary of an assistant professor.

Good, I said, I'm happy. I shook his hand. A great day, I said, Germany collapsing and me at McGill. I'll call MacMillan to discuss the nature of the course.

The Dr. left me. Had to go to a meeting on post-war problems. My post-war problem, I told him, was solved.

Phoned Bess from a pay-station. Strangely enough Rosenstein was speaking to some one from another booth. Must have wanted to keep his talk secret from his stenographer. Bess was elated. Kept kidding about Herr Doktor-Professor Klein. And calculated the number of people whom the announcement would slay. A pleasant thought.

Back to the office. Central Cadillac up five points. And in the mail, a jubilant superlative appreciation of my book by the poet Jacob Glatstein. A great day.

The mood of the conversation with the Dr. is, of course, not conveyed. It was a confused mood. At times I was fond of him, and thought him a great guy, a go-getter, one who looks ahead for the university; at other times I detected the ineradicable snobbery, the Englishman's prejudices, a resentment that he should have to deal with me, and a sort of subtle intention that while he would feign the granting of my request, he really had plans of his own. Certain conversational idiosyncrasies got under my skin; he loved to refer to the world-renowned by their first names, and thus cast upon his association with them an aura of intimacy. 'When Sir Ronald told me' ... 'I was talking to Sir Malcolm Budge, good old Budge.' Picture of an Englishman letting his hair down.

His appearance, too, seems to partake of the dual character of my reaction to him. At times he looked, or made me feel that he looked, because of his height and his comparative youth, like an older brother – one who has travelled, knows the ways of the world, but still appreciates the unprofitable persistencies of his younger brother; and at times, when dislike sparked, his excessive length, and short round black mustached head, made him look in my eyes like one of those animated caterpillars that stand on their culs and sway in the Disney films.

Now that it seems practically settled, I am full of misgivings. I am worried about Dr. MacMillan's attitude. Every time the Dr. had to quote him, he had to preface his sentence with an apologetic: 'Frankly, he thinks ...' I am worried about the students: A Jew teaching English poetry! About students who will have come back from the wars: And where were you all this time? About the subjects I will teach. About what will constitute the measure of success. About the 'experimental' nature of the thing; and then, what? Return to the law? I'll never do that. O, that my father had left me an inheritance.

'The Contemporary Poet'

Statement

The composite poem.
30 to 50 lines in length.
easy to read, difficult to comprehend.

Comment

Reason for abstruseness.
Describe the enveloping of a platitude.
Fear to be understood.
Also due to reaction to the simple lyric.
Itself may soon bring a reaction to simple lyric.

Statement

Typical poem would be *about* something

a man called by name a place a thing of intellectual interest.	The Noun

Comment

Reaction from the dramatic monologue.
Its synthetic nature.
Describe how it's done –
language,
double entendre,
signal characteristics,
static.
Contrast with dynamics of Donne, Browning.

Statement

Anti-lyrical in tone
anti-romantic in spirit
in pt. of view probably anti-middle-class.

Comment

Reason – self-conscious, wants to show that he too can think.
ashamed to merely sing.

Anti-romanticism itself a kind of romanticism – The hard-boiled skill.

Its ingredients
some prophetic sadness of Eliot, little of his music
earnestness & cleverness of Auden
home-made mysticism of Rilke & Yeats
political watchfulness of McLeish or Spender.

Statement
Would appear in a *liberal* magazine
literary journal
quarterly review, & find its way to 3 or 4 American anthologies and one of the English ones.

Comment
Discuss the journals
Nation
New Republic
Partisan Review
Kenyon Review
Poetry Magazine
Sewanee Review.

Statement
Circulation about 5000 people.
mostly poets & college students would read it.

Comment
Compare with mass circulation of radio & press.
Search for a more adequate medium.
Radio. McLeish.

Statement
The man behind the poem.
Read his description.
[ ]

Comment
Comment upon this search for esoteric literature.

What does it show about his own estimate of himself.
Of poetry born of books.

His literary heroes
Chosen by the critics.

I would rather sit on a pumpkin and have it all to myself than to be crowded on a velvet cushion. Thoreau.

101 'The Contemporary Poet'

Qualifications

1) solitariness — I want to be alone.
Solitude – A good place to visit but a poor place to stay.

2) prophetic insight – The best prophets are children and fools.

3) personal unhappiness – O that was a good time, when I was unhappy.
Seventeenth Century.

Owen	over	Brooks
Prophet		Conventional
experimentalist		adjusted

Heroes – Rimbaud
Hopkins
Kafka
Rilke
Soren Kierkegaard.

Introduction to the galaxy.
Tests – Kipling – but note T.S. Eliot — A confusion of les métiers.
– Tennyson – Auden
The I.Q. test – his status as thinker.

The authoritative critic behind the conclave.
Edmund Wilson
R.P. Blackmur
The group critic
Scientific research & laboratory experiments
Semantics
Kenneth Burke
Richards, Ogden.

The common factor of revolt.
Disillusion.
Approach to religion or abstract aesthetic.
But our poet still out of sorts with himself.
Seeks either some spiritualistic black magic or mysticism of the dialectic.

Left behind with various myths
The Marxist
The American Dream.

'Marginalia'

Project: To discover the character of the poet's initial gesture. At a given moment he is not within the poetic process; in the next moment he is, – how is the transition effected? What is the bridge that leads from the static to the dynamic? Is there a poetic attitude? If so, how is it struck?

Medium of investigation: A study of first lines.

Terrain of investigation: Palgrave's *Golden Treasury*. Other anthologies, of course, may be used. Palgrave's is chosen because it is more accessible and because it has acquired, if only through lapse of time, a certain classical character.

Some discoveries: Of the 288 first lines in this anthology, most are couched in the declarative mood. This would indicate that oftenest the poet does not begin by striking an attitude; he begins simply by beginning to speak. He states either that

> Many a green isle needs must be

or

> Most sweet it is with unuplifted eyes

or

> The world's a bubble, and the life of man

or

> The twentieth year is well-nigh past.

Sometimes these commencements are so untransitional that they are made either to read as if they were the poet's *interruptions* of his own thought, or to show that one is plunging *in medias res.*

And are ye sure the news is true?

or

And is this Yarrow? – this the stream

or

And wilt thou leave me thus?

The operative thing, of course, is that *ampersand.*

It is to be noted that while there occur 4 poems beginning with *and,* there are none beginning with 'or.' Poets are not the ones to brook alternatives.

A favoured exordium, more in harmony with the reputation for impoliteness which poets enjoy, is characterized by the use of the imperative. Wilfulness and aggressiveness, it would seem, set a poem off to a good start.

Blow, blow, thou winter wind

(This is the imperative mood conditioned by permissive necessity.)

or

Avenge, O Lord! Thy slaughtered saints, whose bones

or

Awake, Aeolian lyre, awake

or

Hence, all you vain deluding joys.

And more and more of like imperious imperation.

Other first lines would indicate that the poet's first move is to rouse himself from silence to inquiry.

Doth then the world go thus, doth all thus move?

or

> Shall I compare thee to a summer's day?

or

> Why so pale and wan, fond lover?

or

> Art thou poor, yet hast thou golden slumbers?

The total of these is [ ]
The count therefrom is – declarative [ ]
imperative [ ]
interrogative [ ]

It is startling to discover, in the work of a tribe that is considered as being so prone to the hypothetical, that only five poems begin with an if.

As might have been suspected, there is a great frequency of ejaculation. Nineteen O's have been counted in the index of first lines. Only two of the poems begin with Ah! It should make an interesting, if perhaps unfruitful study, to establish the range of nuance between the said Ah and the aforementioned Oh's.

One notes, too, the prevalence of 'how' beginnings – the adverb of wonder.

> How delicious is the winning

or

> How happy is he born and taught

or

> How sweet the answer Echo makes

and how, and how, and how.

Only two of the poems begin boldly with similes.

> Like as the waves make toward the pebbled shore

> Like to the clear in highest sphere

At least 10 of the poems seek to make sure of their destination. The name of the addressee is included in the text. Whether it was the degenerate Douglas, or Cyriack, or Milton who should be living at this hour, or the wee sleekit, cowrin timorous beastie, the poet in each instance makes sure, in the very first line, that the saluted one is identified.

Further statistical analysis is left to those who would qualify for their Ph.D. To simplify their task, I leave them only this hint – all of the first lines are either in the declarative, imperative, subjunctive or interrogative. Quod erat sciendum.

*

The Man with the Hoe

There are poems that are planted and grow; there are poems that are grafted.

This is a grafted one. All the elements in it are borrowed.

Apart from its general inexpensive good-will – inexpensive because no part of the poet's personality is really engaged within the plight of the man with the hoe; the poet really shares the feelings of his contemporaries about the 'brother to the ox' with the 'brutal jaw' and brow slanted back – the poem shows neither original heart nor mind. Its ideology is utopian – Knights of Labour – I.W.W.; its emotion that of the poet who is better than his fellows – for the duration of the poem.

Moved by neither a personal sensitivity or an individual percept, the poet calls upon *rhetoric* to do his work for him. The rhetoric, moreover, is conventional – out of the ancient text-books. First *exposition*:

Bowed by the weight of centuries he leans
Upon his hoe and gazes on the ground,
The emptiness of ages in his face,
And on his back the burden of the world.

Then *interrogation*:

Who made him dead to rapture and despair,
A thing that grieves not and that never hopes,
Stolid and stunned, a brother to the ox?
Who loosened etc.

After the first exordium of interrogation, *declaration*:

There is no shape more terrible than this –
More tongued with censure of the world's blind greed –
etc.

Next paragraph: Exclamation, further interrogation, reiteration.
Final paragraph: Peroration –

> O masters, lords and rulers in all lands.

All the primer lessons of the art of public speaking, down to the tricola:

> To have dominion over sea and land;
> To trace the stars and search the heavens for power;
> To feel the passion of Eternity,

or

> More tongued with censure of the world's blind greed
> More filled with signs and portents for the soul, –
> More packt with danger to the universe.

(As to this last line – More packt with danger to the universe – a worse *prose* line I have not encountered.)

The rhetoric, apart from its observation of the categories, is, moreover, prosodically speaking, incompetent. The tone is never really rhetorical; it is metronomic throughout. Every single line is end-stopped! There is not a run-on in the whole piece. Far from giving the impression of impassioned speech, which necessarily ignores – or appears to ignore – the pentametres, the poem speaks like a grandfather clock!

As for language – the thing is all of clichés compact. 'Weight of centuries,' 'burden of the world,' 'emptiness of ages,' 'the wheel of labour,' 'rift of dawn,' 'dread shape,' 'the suffering ages,' 'Time's tragedy,' 'dumb terror,' 'the music and the dream,' 'silence of the centuries.'

There is some true magniloquence – but it is borrowed. Beginning with the epigraph where God stands sponsor to the poem, the poet continues throughout his work to make use of other people's felicities – Shelley's 'trumpet and prophecy,' Milton's 'dread shape' and 'immedicable,' but above all the Bible which kindly lends the 'Dominion over land and sea,' 'the swing of Pleiades,' 'the whirlwinds,' the 'how will it be with' and the last judgment? Only occasionally does the poet deviate into fashioning something that looks like his own.

> When will you ever
> Give back the upward looking and the light?

The rest is achieved with biblic sonority and, above all, the Bible's parallelismus membrorum.

In fine: photography by Millet; script by Job; direction by Quintilian; music by Toscanini on vacation: up, down, up, down.

E pur muove.

Nonetheless, the poem moves. Why? Because despite the poet's difficulty in making himself understood in his own words, he is understood. He is understood because his audience already knew, as soon as he announced the title of his poem, what he was going to say.

The impression is as of some wonderful orator who can be appreciated only by lip-readers. No voice is heard; but both the moving of his lips and his gestures are wholly beyond reproach.

*

Shakespeare's Dog

Even for the purposes of worship, none but the great ought to approach the shrine of Shakespeare.

For there is not any other act which in its performance is more likely to betray a man's littleness, immediately, – sooner, in fact, than you can say Edwin Arlington Robinson.

Of 'Ben Jonson Entertains a Man from Stratford' Untermeyer says: Here 'we have the clearest and most human portrait of Shakespeare ever attempted; the lines run as fluently as good conversation, as inevitably as a perfect melody.'

Thus is not only Shakespeare's worshipper betrayed, but Shakespeare's worshipper's acolyte.

Edwin Arlington Robinson undertakes to give us a portrait of Shakespeare; he succeeds only in painting the picture of a man who he thinks looks like himself, E.A. Robinson. In about four hundred lines of blank verse, the only 'insights' into Shakespeare's character are

(a) Shakespeare loved money.
(b) Shakespeare wanted to be a duke.
(c) Shakespeare was otherwise very great.

Of (a) and (b) it may be said that, though true, they are facts, if facts, which belong to the category of the merely mentionable; they are not the elements of a full-length portrait. But Robinson here is subject to an idée fixe; he lets all other questions abide, while he ponders, again and again, Shakespeare's worldly assets. The obsession emerges with éclat in the fourth line:

Shakespeare who alone of us
Will put an ass's head in Fairyland

> As he would add a shilling to more shillings.

From these modest beginnings, Jonson goes on to prophesy for Shakespeare even larger possessions:

> But there's a comfort, for he'll have that House –
> The best you ever saw.

For Shakespeare is 'manor-bitten.' Shakespeare is this 'mad, *careful*, proud, indifferent Shakespeare' (italics mine; careful is used in the *New* England sense of the word). And finally Shakespeare's only care, when he dies,

> Will be a portion here, a portion there,
> Of this or that thing or some other thing
> That has a patent and intrinsical
> Equivalence in those egregious shillings.

(Result: Shakespeare is Shylock.)

Complementary to these ambitions is Shakespeare's desire for a dukedom down in Warwickshire, 'which he wants the most.' (Result: Shakespeare *is* Bacon, Lord Verulam.)

The truth is that this pervasive concern with Shakespeare's worldly goods and ambitions (elements which, of course, are [..... .....] to a total portrait – but they are not the portrait) stems from Robinson's own ambitions, the which ambitions having been frustrated, Robinson elsewhere built an entire poetic about the doctrine that Success is Failure. (Result: Shakespeare is Robinson.)

That (c) *Shakespeare was otherwise very great* is an opinion of which the reader has been *elsewhere* persuaded.

Certainly, Robinson, in the body of the poem, does little, beyond a gaping inarticulate use of phrases like 'There was that about him which ...,' to communicate that sense of greatness. Robinson dares to give direct quotes from the lips of the Bard. They are pathetic in the extreme. Concerning women, Shakespeare is made to say 'So few of them are worth the guessing.' It is an opinion which is typical of Robinson, the Robinson who through all the years of his life was scared of a skirt. It is impossible to imagine Shakespeare even thinking in terms of 'guessing.' What is there to guess?... This is not the Shakespeare of Manningham's Diary.

> Upon a time when Burbidge played Richard III there was a citizen grew so far in liking with him, that before she went from the play, she appointed him to come that night unto her by the name of Richard the Third. Shakespeare,

> overhearing their conclusion, went before, was entertained ere Burbidge came. Then message being brought that Richard the Third was at the door, Shakespeare caused return to be made that William the Conqueror was before Richard the Third.

And also before Eddie the Confessor.

Shakespeare is also shown disturbed by matters grand and sublime. Via direct quotation, quotation, of course, not from Shakespeare's works, but from Robinson's imagination. As Jonson pleads that Shakespeare dower the world with more of his writing, we are given the privilege of overhearing the bard, word for word.

> 'There's time enough – I'll do it when I'm old,
> And we're immortal men,' he says to that;
> And then he says to me, 'Ben, what's "immortal"?'

'Ben, what's "immortal"?' One had thought that the tone, the attitude, the insufferable coyness and the innocence which denies itself, all implicit in questions of this nature, was original with Baby Snooks. But no, Shakespeare fathered this, too.

And having put the question, Shakespeare stays to make answer.

> Think you by any force of ordination
> It may be nothing of a sort more noisy
> Than a small oblivion of component ashes
> That of a dream-addicted world was once
> A moving atomy much like your friend here?

(Result: Shakespeare is made a Polonius who did not have a Shakespeare to write his speeches for him.)

There is yet some further oratio recta. Jonson bumps into Shakespeare, down Lambeth way, Shakespeare gloomed and mumbled like a soul from Tophet. Jonson is equal to the occasion.

> 'What is it now,' said I, 'another woman?'

O rare Ben Jonson!

> That made him sorry for me, and he smiled.
> 'No, Ben,' he mused; 'it's Nothing. It's all Nothing.
> We come, we go; and when we're done, we're done.
> Spiders and flies – we're mostly one or t'other –

> We come, we go; and when we're done, we're done.'

Remember this is Shakespeare when, as Robinson takes pains to indicate elsewhere in the poem, he is no more than five and forty, – not in the repetitive dotage.

Jonson interjects:

> 'By God, you sing that song as if you knew it!'
> Said I by way of cheering him; 'what ails ye?'

And Shakespeare makes answer:

> 'I think I must have come down here to think.'

Like a schoolboy in love, Shakespeare aetatis 45, does not know why he came down here. He surmises, however, that there must have been a reason. Yes, that's it: I think I must have come down here – to think! The great bard does not think wherever he happens to be; he thinks only down Lambeth way. (Result: Shakespeare an anticipated Rodin.)

Actually, there was an occasion when Jonson caught Shakespeare in a melancholy mood. It is reported by Sir Nicholas l'Estrange. Sir Nicholas tells of the time when Shakespeare stood godfather to one of Ben's children. (Ben had [ ] of them; he was estranged from his wife for most of his married life.) After the christening Jonson, finding Shakespeare in a deep study, came in to cheer him up and asked why he was so melancholy.

> – No, faith, Ben, not I; but I have been considering a gift for the godchild, and have resolved at last.
> – I prythee what?
> – I'll give him a dozen good latten* spoons, – and thou shalt translate them.

And this, of course, is more like it. None of the business of 'coming down here to think.' Natural human speech, not self-conscious posing; sensible talk, not pompous platitude.

But the payoff, I think, is in Robinson's evocation of 'Shakespeare's dog.' Jonson *loquitur*:

> He must have had a father and a mother –
> In fact I've heard him say so – and a dog,
> As a boy should, I venture; and the dog,

* mixed metal spoons, resembling brass [*Klein's note*]

> Most likely, was the only man who knew him.

Get it? the dog – the only man. Oxymoron, ox-like, moronic!

> A dog, for all I know, is what he needs
> As much as anything right here to-day,
> To counsel him about his disillusions,
> Old aches, and parturitions of what's coming –

This the dog knows, too.

> A dog of orders, an emeritus,
> To wag his tail at him when he comes home,
> And then to put his paws up on his knees
> And say, 'For God's sake, what's it all about?'

Thus is the myriad-minded one made to take counsel of Fido. The entire passage can be regarded not otherwise than as an embarrassing attempt to measure the stature of Shakespeare with the standards of suburban dog-lovers: 'A dog, for all I know, is what he needs' – the personality of Shakespeare is not complete without such companionship. It is significant that Shakespeare had quite other views on this subject. There is not a dog-fancier's line in all his works. As early as [ ] Whiter commenting upon

> The hearts
> That spaniel'd me at heels, to whom I gave
> Their wishes, do discandy, melt their sweets
> On blossoming Caesar.
> – *Antony and Cleopatra*, Act IV, Sc. 12

had this to say:

> [ ]

Not only is Shakespeare, in this poem, everybody that he is not, but even Jonson is not Jonson.

It is inconceivable that the poet who is the first authority on the merds and ordures of the Thames should be able to speak four hundred lines – in a tavern – without once deviating into censurable expression.

It is inconceivable that Jonson, who was a man of singular common sense, should describe himself as 'one accustomed to private outbursts of laughter. This Robinson makes Jonson do not once, but twice. Reflecting upon Shakespeare's ambition for that House, Jonson says:

Good God!
He makes me lie awake o'nights and laugh!

It is to be doubted whether Jonson of the Mermaid Tavern *ever* suffered from insomnia, let alone insomnia accompanied by cachinnation.

Again, fifty lines later and touching the same House:

D'ye wonder that I laugh?

It is inconceivable that the Jonson described by Drummond of Hawthornden should entertain the naïve views about women which Robinson makes Jonson entertain. Jonson knew a thing or two.

[ ]

– Drummond of Hawthornden

It is inconceivable that Jonson would talk as he talks, or that he make Shakespeare talk as he does make him talk. After all, Jonson, unlike Robinson, knew Shakespeare.

> Which two (Jonson and Shakespeare) I behold like a Spanish Great Galleon and an English man-of-war: Master Jonson (like the former) was built far higher in learning, solid but slow in his performances. Shakespeare, with the English man-of-war, lesser in bulk but lighter in sailing, could turn with all tides, tack about, and take advantage of all winds, by the quickness of his wit and invention.
>
> – Fuller's *Worthies*

It is inconceivable, finally, that Untermeyer proofread his galleys: 'Clearest and most human portrait of Shakespeare ever attempted ... good conversation ... perfect melody.'

Previsions

The prophetic and poetic are kin.
Also upon the high places of poetry are there false prophets and true seers.
Not all previsions are inspired.

In 'Ben Jonson Entertains a Man from Stratford,' the 'entertainment' takes place in the year 1609. 'He's' (Shakespeare is) 'five and forty.' Nonetheless Robinson puts into the mouth of Ben the following proleptic lines:

> And I say now, as I shall say again,
> I love the man this side idolatry.

Obviously it is Robinson, who now knows the paragraph of tribute to Shakespeare in *Timber*, who makes the remark, hoping to titillate the reader's sensitivity for the apt; and not Jonson, who can hardly be expected in 1609 to quote himself as of the works of 1623. The parenthesis is factitious; one must resent it as Robinson's ex-post-facto wisdom; it is foresight which is incredible because it sees too much.

Of the same facile nature is the remark in which Ben foretells – not his own intended works – but Shakespeare's. Shakespeare's gloom, Ben prophesies, in 1609, will not

> shut quite out
> A cleaving daylight, and a last great calm
> Triumphant over shipwreck and all storms.

Ah, of course, *The Tempest*!

It must be considered restraint on the part of Robinson that he refrained from indicating the *dramatis personae*.

How different, how much more convincing are the previsions of Eliot's 'Journey of the Magi.' They see, and yet they do not see; what they see, they see with their own eyes, not Eliot's; what they do not see, the reader sees. The poet Eliot is everywhere poet, and like Robinson a régisseur prompting his protagonist from private documents that the protagonist has not yet seen.

> Then at dawn we came down to a temperate valley,
> Wet, below the snow line, smelling of vegetation;
> With a running stream and a water-mill beating the darkness,
> And three trees on the low sky,
> And an old white horse galloped away in the meadow.
> Then we came to a tavern with vine-leaves over the lintel,
> Six hands at an open door dicing for pieces of silver,
> And feet kicking the empty wine-skins.
> But there was no information, and so we continued ...

'Eyes they have, but they see not.' The wise men, thus reporting, report complete revelation.

'The wet,' 'the running stream,' 'the water-mill beating the darkness,' announce to others, if not to the Magi, the passing of drouth and paganism.

[ ]

There is a birth 'smelling of vegetation.'

There are 'three trees on the low sky.' The Magi are of Matthew, Chapter 2, but the three trees of Matthew, Chapter 27.

Even the 'old white horse' is a quarter of an apocalypse.

'Tavern with vine-leaves over the lintel':

[ ]

'Six hands at an open door dicing.' As in Matthew 27:35, *casting lots*, but not as yet for the garments; they are casting lots (six out of the twelve) for the role of Judas and the pieces of silver. (A profound intuition! Daring, but not unfounded; even Peter denied.)

And of course everywhere the 'wine-skins' and their miracle repudiated.

The very landscape was prophecy – 'but there was no information'!

The difference between the 'Ben Jonson' and the 'Magi'? The one is vision; the other is only allusion.

*

The Classical Simile

> Thus Satan ...
>   in bulk as large ...
> As whom the fables name of monstrous size ...
> Leviathan which God of all his works
> Created hugest that swim the ocean-stream.
> Him, haply, slumbering in the Norway foam,
> The pilot of some small night-foundered skiff
> Deeming some island, oft, as seamen tell,
> With fixèd anchor in his scaly rind,
> Moors by his side under the lee, while night
> Invests the sea, and wishèd morn delays.

The purpose of a simile, as Aristotle early perceived, is to extract similitudes. Two disparate objects are compared one with the other in that they possess some common point or points of resemblance. Satan in bulk as large as Leviathan – once that is stated the co-ordinate logic or the superimposed geometry of the image is achieved. The poet or the rhetorician has made his point, adding, with both logical and spatial pertinence, that this Leviathan was created hugest that swim the ocean stream.

But what, it may be asked, by logicians justly asked, has the Moby Dick incident of the next five lines to do with the matter in hand, namely, Leviathan's proportion. True, he to whom Satan has been compared is himself compared to an island; but of what relevance here the nautical errors, the time of day, the condition of the ship, and the quality of the Leviathanic carapace?

Milton was following the conventions of the epic; the classical simile he borrowed from Homer. But why did Homer, whose narrative is so unmystical in all other respects, affect this diffuse method of comparison?

Can it be that it was because Homer was blind? Is it not a tendency of blind men, conjuring a scene, to seek to dwell upon all its details – nothing is irrelevant – and thus to compensate for the undone fiat of their days? Did Milton – blind man touching blind man – discover for himself these secret rewards of the classical simile?

But Vergil? He merely imitated. He did not find the thing incongruous, nor do I, seeing, find it so. For we are all, in the light of the poetic illumination, a little blind.

Investigate whether such similes appear before Homer.

*

'I don't know much about poetry, but for me it is enough: he reads it so beautifully!'

For me it is not enough. For me, in fact, it is a detail – this beautiful reading – which puts under suspicion the whole estimate of the anonymous bard. *Beautifully!* It is not difficult to imagine him, the ethereal being – for that surely was what the coiner of the adverb implied – as he sits there amidst his innocent admirers, diffidently gesturing his too too solid flesh away. What his audience expects of every poet he knows: to be, if not totally disembodied, at least one-dimensional. Out of this world. Good! He will give them – since that is what they must have to know that they have met a real live poet, a real quasi-live poet, he will give them the insubstantial.

I see him – it is as if I was there, and, in sorry fact, not once but many times have I been there – I see him as he withdraws, almost with a purposeless gesture, the manuscript, distastefully warm, from his bosom pocket. He regards it: that paper should be of such a thickness gross! However ... one lives among *things*. Somehow this paper, nonetheless, has lifted itself to the level appropriate for reading. Directing from behind the veil of his eyelashes a last look at his listeners, he takes his spiritual leave and in a moment is far, far away. He is reading, for his lips seem to be moving; his voice, of a softness that is not on land or sea, barely touches the delicate syllables that frailly slant upon his aspen sheet; his poem is being overheard. No sentences, of course, emerge mundane and comprehensible and crass, but only a flitter of phrase, a white incantation, a slight undulation of air-wave ... Then pause ... Is it a rhetorical pause, or is he really finished? Yes, the glaze is lifted from his eye. He has, indeed, come up for the third time. He is done. Beautifully! ...

*

$x^2 + 2xy + y^2$

Successful is the poetic statement only then when each of its constituent words acquires through juxtaposition a significance equal to at least the square of its value in isolation.

Let *a* and *b* represent any two words in dictionary isolation. It is contended that when juxtaposed $(a + b)$, they do not become poetry unless such juxtaposition effects a raising of their power to $(a + b)^2$; i.e., juxtaposition must give them the value of $a^2 + 2ab + b^2$.

> Will all great Neptune's ocean wash this blood
> Clean from my hand? No, this my hand will rather
> The multitudinous seas incarnadine
> Making the green one red.

The multitudinous seas incarnadine: By itself, *multitudinous* is simply an adjective of indefinite great number. Placed, in the present context, in appositional relation to *seas*, its purpose is not merely that of enumeration without summation; its purpose is also to effect a metamorphosis; the *seas*, it is observed, since they are not seven but multitudinous, are really waves, by their adjective magically magniloquized to oceanic proportions, and perhaps, also, to ochlocratic violence. *a* has at least been squared.

Similarly *incarnadine*, almost a technical term, painter's jargon, a *b* most algebraic, incarnadine is, in this place among these words, enhanced to meaning in the second degree. For it communicates to the reader not merely the notion of colour – any other sanguine word might have hoped to do that – but it vibrates also with the resurrected potency of its elsewhere forgotten etymology: here, amidst flesh murdering and flesh murdered, it is crimson, indeed, but crimson of the flesh. b^2.

And, of course, multitudinous seas incarnadined are more than merely many waters plus a coat of red, and more than merely dashes of red, multiplied; they are a welter of blood. One must mention also, if only to elicit the 2 of the 2ab, the effect of the Latin polysyllables overwhelming between them the monosyllabic *seas* – crests and trough.

Making the green one red. It is as if the poet were now converting his algebra into arithmetic to give us, by way of perorational relaxation, the numerical values of *a* and *b*.

*

The Ballad of Sir Patrick Spens: A Scenario

A throne-room and banqueting hall. Closeup of

> The king sits in Dumferline towne
> Drinking the blood-reid wine:
> 'O whar will I get a guid sailor

To sail this ship of mine?'

Camera moving over faces of guests, finally rest upon

an eldern knicht
Sat at the king's richt kne:
'Sir Patrick Spens is the best sailor,
That sails upon the sea.'

Closeup showing eldern knicht eminently satisfied with his cunning. Fade out. Change to

Sir Patrick Spens
Was walking on the sand.

In distance, horseman, gradually increasing view. Descent of horseman.

The king has written a broad letter
And signed it with his hand.

Closeup to Sir Patrick:

The first line that Sir Patrick red
A loud lauch lauchd he
The next line that Sir Patrick red
The teir blinded his ee.

'O wha is this has done this deid
This ill deid done to me
To send me out this time o' the year
To sail upon the sea!'

Fadeout, and change to Harbour scene:

'Make hast, make hast, my mirry men all
Our guid schip sails the morne.'
'O say ne sae, my master dier
For I fear a deadlie storm.'

Flashback:

'Late, late yestreen I saw the new moone

With the auld moone in her arme.'

Camera, in turn, at a harbor, a forewelling, a ship, a lowering sky, and a crowded deck.

Closeup of Sir Patrick and first mate on forward deck.

'And I feir, I feir, my dear master
  That we will come to harme.'

The high seas. A storm. Closeup of

O our Scots nobles were richt laith
  To weet their cork-heild schoone.

Storm. Empty view of sea. Calm. Closeup of

Their hats they swam aboone.

Return to the harbour:

O lang, lang may their ladies sit
  Wi their fans into their hand,
Or eir they see Sir Patrick Spens
  Come sailing to the land.

Fade out, to the castle-towers of Scotland:

O lang, lang may the ladies stand
  Wi their gold kems in their hair,
Waiting for their ain dier lords
  For they'll see them na mair ...

Fade out, and then final scene, submarine, arranged so as to be reminiscent of Scene 1:

Half oure, half oure to Aberdour
  It's fiftie fathom deep
And thair lies guid Sir Patrick Spens
  Wi the Scots lords at his feet.

*

Is it really a part of speech – this comma? So pregnant with meaning that its insertion in the place ordained for it by its commadore must, of its very self, illuminate the context with significance beyond the reach of mere vocabulary? And of itself so connotative that even its omission from the poetic sentence aches oracular with meaning?

> I speak this poem now with grave and level voice
> In praise of autumn of the far-horn-winding fall
> I praise the flower-barren fields the clouds the tall
> Unanswering branches where the wind makes sullen noise

Thus Archibald MacLeish, in his comma-less period, before his style was inoculated with colons. And it cannot be denied that this designed exclusion of punctuation achieves its effect. The comma, being by definition, a dépassant of speech, its excision is the proper complement to 'the grave and level voice.' Moreover, it is the uncomma'd sentence which provides all the gratifying ambiguities: the far horn is thus sounded in accompaniment both to autumn and to fall. *I praise the flower-barren fields the clouds the tall* – for a fleeting moment the reader imagines that it is the height of clouds that is being praised, but further reading dissipates this tentative illusion to reveal the *tall unanswering branches*. Thus is the mind pleasurably filliped, to vibrate with conjured alternatives. Adjectives do double duty; and this – comma fecit.

With Mr. Cummings, however, it is not the absent comma, but the comma present, – curled and clairvoyant, that is exploited for the poem's sake. Not a mere aid to elocution is intended, but a new integer of speech, the vocable inarticulate.

> O sweet spontaneous
> earth how often have
> the
> doting
>
>   fingers of
> prurient philosophers pinched
> and
> poked
>
> thee
> ,has the naughty thumb
> of science prodded
> thy
>
>   beauty   ,how
> often have religions taken

thee upon their scraggy knees
squeezing and

Certainly it is not to announce a pause that Mr. Cummings dropped that first curlicue where he did; that pause was already achieved by the economy (sic) of his spacing. The thing must have some other function, appearing as it does, not so much *after* a phrase as *before* a new half-sentence. Symbol? The poking finger? The naughty thumb? Then what, it must be asked, is the function of that second comma, standing as it does, a leper's distance from the word *beauty*?

Perhaps it is a new kind of mysticism, the cabala of the printer's devil?

Quaere: Whether, given marks of punctuation as parts of speech, a poem can be written made up entirely of such marks?

Example:

?
:
,   ,
!

Here, in the very first line, a line moreover unencumbered with verbiage, the essential question is put. That question, like most questions, is subject to ambivalences; and we see them, these ambivalences, bandying their schismatics over the fence of a colon. But not everything is as cut and dried as it might appear; often what is perceived as dual is in fact trinitarian. With what subtle innuendo is this triple possibility suggested by the two commas winking at each other! And, indeed, as is clear from the last line, the commas have hit upon it. Basta!

I must admit that I prided myself on this little cherrystone of scratched verse until – until I discovered that it had already been done, and by Mr. Cummings. In Poem 98 of his Collected Verse, I found, alas, these rhetorical lines:

?
??
???

But this, of course, is an entirely different poem.

*

Prose is concerned with denotations; poetry with detonations.

*

A poem complete in itself is a contradiction in terms. Every successful poem involves a talented reader. The effective force of a poem only begins at the moment when its last line has been read. If its effectiveness is completed with the last line, it is not a poem; it is only a rhymed [ ]

*

Of the imitators of Eliot: They write under mesmerism. They compose in their sleep. They have been bitten by the TSE-TSE fly.

*

No one, really, should be impressed by the manner in which things turn out so pat at the end of a novel. If you're God, it's easy.

*

The lunatic, the lover, and the poet
Are of imagination all compact;

Having named the three imaginative types, the poet now proceeds to describe them. In this he may adopt either a progressive or regressive order, going from lunatic to poet, or from poet back to lunatic.

One sees more devils than vast hell can hold.
That is the madman.

The poet finds it necessary to state, explicitly, that is the madman. It is as if he were saying: Not knowing the order which I am to follow, you might have thought that the one who sees more devils than vast hell can hold was the poet; the error is so understandable that I find it necessary explicitly to correct it. That is the madman.

*

To what purpose the writing of verse when the atomic bomb has already achieved the ultimate onomatopoeia – *boom!*

*

Mr. S., the enlightened publisher, really prefers to publish poetry. The linotype costs are smaller.

*

123 'Marginalia'

The poet's strength – Beelzebub's gift:

> that fixed mind
> And high disdain from sense of injured merit.

*

Fiat of metaphor, O silvered glass
Propelling out of the blank and shine of naught
Worlds, satellite similitudes,
The planetary parables.

What is the x of which this world
is metaphor?

*

In the writing of poetry it is not necessary to be sincere. It is necessary only to give the impression of sincerity. To this end, being sincere may help; but it is not sine qua non.

*

Poetry as diplomacy – use Clausewitz's vocabulary.

A poem is made up of words evoked and used for diplomatic effect.

Every poem should have a foreign policy.

Internal structure, of course, affects foreign policy.

The purpose of politics is to bend another's will to your own; the purpose of poetry is to intertwine another's mood with your own.

*

Sonnets – neat, compact, residential – like self-contained cottages. Standard Petrarchan specifications: ground floor – an octave, topped by the sleeping quarters of the sestet. 14 rooms 14. Note the southern exposure of the climactic line. Apply Poetry's Suburbia.

It is no wonder that my contemporaries sneer at the sonnet. It is part of their general antipathy to the bourgeois. To them the sonneteer is the last degradation – a man of property: a promoter of real estate developments.

How much goodlier, O Vers Libre, are thy *tents*?

One must admit that too many sonnets, because of the very needs of their architecture, are conspicuous more by their cloacal gadgets than by their liveableness. Nonetheless, even the nomads must concede that there are sonnets which, like good addresses ...

*

Even Milton was not pure in thought: else why did he write

> Th' enamel'd Arras of the Rainbow wearing

instead of, as he originally wrote,

> Orb'd in a rainbow, and like glories wearing?

*

The purpose of rhyme is to afford the poet the thrill of living dangerously. Trapeze without net.

*

The Proper Eating

Cliché – it is not what a poem says as how it says it which makes the poem. Reaction against verses with a message, the tales that point a moral. Compromise upon verses in which the message is latent in each line, and not tagged as a conclusion.

But can one really divorce form from content? Does the above-referred-to cliché of criticism really state an absolute law?

Imagine a poem, for example, which expressed in ineffable unsurpassable nonpareil ne plus ultra speech, the pleasures of gustation – simple, sensuous, and in places, perhaps, even passionate, such a poem as Shakespeare might have written describing the viands and dainties of an Elizabethan feast, imagine it as couched in divinest language moving from felicity to felicity, and then imagine that its last line reveals that the menu has consisted of – a human body. Cannibalism. The proper eating of mankind is man.

Does, in such case, form still remain pure and untouched by content? Or does not rather the nausea of the ultimate regurgitate back even upon the ne plus ultra felicities?

Obviously it is not an absolute rule. Complete amorality is impossible, even in poetry.

'Towards a Psychoanalysis of G.M. Hopkins: The Art of the Rorschach'

Obviously one must reconcile oneself to the impossibility of the usual techniques of the questionnaire, the hypodermic needle, the couch, the electrodes.

The first objective, therefore, must be to find among the 'remains' of the subject some materials which may have psychological implications. It is conceded that all creative writing has psychological significance; what one is seeking now is something which may substitute for the modes of investigation which the subject's absence renders impossible.

Materials: The poetry
The letters
The notebooks
Some drawings.

A study of the thought-sequences and mental-associations of the subject does not, considering his theme, promise to be very fruitful of results. His ideas are bound together by the usual connectives and nexae of the Catholic mind; when one reads of the Son, the Father and the Holy Ghost are sure to follow.

Nonetheless one cannot escape the impression, as one goes through these pages, that everywhere one is encountering the products of some insidious mental agency. One senses peculiar pattern everywhere. It is as if one were being looked at by a squint-eyed man.

Detailed examination has revealed the pattern. It is ubiquitous. It is the pattern of the Rorschach.

In fact here the Rorschach, instead of being merely a method whereby one may arrive at psychological conclusions, is itself a psychological revelation.

This subject, without being asked, consistently proffers his Rorschachs.

With Hopkins the Rorschach is not a measure, it is the mind.

By a Rorschach mind is meant a mind which rejects, wherever possible, concepts of clear and regular outline; the definite and the circumscribed holds no attractions for it; it considers the design of the Rorschach – blot, blur, and symmetry – as the most satisfying exemplar of beauty.

It is the eyes that usually betray this mental idiosyncrasy. The subject afflicted by (or endowed with) this peculiarity will invariably seek out, for his vision's delight, things which are checkered, frilled, furred, mottled, veined, – things which titillate the forms, which taunt geometry. This must not be understood, however, as a love of the amorphous; always the passion of this mind for the speckled and the numinous is accompanied by an equally strong infatuation with the symmetrical. It is only the bounded, the precise, which is avoided.

Images: Its first manifestation is in the language, the single phrases, the uniformly torn and toothed objects he evokes – things that are 'tatter-tassel-tangled,' life in its 'skeined stained veined variety.' One encounters a 'windpuff bonnet of fawn-froth' and a west that is 'dappled-with-damson.' 'May / Mells blue and snow white through them, a fringe and fray / Of greenery.' It is with 'trickling increment' that God veins violets. The 'mazy sands are all water-wattled.' An elder brother's life is 'love-laced.' The starlit night is full of 'fire-folk,' 'elves eyes,' 'flakedoves.' 'Mankind's medley' is 'seared with trade, bleared, smeared, with toil.' Spring is 'when drop-of-blood-and-foam-dapple-bloom light the orchard apple.'

Epileptics are 'fallers in dreadful frothpits.' Himself he is agitated by 'selfyeast of spirit,' and when he prays 'he puts his lips on pleas / Would brandle adamantine heaven with ride and jar.'

Everything is a Rorschach blot, stained, veined, flaked and frothed.

Akin to the above designs is the design which unwinds from the circular, which, like the psychologist's stain, unfolds to wavering erratic continuations of itself. The world's business is 'all that toil, that coil,' and the world itself 'the ruck and reel which coils and teases single sight.' Spring is the time 'when weeds, *in wheels,* shoot long and lovely and lush.' In a storm, the snow is 'wiry and white-fiery and whirlwind-swivelled.' The grandeur of God flames out 'like shining from shook foil.' The 'stormflakes were scroll-leaved flowers.' When the lark ascends, Hopkins hears 'his rash-fresh re-winded new-skeined score / In crisps of curl off wild winch whirl.' The things that cry: '*What I do is me: for that I came*' are 'like each tucked string tells, each hung bell's / Bow swung finds tongue to fling out broad its name.'

The notebooks, too, contain instances of this tendency: 'Feathery rows of young corn.'

[ ]

The drawings:

[ ]

This list could be augmented; the meaning of this list, made explicit in 'Pied Beauty,' is everywhere. Hopkins' eye (or his mind, or his personality) reduces all things worth commenting on to but one form – the Rorschach blot, the model of internal symmetry frayed with peripheral ambiguity.

The Jesuit sees each thing with a nimbus around it.

The Aesthetic: Nor was Hopkins completely oblivious to the existence of this his predilection. There are two concepts for which he himself has provided definitions which may be treated as the key-words of the aesthetic: *inscape*, and *sake*.

'"Inscape" is any kind of formed or focussed view, any pattern discerned in the natural world' and, says Mr. Austin Warren, 'the prefix seems to imply a contrary, an outer-scape – as if to say that an "inscape" is not mechanically or inertly present, but requires personal action, attention, a seeing and *seeing into*' [ ]; that is to say, the core of the Rorschach blot.

Sake: 'I mean by it the being a thing has outside itself, as a voice by its echo, a face by its reflection, a body by its shadow, a man by his name, fame, or memory, *and also*, that in the thing by virtue of which especially it has this being abroad'; that is to say, the Rorschach blot's spotted ambience.

The inked: and the inklings.

The Prosody: The Sprung Rhythm of Hopkins, too, follows true to the general pattern. It is arrived at, as may be gathered from Hopkins' preface to his poems, by an analysis of Counterpoint Rhythm, 'two rhythms ... in some manner running at once, ... something answerable to counterpoint in music, which is two or more strains of tune going on together.' It is a rhythm which unlike the conventional will not become 'same and tame.' The Rorschach symmetry again, this time rendered in rhythmic terms.

As if to further emphasize the formative design, this Sprung Rhythm, too, has its frills and tassels. 'Remark,' says Hopkins, 'that it is natural in Sprung Rhythm for the lines to be *rove over*, that is for the scanning of each line immediately to take up that of the one before, so that if the first has one or more syllables at its end the other must have so many the less at its beginning; and in fact the scanning runs on without break from the beginning, say, of a stanza *to the end and all the stanza is one long strain, though written in lines asunder.*'

Just like the Rorschach.

'Two licences are natural to Sprung Rhythm. The one is rests, as in music.' (Flecks and whitenesses, as in the folded blot.) 'The other is *hangers* or *outrides*, that is, one, two, or three slack syllables added to a foot and not counting in the nominal scanning. They are so called because they seem to hang below the line or ride forward or backward from it in another dimension than the line itself.'

The Rhymes: These, too, much to the consternation of Dr. Bridges, are occasionally achieved by folding over.

She drove in the dark to *leeward,*
She struck – not a reef or a rock
But the combs of a smother of sand: night *drew her*
*D*ead to the Kentish Knock.

or

A bugler boy from barrack (it is over the hill
There) – boy bugler, born, he tells me, of *Irish*
Mother to an English *sire* (*he*
*Sh*ares their best gifts surely, fall how things will).

Assonance: For the purposes of the equation being established, assonance may be considered as a duplication on the left side of the blot of the sound heard on the right. It is the same sound but being in a changed place, a sound somewhat, but only somewhat, different.

Rhetorical and Syntactical Devices: Here, too, that which is most unusual in Hopkins' work is the result of the Rorschach obsession. Probably the most infrequent rhetorical device in English is the *tmesis;* certainly it appears much more native to the Latin tongue: *Saxo cere- comminuit -brum.* But Hopkins appropriates it and writes 'brim, in a flash, ful' for 'brimful in a flash,' and 'wind- lilylocks -laced' for 'windlaced lilylocks.' The Rorschach is the tmesis of the visual.

Similarly Hopkins cultivates aposiopesis:

But how shall I ... make me room there:
Reach me a ... Fancy, come faster –
Strike you the sight of it? look at it loom there,
Thing that she ...

The uncomplete and unfortellable design!

Even his audacity with the possessives of speech is of a piece – frill upon frill, mark dwindling to lesser mark itself mark-dwindled, e.g., the longest genitive in the language:

Our hearts' charity's hearth's fire, our thoughts' chivalry's throng's Lord.

The Biography: The contrast, if contrast, between Hopkins the Jesuit and Hopkins the poet has been noted by all of his biographers. Ascetic in life, he is almost sybaritic in his love of the lush, the rich, the sensuous. Some even go so far as to say that the ambivalence of his character further exemplified itself in his homosexuality. The Rorschach of the flesh.

But here I have been concerned only with Hopkins' art.

Untitled Novel

CHAPTER ONE: HAPAXLEGOMENON

The voice of God pronouncing the commandments was an especially created voice. – Philo of Alexandria

Hapaxlegomenon!

The man articulated it, syllable by syllable, as if it were some mystic incantation; and Pimontel knew then that his decision had been made for him, that the word, the crossroad omen, which thrice in the past had augured a turning point in his life had again presented itself to announce, through its vocables of mingled harshness and fluidity, some new and as yet enigmatic advent.

This sense of premonition, he assured himself, he could justly entertain. He had come a long way – had he not? – from his mother's interpretations of signs and portents: *The cat is washing herself, we will have guests! The dream was of water – that means life! The pregnant belly is not rounded, it will be a boy!* and it was with pride that he thought of himself as the rational animal immune to the blandishments of coincidence. Yet the fact that the man should evoke at this particular point this particular word seemed to him to have some cabbalistic significance. Through his mind there echoed the various occasions when the word had brought to him its esoteric message:

... He was in the Bible class of the Kerem Israel Talmud Torah, the class of the twelve-year-olds. It was Sunday morning, and the venerable Rabbi Glazer, followed by a retinue of school trustees, scholars, men busy in the communal interest, has come from his sacred preoccupations as head of the rabbinate to give ear to the sucklings of Torah. Mr. Herscovitch, the teacher, is very excited; his thin home-made cigarette, set between the hairs of his beard and his mustache, glows bright, like Moses' bush. Burnt down, he drops it to the floor and stamps it down, wisp of tobacco and leprous stain of ricepaper. Mr. Herscovitch finds the presence of the honoured company extremely disturbing; he keeps moving his skullcap back and forth over his head; he smiles, ingratiating; he is apologetic; and, finally, he proceeds with the text in Genesis. The word *tzohorayim* is reached.

'Is there any boy here who can tell us why *tzohorayim* means noon?'

It is Rabbi Glazer himself who puts the question. The worthies who have escorted him smile benignly one to the other. Even Mr. Nathan Gordon, the distinguished lawyer of whom it is said that he is 'learned in the jots and tittles' and that it is this very erudition which has made him the brilliant jurisconsult that he is – all gentiles, it seemed, were foredoomed before so irresistible a Talmudist – even he appears to be impressed. A good question: one will see whether the little heads are of the true line, whether the apples do indeed fall not far from the tree.

There is silence. Some of the boys demonstratively knit their brows in concentration. Suddenly the boy recently arrived from Europe – he enjoys in Holy Writ, therefore, an unfair advantage – is waving his hand frantically. His palmful of knowledge will not be contained.

'From *tzoroh* – trouble? Because at noon it is very hot?'

From the expression on the faces of the elders it is clear that the answer is wrong. The immigrant boy falls back crestfallen ...

And he – Pimontel remembered this distinctly – he had rejoiced at his rival's discomfiture; so early had displayed itself his avidity for intellectual pre-eminence, his corrupting cursed pride of mind. But no one had noticed it then, not that day in the classroom; later, a year later, his father was to suspect it, as he did that Simchas Torah when his son, in the arrogant piety of his confirmed thirteen years, had come home, after having visited five synagogues in each of which he had been accorded an aliyah *and* the ritual glass of wine, and in his drunkenness and with a very wide gesture had declared to his father that he, Wolf the son of Kalman, designate Pimontel, was the Messiah. He could not but smile at his father's response to this annunciation. 'Yenta,' he had said, addressing his wife, 'give him a sour pickle, and let him go to bed!' ... He remembered, too, how then, as for many years later, the very name of his mother had been an affront to his sense of dignity – Yenta, the name of a chattering argumentative virago of a shrew – and he, the son of! It had been – such was his obsession with words, names, designations, and the aura which hovered about them – intolerable; intolerable until he had discovered that the name came ultimately from Ianthe, a classic personage!

[ ]

His mind reverted back to philology in the Kerem Israel where Mr. Gordon was asserting that this last had been a good try, but that in *tzoroh* the *hai* followed the *resh*, while in *tzohorayim* it was the other way round. This, then, was the clew: one must look for a word in which the *hai* was before the *resh*. *Tza'ar*? No, that was with an *ayin*. *Tzir*? That was with a *yud*. Ah, *tzohar*!

He was a young boy again, raising his hand in triumph.

'From *tzohar* – a window. Because at noon it is very bright.'

The countenances of the old men light up like shining fenestrations.

'And how do you know that *tzohar* is a window?'

'Because it is written: [ ]

They glow with racial pride, these elders, looking down at the shoots and sproutings in their garden. Rabbi Glazer advances and strokes affectionately the prodigy's cheek. Mr. Gordon, too, praises an ingenious derivation, nor can he resist an excursus of his own. There are other words, he says, which might have been adduced: *zohar*, splendor, *sohar*, the moon; and in Mr. Herscovitch's Pentateuch he seeks examples. The boy's mind wanders off in a rumination of possible English parallels – window, noon-do, moon-dawn – while Mr. Gordon continues to wet his finger to turn the pages to find the quotation to show the hues and uses of the chatoyant word.

'But who' – exclaims the lawyer suddenly, interrupting his spittled researches, his finger in mid air – 'who will give me the derivation of *apiryon*? ... And what does the word mean?'

The sounds sound familiar, but no one is able to identify their origin. There is a depressing silence. Mr. Herscovitch frowns.

'Does nobody remember,' Mr. Gordon hints, 'King Solomon's *apiryon*?'

One of the older boys snickers.

'From the *Song of Songs*?'

The *Song of Songs*? This he, Pimontel, knows. Does he not recite it every Friday night, in the company of his father, to usher in the queenly Sabbath? *Apiryon*. Of course he remembers it, he always stopped at it, it reminded him every time of Apollo. Murmuring to himself the introductory verses, he at last recites out loud:

'King Solomon made himself an apiryon of the wood of Lebanon. He made the pillars thereof of silver, the bottom thereof of gold, the covering of it of purple, the midst thereof paved with love, for the daughters of Jerusalem.'

'Very good! Very good!' Mr. Gordon praises. 'Now what is an *apiryon*?' He pauses. 'But the question isn't really fair. Nobody knows for certain. Some translate it a chariot, others a palanquin, others [ ]. And there is no derivation. *Apiryon* belongs to that class of words in the Scriptures known as *millot bodedot*. Isolated words. Lonesome words. They occur but once in the whole Torah, and are related to no other word. In English, or rather in Greek, they are called hapaxlegomena, words of single occurrence. Once, only once, do they appear in the Bible, and then are not heard from again ...'

The scene faded from his mind, Mr. Gordon's haunting voice melted away like the ghost that it was, the circle of beards faded slowly as into the general smokiness of some rembrandtesque painting. Throughout the years he had remembered that word, and remembered also, sometimes with pride and often with embarrassment, the use which Rabbi Glazer that day had made of it. Always there was, the Rabbi had said, in every group, or congregation, or community, some one person who, too, might be called a hapaxlegomenon, – a man who for learning, or piety, or good works, was single of his generation. These of mankind were God's especial gems, even as were gem-like the unique words set in the crown of Torah. Towards such singularity to strive was a good and meritorious thing; he hoped that in this classroom there was one who was destined for such distinction. And here it was that there had been made personal for Pimontel the reverberating word, for the Rabbi, seeking through flattery to set the boy athirst for Torah, had then turned his homily about the bright answers that Pimontel had made and had prophesied that if he kept along the path which he seemed to be taking then he might one day be a great one in Israel, a scholar, a rabbi, an eminence of The Law. There were no heights which couldn't be scaled; there had been, indeed, a rabbi who was so holy and wise that his contemporaries had called him Sinai. But to achieve such heights there was required not only God's gift, but also unrelenting application. 'To what do you attribute your genius?' the Gaon of Wilna had been asked; and had replied: 'To my name: *Wil*ner Gaon – do you but will it, and you will be a gaon!'

Perhaps it had been this childhood's unction thus laid to his soul which had persuaded him to study for the rabbinate and had stood beacon for him throughout his journeyings through those territories called by the Talmudists the PRDS of knowledge. Nostalgic warmth stirred him as he recalled the geography of that Paradise – the easy levels of the simple Pshat, the echoing canyons, yclept Remez, echoing with hieratic innuendo, the lofty altitudes of homiletic Drash, and Soid's mysterious thickets, with sacred whispers sibilant. That he had liked; the journey, certainly, had been to his taste; but the destination – it was not long before he realized that the rabbinic office was not for him. He did not have the vocation. The rabbinic discipline appealed to his mind, but his spirit revolted at it; they were too many and too onerous, the prohibitions and behests heaped upon the man who would be religious mentor to his people. The fact was that he was not good enough, not godly enough, not godly at all. Worldly doctrine, moreover, had come to seduce him away from the arbitrary rigors of tradition.

It had been at about this time – his zeal for ordination abated, he was following now a course in Arts at McGill – that he had begun his at first careless and later systematic breaking, not of The Commandments (God forbid!), but of those proliferative other unthundered precepts of the Law. He had begun to desist from the putting on of phylacteries; to fail in attendance at synagogue, both on week-days and on the Sabbath; to interject cynicisms between the exclamations that punctuated his mother's narratives touching the wonders and works of wonder-working rabbis; to praise, in his father's presence, the wisdom of gentile sages; to question, mock-innocently, the wherefore of certain biblic laws, such as those of the red heifer and of the ordeal of the woman suspect in adultery; respectfully to sneer, to quote enigmatically, ironically to perform ... in a word, to kick and buck like a Jeshurun waxed fat.

The whole thing had come to a head, and the full extent of his relapse had been revealed, that day when his mother had discovered him sitting over his books, *bare-headed*! Shocked at such heathen nudity she had reprimanded him, had spoken of her shame before God and gentry, had knit and bent her fingers backwards in gestures of despair and humiliation; and it was when he had tried to remonstrate with her, tried with texts blasphemously rendered to joke away his offence, that her anger had summed up, in a phrase, the full abomination of his impiety. 'Liver-and-sourmilk!' she had shouted at him. 'That's what you are! Each a good by itself, but together a sickening, disgusting, trefah combination! Worldly knowledge – of course that's good; and Torah – of course and of course; but put them together, mix them up, and what do you get? Scoffing and unworthiness and a teasing of God – Oh, may the Heavenly One forgive us!'

Yet most earnestly had he desired to serve at the altar. His religion, he had realized, was no longer his mother's religion, with its tabus and superstitions, its cherishing of bottles of healing holy water sold by saints, its hanging of talismans in the rooms of parturitive women, its tearing of grass from graveyards, its shun-me scarecrows and its kiss-me fetishes; but still it was something which to him was valid, important. He wanted, even now, to justify – perhaps in a secular way? – the high hopes that Rabbi Glazer had entertained for him, to fulfil through a variant thereof the prophecy with which he had blessed him.

And a way had indeed suggested itself: it would be with words, themselves a kind of deed, that he would serve his Author. With little verbal fiats of his own would he pay his tribute to him Who had uttered the fiat, first and all-creative. Yet, while he had toyed with the notion – wordship and worship, – who praises, prays – the realization of the brazenness of his impulse frightened him, and he had accordingly modified and restrained his resolve. Not fiats would he issue, – that was for the truly God-inspired, the chosen doves murmuring beneath the wings of the Shechinah – but only their echoes. He would English the sanctities of the Hebrew poets of the post-exilic era.

It had been a wonderful year, that year, with its savouring of the vocabularies of the mediaevalists – this word is allusive, and, ah, this is neologism – and its palatal search for the equating English style: a wine-taster's holiday. But that had been only part of the experience; his had been also a kind of service in the Temple, the lamentations of the elegists of Fez and Kairuwan providing the burnt-offerings, the rhymes of the Andalusians an incense sweet to the nostrils of God, and the hereditary poets of the Kalonymos clan a priestly line of succession. In Toledo, at Rome, in Mayence, they stood on their far-flung stances, these Levites in exile, singing the Lord's song. And he, like some prodigal returned from the north, had stood in their midst, bringing back the echoes that their words had made against his Canadian forests and the resonant rock of his mountains.

Not an easy task had it been, but a ceaseless unrelenting struggle: again and again they stood in opposed deadlock, the intransigent Hebrew meaning, the Saxon syllables aloof and unaccommodating. But the struggle had not been without its own reward, for it had been a wrestling with an angel. And though foredoomed to defeat, who would not wrestle with an angel? One stood, surely, in danger of the thigh-bone wrenched, but what blisses, what nonpareil felicities there were in such grapplings and embraces! O the sweet odour of the beating wing! The ineffable musk of the angelic sweat!

At last it had been published. With a not disinterested tolerance Pimontel recalled the pride with which he had considered his own virtuosity. So as to communicate the archaic flavour of the original Hebrew, Halevi he had translated into Chaucerian English; Alharizi's poem – the one in which every line begins with the letter Resh – he had Englished into a rumble of recurrent r's; he had imitated the couplet of the rhyming homonyms; he had reproduced acrostics, horizontal, vertical, and transversal; and for the purpose of communicating to the gentiles some feeling for the language which had no vowel letters, but only vowel pointillation, he had boldly made use (but only in one rendering) of a disemvowelled prose – he could not but smile now at the splutter with which the Psalmist, quoted in one of the pieces, had issued from his pen: Fr thr is no fthflnss in thr mth; thr inwrd prt is vry wickdnss; thr thrt is an opn splchr.

And he had waited – temeritously, he now realized – for the reviews.

The Hebrew press had altogether ignored the book; it had the originals. Most of the English literary journals, not able to make head or tail of these biblic macaronics, this procession of dainty-stepping gazelles and hinds, these invocations – in several dialects – to an all-comprehending deity, had contented themselves with a simple acknowledgment among their BOOKS RECEIVED. Only one reviewer had condescended to expatiate upon the book, but the consolatory length of his essay was somewhat vitiated by his declared refusal to believe that they were translations which he had before him. He could not imagine, he had asseverated, that these 'renderings' really had had originals. Throughout the review, therefore, he had persisted in treating the poems as experiments – as the perpetration of a hoax: modern poetry disguised in an exotic mediaevalism – and had accordingly condemned the book as a horrible example of the two tendencies which were corrupting *our* literature – the tendency to Semitize which had begun with Milton's deplorable orientalisms, and the altogether modern tendency to subject words to plastic surgery. The translation of one of the poems had required the 'rendering' of the names of the Hebrew letters so as to constitute an alphabet of affectionate diminutives: alephule, bettikin, gimlet ... iotajot, tessitittle, memimum, nunnicle, paipetit, and so on – and this series the reviewer had adduced as an illustration of the both tendencies exemplified in a single stanza. Then he had continued:

'We EXPOUND. We will not say that poetry of this kind, whether admitting its authorship, or hiding behind non-existent originals, ought not to be written. Only that it ought not to be read! We are not opposed to forgeries. *Cf.* Chatterton, Mangan. But we do not – positively – want Yidgin English! Such a book as Pimontel's may perhaps be allowed – once! Once – and *basta!*'

So there it had come again, the *hapaxlegomenon,* this time wearing dagger and Italian cloak. Meekly had he taken it, then, as an omen, auguring change of vocation. The Hebrews would not read him, the gentiles could not understand him.

There must be in the Jew, Pimontel reflected, some hereditary instinct towards legislation (wasn't the Torah the Law?), some atavism of the Mosaic, for how otherwise could he account for his decision, made at this point, to qualify for the Bar? He could not serve at the altar between men and God? He would serve, then, in the courtroom between men and men. That, too, would be a sacred service. The hard rock of jurisprudence would he strike, and the fresh and liquid crystal of the prophets would flow forth!... He had long ago realized his naiveté. That law and justice were not things synonymous was the truism of old wives; but how life conspired always to prove its truisms true! The heart said one thing, the code as a rule echoed it, and then, when these sounds were coursed through a courtroom – with circumstance distorting them, and the human voice recording them in prejudiced fortissimo, in self-protective pianissimo, how strange, how unrecognizable, the original high principle issued! Through the decade of his practise Pimontel had gradually learned that justice was never really blind, but only astigmatic; that litigation was of the act of war rather than of the abstract science of spiritual truth; and that judges were humans permitted divinely to err. He had learned, above all, that his function, not sacred, was pre-eminently secular, and of the world, worldly.

And here, too, there had interposed a series of events which had proclaimed his unfitness for the trade. It had taken place but four years ago when he had brought to court, one after the other, a number of important cases, convinced that in each of them his client's cause would irresistibly prevail. For each of these cases fell, he had been sure, foursquare within the provisions of some definite and inescapable paragraph of the Code Napoleon; the judge, no matter how recalcitrant or obtuse, could not avoid – he was convinced – giving him favourable judgment; the judge would have before him an ineluctable equation, and all he would have to do would be to write down the answer. Yet in each instance he had been frustrated by means of the same device; in each instance the judge, obviously embarrassed by the dogmatism of the code, had freed himself from its strictures with the same cliché of escape. For each judgment had in it the same devastating *considérant*: attorney for plaintiff was right as a matter of principle, but – but the case before the court offered a special set of circumstances – here there had followed some pseudo-subtle nugatory distinction – it was *sui generis*, unique, it was a *cause d'espèce*.

The phrase, Pimontel reflected bitterly, had had a familiar ring; and had seemed to enjoin once more a change of climate. If his cases were so frequently to be dubbed *causes d'espèce*, and were to be subjected, therefore, to one man's arbitrary discretion, and that man, being human, a weathervane rotated by meteorological conditions he couldn't even surmise, let alone control – then he might as well give up, or play the horses, or, relying on the law's glorious incertitude, take only cases that seemed to him to be bad.

It had been out of the dismissal of his last case that an opportunity for a new vocation had presented itself. This had been an action in damages directed against certain officers of the *Sûreté Provinciale* who had unjustly arrested, fingerprinted, and held in detention a suspect against whom no further legal proof had been forthcoming; and although Pimontel had been defeated in his attempt, he had succeeded, in the course of protracted litigation, in establishing a kind of friendship with the head of the detective bureau who seemed to have been impressed by his conduct of the affair. The usual malice engendered against an opponent had failed, indeed, to make its appearance, for the detectives, for some reason, perhaps the natural courage of righteousness, seemed never to stand in fear of losing their case. Just the same, Pimontel had been somewhat surprised when, at the termination of the case, the captain of detectives had asked him to join the force – in a capacity, of course, worthy of his talents – the department needed a Jew, and he felt sure that he would make a success of criminal investigation. Pimontel, for his part, had been ready for a change; nor can it be said that he had not again deluded himself – his irrepressible sacerdotal passion rising to the fore once more – into believing that the detection of crime, too, was a priestly office involving the daily asseveration of right order and the administrative implementation of the will of God.

There had followed, then, three years of a most fascinating discipline. It had been like Torah and like Talmud – like Torah for its enunciation in practise of the basic laws, like Talmud for its involvements and unravellings. He became proficient in the hermeneutics of bullets, expert in exegesizing from its effects a poison, and like the veriest Talmudist in the building up from the mere straw of a clew the cities of Pithom and of Rameses. His especial forte, it had soon turned out, was organization, and time and again had he been called upon to direct investigations where he stood, like some master-commentator, compiling and comparing the reports and commentaries of his various sleuths.

It had been an experience completely exhilarating – for the brain, not for the soul. (He never used the word, he only thought it.) For it had soon become clear to him that no matter what his own predilections were, the Department never, never got itself exercised over the moral principles involved in any matter under its attention. That sense of outrage at iniquity rampant, which to Pimontel had seemed of the essence, was here entirely absent. It was all a game: an incident took place marked by certain elements known and unknown. Problem: Find the unknown. The unknown, of course, was the particular incident's author. Find him, then proceed to the next problem. It was a sport, and the members of the force, in their various categories, were but Nimrods of a greater and lesser aptitude in hunting.

And into this discontent had it been that the man had come with his oracular word and his ceaseless persuasion. Caught in a trance of introspection, self-hypnotized with reminiscence, it was as through a mist that Pimontel could hear the man continuing with his argument. Though he tried now and again to concentrate upon the words which the man was uttering and which he heard as from a great distance, he could not, he could not escape from the narcissism of autobiography into which the mystic syllables had induced him. It was only when the man repeated it again that the spell having come full circle seemed to have been broken. Now he heard him; he was back now in the midst of dialogue, and the man was speaking: 'This is no mean assignment,' he was saying, 'that I ask you to undertake. I am asking you only' – the man put a very flattering irony into his pronunciations – 'only to step into History. That's all. There aren't many we could ask to undertake this job. We – we trained nobody for it. But you have the knowledge, the experience, and I know that you are with us in our struggle. You must accept! You will be the first of that function in two thousand years! You can't refuse! The first – a great, glorious, unprecedented hapaxlegomenon!'

CHAPTER TWO: ADLOYADA

Mystic as had been the word in which the man had couched his message, equally inscrutable and unannounced had been his coming. Pimontel had not expected that blustering March day when he had driven up from the offices of the Sûreté to the Chevra Thillim Synagogue to attend at the Reading of the Scroll of the Book of Esther that the day would be climaxed with his receiving yet another, a grander, summons and vocation. Like some strange emissary come from an Eastern land, the light shining from his face and his lips trembling with secret tidings, that man had come to him, had touched him on the shoulder and had changed, it would appear, the course of his life and the very texture of his days. But as Pimontel drove through the slush of the Montreal streets, it was only to his father's old synagogue that he was directing himself; of the oases and the groves that unseen reared themselves about him he had neither suspicion nor forecast.

And to the synagogue he had come this day not in any upsurge of piety, but because Purim of all the festivals in the calendar was the one he favoured most. It was his childhood. The High Holy Days, the Days of Awe and Contrition, the Sabbath, and the Sabbath of Sabbaths – these, with their menace and mortifications, lay burdens on his heart; but Purim, the feast of the casting of lots and purparts, feast superlatively festive, feast-day upon which it was of merit to get so topsy-tipsy, so purblind drunk, as not to be able to distinguish (Adloyada!) between Mordecai blessed and Haman execrate (not that anybody did; it was its permissiveness that was so exhilarating); Purim commemorative of the enemy in his purpose frustrated; triumphant Purim, and the ten unspeakable sons of Haman enumerated, as they hung from gallows and purlins and rafters, in one single sibilance decabarbaric; full of gaiety, with its Purim players in mock purfled purpur: Ahasueros, poor royal fool, and perfumed Vashti, and Esther pure and noble, and Mordecai maintaining defiant port against imperious Haman – this was the holiday above all others that called to him, persuasive, peremptory, from the purlieus of his youth.

It may also have been that at the back of his mind he was dimly aware, as one is aware of clamour issuing from deaf-mutes argumentative amidst a hush of fingers, that in the Book of Esther there is no express mention of the name of Providence.

At his entrance into the synagogue, Mr. Joseph, the shamash, friend of his father, Jehovah's ancient, had given him the large and bantering welcome.

'Blessed be the comer! A guest! A guest! Already a long time have not seen – not since your father's yahrzeit – a guest, indeed!... Never mind, it wouldn't hurt you if you ran in, now and again, and snatched a short *Shmoneh Esreh*! Your father – upon him, peace! – your father more than deserved it. Prayer brings rest to the departed soul, lights up a new light in Eden, brings honour to the deceased. See, his friends in Eden say as they see the newly kindled prayer shining about them, see, what a son he has left below!... What's the matter – you're carrying a mad on God?'

'God forbid!'

'So let us see you oftener, and not only on Purim ... After all, moving around all day with the detectives, with cutpurses and cutthroats, it should be a pleasure to come into the clean House of God.'

Pimontel assured him that he was right, and that he would put it on his diary.

As the shamash, with aged faltering steps, led him forward to the eastern wall, Pimontel recognized the place where his father had used to sit when he was yet a little boy, standing at his father's side, following slowly, syllabically, the prayers which the elders about him despatched with such impetuous speed, halted only here and there by some erratic lingering over some favoured or dearly melodious phrase.

While the Jews about him were waiting for the service to begin, and as the congregants congregated and the urchins bearing gragers grew gregarious, small talk was made.

'How different,' said the man with the folded copy of *The Jewish Eagle* – 'how different this Purim is from the Purims – recur they never! – which we have known these past fifteen years! The Megillah, for a change, is a fact, and not a grandmother's story told to taunt us in our misery! The enemies of Israel, thank God, have burst like an abscess, the Nazis lie nine yards under ground, and Hitler – be blotted out his memory and name! – Hitler is ash, and even the worms, that will feed on pig, will not feed on him!'

The perverse-faced Jew beside him – you knew at once as you noted the cynical cast of his countenance that if you would say *day* he would say *night* – interrupted:

'And what about the six million? That's nothing! They don't count, eh? What kind of Purim have they known about? I ask you: insofar as they are concerned, who won, Mordecai or Haman?'

'So why do you come to the reading of the Megillah?'

'I come,' the Jew answered wearily, 'because I come. God knows why. It's a habit, I suppose. Maybe I'm like the Jew who sat through a movie for three shows in a row – he wanted to see how the serial would end ... I come because there's nowhere else to go, because the soul is ever hungry for a piece of consolation, because I think, maybe ... maybe ... But don't tell me, while a great emptiness yawns in our midst, of miracles and salvations.'

'You think then, perhaps, that you are the only one who mourns for the missing, the only lamenter of "the fracture of the daughter of our people." We all mourn. A great calamity has befallen all of us. Not a house is there, anywhere, that has not its losses. Certainly there has been a terrible cutting-off, but think, think what might have been! Like Haman he came "to destroy, to kill, and to cause to perish, all Jews, both young and old, little children and women." That's what he wanted, to wipe us out off the face of the earth, in one wiping, like a teacher a blackboard. Finish! That was his thought – may the brains of all who likewise think trail from their ears and dangle from their sockets! But what did the Almighty one do? At the last minute, when the pride of the oppressor was at its highest, he dashed him to the ground! Dashed him to the ground and saved a remnant. The remnant will yet be for a great people, strong and many!'

'The Remnant! And tell me, now, what is happening to that Remnant? Are they finding a place of refuge? Is Bevin letting them into Palestine? Tell me, tell me!'

'Bevin, too, will have his day. You just leave God's business to God. Don't stand over his shoulder, kibitzing. He has not at all done badly by us. True, there has been suffering and death, things we can't understand, but – when we will, after a hundred and twenty years, appear before the Heavenly Court, we will make our interpellations, have no doubt of it, and we will have the answers. In the meantime, all we know is that, Israel's enemies in despite, Israel exists and persists!'

'Such a persisting for our enemies be it provided! Pitiable Jews, broken, destitute, sick, longing for a resting place in Palestine, wander and vagabond it through country after country, crowd themselves like marinated herring into stinking ships, spit out the green gall before they see the blessed shores – and then, then comes Bevin, catches them like minnows and packs them off for Madagascar or Cyprus. Do you call that –'

'Do you know what I read in the paper?' It was a third Jew interposing to give the altercation a milder tone. 'That Bevin's sick. And do you know what his sickness is? Haemorrhoids!'

Everybody grinned. The man, pleased, continued.

'The reporter who brings the report – the places these reporters can get to is beyond me – this reporter says that it's like the Bible all over again, when the Jews were fighting the Philistines who also wouldn't let them into the land. What happened? The Almighty one intervened. You won't let my Jews sit each one under his fig-tree, each one under his vine? Allright, then *you* won't sit, too. Haemorrhoids. As the psalmist sings: And the Lord smote them in their hinderparts. As it is written: And he smote them with emerods, even Ashdod and the coasts thereof ...'

'But in the meantime,' said the cynic, 'he sits on us.'

'Don't worry,' said the Jew with *The Eagle*, changing his role of polemicist to consoler, 'we'll survive him, too. All of us will yet partake of the messianic feast. The signs of it are everywhere. We have reached such darkness that the only change now due is a change to light. Maybe now it's being prepared somewhere – the great leviathan, couched, scaled, gutted, and splayed, ready to be fried and roasted by a redeemed Israel, and the wild ox, caught in the branches of some tree, waiting for the true blade, blessed and without flaw, to make him fit food upon Messiah's board. Ah, will that be a banquet! And how it will be quaffed that day, the wine cherished and hidden, from Noah's day throughout the ages aging, just for this great day! If we will have years, and we will have merit, we will yet see it!'

'I don't know about Messiah's feast,' said Bevin's diagnostician, 'but I would like to see the day when we could arrange a preliminary banquet, without miracles, to celebrate in our tradition the repeated discomfiture of our foes. I don't know what roast leviathan tastes like, or wild ox, for that matter – the Messiah, it is clear, is no vegetarian – but I have a menu that would be almost as tasty, and certainly as satisfying.'

He waited to be invited to give the details of his wonderful menu. Both the Jew who had watered his mouth with prospect of leviathan-cutlet washed down with old vintage, and the Jew who thought all celebration premature remaining silent, he continued:

'A full-course dinner! Side-dishes, as from the hand of a king: Nebuchadnezzar salad, Seleucid olives. For entrée – Teutonic herring – Bismarcks without heads. Soup – a choice of either a Pobodonostyev borsht or a purée with crouton of matzo. The main dish – the pièce de résistance – meats, of all kinds – auto-da-fé steak, or fatima ishkabob, chicken à la Czar, Golden [....] turkey. No lamb. And rich sauces. And of course Chanuka latkes. Cakes. Braided bread. Haman taschen. And Hitler baigel – as mementos of zero.'

'Mister, you make me to vomit.'

'The Golem'

CHAPTER ONE

On this twenty-second day of the month by the gentiles designated August, in the year by them numbered one thousand six hundred and nine, the which day, after our own true reckoning *anno mundi* is the eighteenth of Elul of the three hundred and sixty-ninth year of the Sixth Millenium, I, Sinai ben Issachar, aforetime scribe, secretary, and amanuensis to the erst deceased and deeply mourned rabbi, the Hohe Rabbi of Prague – O wound still open! – Rabbi Judah ben Bezalel Löw, having in piety and humbleness of spirit prepared myself to the accomplishing of the charge that the great Cabbalist, dying, laid upon me, do now, within the twenty-four hours his soul was exonerated this burdened world, commence the relation of the marvellous strange wonders which he in his lifetime worked.

The hand trembles, the soul shudders at the awesomeness of the task; here is a way full of hazard and peril. For it is not the telling of some simple fable of foxes that has been enjoined upon me, but a narrative touching things human and divine wherein the slightest stumbling may push all other merit over the brink, a word misplaced set holy purpose all to naught, a slip of the pen give Satan, eavesdropper ever-present, occasion again and yet again to open wide his mouth.

I pray the Lord, therefore, that He permit the spirit of my Master and Teacher, whose bidding I now write, ever to rest upon me, so that he may guard me against falsehood, and defend me (the heavens know my heart!) from unintended heresy, and save and warrant me free from all error and taint. May they come to me clear and shining as at the times they happened, the events whereof I write; may I be shielded against the pranks of demons, if any there be that beset my path, that they spill not wantonly my ink, nor cause my thoughts to go astray, nor with midnight scrawlings corrupt my text. May angels, rather, and the heavenly ministers whom once we called down upon the banks of the Moldau, stand sponsor to my *aleph* and my *tau*, my *beth* and *shin*, and may it be given to me, in undimmed recollection and with understanding, so to set forth the high argument of this chronicle that it may serve as a smiting-down to the unbeliever, a hope for the sorely tried, for the froward a lesson, and for those who mourn Zion and other happiness lost a sure and strengthening consolation. *Amen* and *amen*.

And it came to pass, say the Scriptures, ever announcing with this phrase, as our commentators aver, either the imminence of calamity or the advent of salvation – but at what curve of this revolving circle, this coming and passing and coming again, at what tangent shall I snatch? Where shall I cry *bereshith, in principio, thus in the beginning it was*? I envy, against all our custom, the calligraphists of the gentiles who herald their texts with the initial ornate, some single letter in the curlecues and branchings whereof there is already shadowed forth, not only the emblem, but almost the whole narrative of the illumined page. There was a scribe out of Hibernia whose leaf I saw once at Tergesta – the script was from Genesis, the chapter beginning, *Sed et serpens*. How cunningly colubrine that S was shaped, sinuous, undulant, nowed, the subtlety of the old serpent symbol'd in every spiral and twist of that sigmoidal letter! And within its daedalian convolutions, about its rampant head and sleek ophidian tail, how helplessly was caught our Mother Eve! Surely in that coloured letter, with its rings of gold and gorgets of minium, the third chapter entire found its likeness and similitude! With what image, then, shall I adorn my own first letter of exordium?

I think that were I to discard the mark with which my friends the Soncinos – may their publications flourish! – give key to their press (those two rabbits couchant within the hollows of their consonants), it were, alas, with the miniature representation of some charnel house, a cemetery's slanting perspectives, that I would darken that first informing majuscule. I would mean thus to signify that it is not only over this my present writing that there lean the tombstones of Prague's hallowed acre, but that all of Israel's folk, abiding everywhere in exile, dwell, as it were, in some vast and dismal necropolis. Our very ghettoes, whether in the Saxon, Austriac, or Sarmatic lands, or beyond the Alps, westward and southward, in Francia or the papal states, are boneyards and golgothas whose denizens, though upright still, stand caught in the fixed catalepsy of death.

Go to that crowded field beyond the synagogue and scan the funeral monuments there, their figurings and gestures. Mark the two hands of the Cohen, fingers wide outspread, confirmed forever in his benedictive stance; or the Levite, bearing ewer, his service now eternal; or simple Israelite, his monument graven with the grape, that withers not, nor yet does ripen. Behold, too, that female figure sculpted out of stone; its left hand is raised upward, grasping a carven rose: beneath in an unceasing nuptiality there lies a virgin bride. Grey and weather-beaten stands the cemetery stone, as if it were an autumn mist that froze. All here is caught as in a trance, a trance for which the magic quickening word has been forgotten.

Now turn, return beyond the lych-gate, and through the alleys of the Judenstadt wend your way. Here life dons its vivid semblances, yet is it no less a cemetery, here, and in all our captivities wherein we are squandered up and down the world, preserved in life only to taste a bitterer death, since this is a death not assuaged with peace, but a continual turmoil, and panic, and breathing by another's leave.

I would have the sombre pictured letter stand at the head of my writing to yet another purpose: that it be for a notation of memorial to recall to me, like some votive lamp, that it was upon this very day that the great Rabbin, my teacher, was brought to his eternal rest. It was but eight hours ago – how great a darkness has since fallen! – that we bore his last mortal remains from his home to the Altneuschule, the synagogue where he had ministered and taught and raised up three generations of scholarship. The candle flickers on my table, lights up these words, and sets small rainbows in my tears; it is as if I were still beside the coffin before the Ark of the Covenant, where, since he was purity and incorruption, we had brought him for his last summons to Torah.

Still can I hear the opening outcry and lamentation of Rabbi Solomon Lencyz, as from the clenched wrenched heart of Jewry he delivers the funeral oration: 'Weep, weep, O congregation and auditory of Israel, for the Tablets have been broken! Weep, for we have been orphan'd, and left to the mercies of strangers! Cease not from your weeping, for he in whose merit we lived is taken from us! The mighty Rabbi Judah Leib ben Bezalel, the Lion who stood our shield and our protector, is gone – he is no more! Who knows what jackals gather now?'

I hear Rabbi Solomon still as he recounts the virtue of our fallen prince, tells his inexhaustible lore, his inexhaustible devotion to his people, his selflessness. Like pearls of great price upon a golden string, he numbers off the years of Rabbi Löw's life, to each attributing its memorable exploit, to all, even to his four-score and nine. At every one of his remembered intercessions, the people break into a sobbing. The voice of Rabbi Lencyz itself breaks, but, against the constriction in his throat he continues until, suddenly, as he points his quivering index finger upwards in the direction of the synagogue attic – the sealed attic! – he loses himself, seems incoherent, inarticulate:

'... And – *sod sodoth* – arcana of arcana – that which is hidden there!'

I can still see him in that attitude, held to that gesture which transformed into an eloquence the lump in his throat; and see the people hushed now, transfixed as by some fearful recollection, their gaze – the hundreds of rapt faces! – cast upward toward the vaulted ceiling and the attic door. The Rabbi, recovering, moved to another subject; but we knew whereof he had meant, but had not dared, to speak. Now it was a mystery and a darkness, not to be mentioned save by way of allusion, but a time there had been, and many remembered it, when from that attic had come the salvation and illumination of our days.

We bore his coffin through the streets of the Judenstadt. Every house in the ghetto was emptied of its folk, as men, women, and children came out to escort the saintly remains to their last – until the ram's horn blow and raise up all our dead – abiding place. Alas, many who had stood at Rabbi Löw's side in the days of his triumphs and who this day had walked worthy pallbearers to his couch had themselves been called forward. Noting their absence, I imagined them as standing on the yonder side of the Curtain, the Paragud dividing this world from the next, waiting there in a proud expectancy for the soul of their mentor to burst into their presence – a great new light.

There, among the predeceased, I saw, as through a veil, the noble Mordecai Meisel, philanthropist, builder of synagogues, magnate of wealth so great that men averred he had stored enough to go unhungry until the coming of the Messiah, the incomparable Meisel, who, despite his ventations of fury, a by-word in his day, had ever given the Rabbi the full strength of his temporal arm; there, attendant, I imagined also the unknown itinerant from Cyprus, he who had first winked and hinted the Rabbi to his redeeming purpose, and from whom, these seventeen years, we had received no intelligence; there, too,

[ ]

Without them, but surely towards them, the procession wound its way along the narrow cobbled streets to the cemetery gates. Upon the terraces mounting towards the Hradčany Castle, the citizens of Prague had stationed themselves to watch from a distance the moving, wailing concourse. Here and there, dangling their legs from rooftops, or perched upon gables, the small children of mischief mocked the alien obsequies, but they were soon reprimanded and hushed: their elders remembered the magus of the Jews. Whether it was fear, or a strange veneration, or some spirit confounding in their minds the image of the deceased rabbi with the images of the Patriarchs painted on the walls of their churches, I do not know, but awed and respectful they were; I think I saw them doff their caps. It is also possible that I heard the bells of the church of St. Vitus tolling, as it were, a muffled peal of sympathy; but to assert this positively I can not.

Eleven successions of Jewry lie interred in the one acre of the Prague cemetery. Into ghettoes huddled while living, we are begrudged also the room of death, and must needs in depth bury our kin, grave upon grave, man upon man. They sink into the earth, the triple and quadruple tenements of our last home, they lie heavy one upon the other, the disrespected corpses of our folk. Deeper, descend deeper, even into the bowels of the earth, says the evil edict, forbidding us the last bed's privacy. Even our tombstones shuffle and elbow one another, lean each upon another, and, often, as if stirred and troubled by the uneasy throngs below, fall to the ground.

But our dearly cherished, dearly beloved Rabbi, him we buried in a plot all his own. Come the day of the Messiah, and his would be the body to stand up resurrected first, his congregation, flinging boards apart, pressing at his heels, climbing up and sallying forth – the four-tombed earth about them no heavier than a puff of dust!

The coffin was lowered into the grave. The earth was thrown back, clod upon clod, the world's last stones flung against him. Then was the voice of the cantor lifted in lament: *El Moleh Rachmim*, O Lord, Full of Compassion. The cantor's words, his syllables, – our breath, too, supported them on the trembling air, and they were as a shivering levitation to raise the soul of the departed one, higher and yet still higher, mounting, ascending, soaring, until at last we seemed to hear, as one hears the encounter of winds, the coming-together of the soul and the sweet Shechinah's wings!

Yesterday he was alive and spoke to us. To the very last pulsebeat, his eye remained clear, his brain quick. We stood, a ward about his bed, and our hearts within us ached to see that height and tallness of his – for from his shoulders and upward he was higher than any of the people – now stretched helpless upon the couch from which he would not rise. A fever, like some seraph's shadow, flushed blue upon his brow. He, too, knew that his hour had come.

We stood silent. As he stared into space, his eyes bluer with remote vision, we were at a loss to guess whether his mind was fixed upon some high event of the past or reigned already in the midst of the goodly company that surely was hereafter to be his lot and portion. At last, he spoke, as if to himself:

'Did I do right? Did I do wrong when I summoned him from out of chaos?' He lay there, meditative. 'Was it an audacity as shameful as that of the generation of Babel, or an intervention – God forgive me the comparison! – worthy of Elijah?... To-day I do not know. Once I thought I knew.'

His words were precious to us, and we would not interrupt him. As if to answer our unspoken query, he continued:

'To speak the Unutterable Name! And for what? What did I change thereby?... I crawl to the Gate of Judgment, and my cause is unprepared.'

We approached closer to his bed, and one of us addressed him:

'Rabbi, Rabbi, do not speak like that. You will be with us yet for many years to come. We need you. We cannot live without you. This will pass. It is a fever, and it will pass. You will see, Rabbi, you will celebrate the New Year with us.'

He lifted up his eyes, and looked at us directly, as if to say: Never before did they try to deceive me, but now, when I am eighty-nine and at death's door, they commence deception.

'I do not fear death,' he said. 'It is what I have done with my life that I fear.'

Come, world, and see: the saint on his death-bed, whom the speck invisible terrifies!

'For a rending doubt tears me. Now, when only certainties should make up my baggage, a great doubt assails me.' He seemed to weigh it. 'Would it not have been better, altogether better, had I allowed the Lord's occasions to take their intended course? Was it not an evidence of lack of faith in God's conduct of the world, on my part an arrogance, a stiff-neckedness, to seek to prevent His will with my vain mediations?' He paused, and then returned to his remorse. 'And for such daily purpose to use the Ineffable Name!'

'But thereby, Rabbi, you brought us a deliverance!'

Ceasing his introspections, he now spoke directly to us. 'And thereafter? Have you forgotten what happened after that – that deliverance? I have not forgotten.'

'That, too, was remedied ... And is now the time to –'

'Now is the time, and always is the time. For this is the one controversy that from the days of the Tannaim rages across the centuries: In the accounting of heaven, which of the two prevails, the intention or the act? The Lord is my witness that my intention was ever pure; but, see, to what a pass it has brought us!... Intention or act: it is too late for me now to resolve it. Only at the Lord's footstool shall I find the answer.'

He fell silent again. His disciples, we refrained then from molesting him with protestations he would not believe. Suddenly he roused himself, and, addressing himself to me – to me! – he said:

'For the old Rabbi Löw it is too late. But you, my faithful servitor, Sinai, you who were with me through all these happenings, you I command! Write it down in a book, all, as you saw it!... Scribe, write it down! Add not, nor diminish therefrom, but tell, according to your lights.' He dropped his hand upon the coverlet. His wrist, sheer-skinned, veined, quivered. He several times nodded his head, as if in asseveration.

'But, Master' – the commission appalled me – 'I am in every way unfit for such holy purpose! Who knows better than you, my teacher, my sudden scepticisms, the weakness of my spirit, the infection that is in me from the schools of the gentiles? In my heart I will mean to write righteousness; I will think to have written it; and, behold, it is blasphemy ... Rabbi, not I am the one to unseal the attic and its mystery.'

Rabbi Löw smiled. It was like a patting on the head.

'My son, it is precisely such a one as you whom I would have. A waverer, you call yourself? So much the better. This is not a theme to be unfolded by the fixed fanatic mind. A little of the leaven – that is what is needful – to silence the mouths of the unbelieving. Sweetness from the lion's sweated fell. The truth will issue from the doubt. And' – his look was like a laying on of hands – 'and worse sceptics than you we should not have ...'

'But, Rabbi, I am neither a compiler of tracts, nor a writer of treatises, nor a chronicler. I am a scribe and copyist. How shall I know to select from among the trivial that which is of import, to make choice of sequence, not to confound effects and causes?'

'Follow no other than the rules of your own craft. You know what the rules of the scribe are. You were the one who penned me my dissertation on the laws pertaining to *The Holy Vessels, Mezuzoth, The Powders of the Incense, The Vestments of the Priesthood,* and – *The Writing of Scrolls.* Go over therein the eight rules to be observed by one who copies holy writ. They are rules, it is true, for simple scribe, but they will make you author. For the rest –'

With great effort he shifted in his bed. His breathing was heavy. He was very tired.

As he lay there, serene of countenance, his long white beard curling over his chest, he seemed the figure of resigned content, he seemed like one who calmly weaves together this world's warp to the happier texture of the next.

His lips were moving and, intent, we heard his words:

'I acknowledge unto Thee, O Lord my God and the God of my fathers, that both my restoring and my death are in Thy hands. May it be Thy will to send me a healing complete, yet if my death be fully determined by Thee, in love at Thy hand do I accept it. O may my death be an atonement for ...'

The rest of his prayer was inaudible, for he spoke the words as if to some unseen listener. Only at the end did he summon last strength to declare formally, with scrupulous precision, between gasps, slowly:

'Hear, O Israel, the Lord our God, the Lord is One!'

We heard no further speaking from his lips. We stood about him in silence. One of us smoothed the pillow about his head. We thought that perhaps now he would fall asleep and rise up in the morning, as from a dream. I watched the glory of his beard, its curls and fine white ringlets like the delicate loops about the square inked letters of our scrolls, rising and falling upon his coverlet.

Suddenly, he turned on his side, sighed, and closed his eyes.

Scroll of the Torah consumed in flame!

We rent our garments, we lifted him from his bed to the hard ground, we covered him, and, as we proclaimed blessed the name of Him who giveth and taketh away; we wept.

CHAPTER TWO

Though it was in the ghetto of Cuneo, inland, at the other side of the peninsula, that I first saw the light of day, Venice, whither my father had removed, was to me, from my second year on, the world and all its water. It was as if my father had brought me to some complicated toy, some glittering construct, gift of a mariner, tied in a ribbon of silver.

Here, the years of my childhood, like some iridescence of blown glass, had tumbled and preened themselves beneath the changing sun. Here, when young, I sat by the wharf of the *Giudecca*, and Venice was a cloud of wonder, a city builded out of foam, pillar'd of shafts of sunlight, – a shimmering vision resting half in the insubstantial air and half in the wavering water.

For hours I watched its horizons, entranced, as if they themselves were made of painted sail. Here, I dreamed conjurations of far-off places; and, because I learned Venice while I learned my Bible, these dreams seemed always to float down the reaches of the sea always to settle at last over the hills of Palestine.

It was a city out of the Scriptures, this Venice, a commentary on all that in the Scriptures pertains to the sea; it evoked for me, as I watched the unburdening of the strange cargoes of its galleasses, the apes and peacocks of Holy Writ; its mighty traffic and great navigation, its captains and its pilots, its mariners, its caulkers, its hustle and bustle – this was Tyre restored again; Venice made even the thirty-ninth of Job, that gloomy writer than whom none knew better the ways of waves and water-courses, or the pitchings and rollings of leviathan, or the sweet influence of the Pleiades, it made even those whirlwind verses things local, known, diurnal. I sat by the Grand Canal and it was as that first river that comes out of Eden to compass a land of bdellium and onyx.

Once when I got lost on the Rialto, I caught a glimpse of the Doge, his brocaded robes covering, I was sure, his tail and hooves, his hood suppressing horns, and I thought that parchment face the face of Asmodeus who, with Solomon's seal, had brought into being these castles on these streams. The multitudinous and variegated hues of this maritime fabric dazzled me, and I imagined that Noah's rainbow had been drawn down from the heavens and carved into a city. Wonderful were the mounting coruscating facades of the Venice of my boyhood – I thought some Joshua had blown resurgent trumpets to raise by the sea the walls of this Jericho. And often I suspected that this city was no city at all, but a sorcery, a spell cast upon the waters which some sudden storm would one day shatter.

I moved through these years of my life, happy, without care, every day rich with weather. Nor did I breathe my days empty away, for soon, having acquired the Pentateuch and the Prophets, I was advanced to the study of

Talmud. Venice is a metropolis of learning – are they not treasured abroad, the sacred books marked *Printed in Venezia the Renowned*? – and my father set me at the feet of rabbis the most learned. The Talmud, my father maintained, was the true discourse of our tradition, and, punctilio and proviso, it had been to us an investiture stronger than armour. Its was a lore, moreover, which had also uses profane; for it exercised the mind, and made one sharp. The tractates touching monetary transactions, *The Three Great Gates*, these he especially held to be of a proper apprenticing to business, for they taught one the custom of trade, helped in the interpretation of contracts, and, as commented upon by scholars, rendered one perspicacious to perceive trickery ere yet it was planned. They aided one towards the resolution of ambiguity; they gave one skill to forestall evasion. My father would go on in this way, belauding the shrewdness of the masters of the Talmud, men who, though dedicate to pursuits holy, lost not ever their touch with merchantry.

I betook myself to these studies with zeal and pride. At the same time I attended every day for several hours at my father's manufactory – he was a weaver of silks, employing about forty men of the craft, spinners, throwsters, dyers – and over those years, too, there shines the sheer and shimmer of my youth. I kept my father's ledgers, I conducted, that is to say, I penned, for I wrote a fine hand, his correspondence with our factors and merchants of the Levant; sometimes I oversaw the shuttling of our weavers. But they were the silkworms, in their well-lit rearing chambers, who were my constant delight.

Composers of delicate distich, they were my first *payttanim*, these silkworms. Gilgul and metamorphosis of the winged moth, in the orchards on the mainland, on the leaf of the mulberry, we fed them, coupling thus the earthy and the aerial; we watched their hatchings; we measured their changes; and when, in the fulness of time, their little heads, as each fashioned its cocoon, its stanza, began to whirl, and whirl unceasingly for three days, we uttered benediction. These were, indeed, vermicules of the true inspiration! From the head and inward they wrought; the memory of their several transmigrations entered into their reelings, as with the floss and blaze of filament they breathed forth the raiment of a princess. Then they perished. Like small pharaohs in their sheaths they lay there, until our skilled men, like pious priests, disrobed them, twisting and reeling and weaving and dying the spool of their mummification into something bright and quick.

From these labours we won our sustenance; by God's grace our lives were stablished upon the thread of a worm.

Thus I divided my days between my studies of the Talmud and my duties of commerce. My teachers were the erudites Azriel Bassolo, Hezekiah Galico, and Samuel Archevolto, pedagogues who greatly affected that manner of Talmudic explication which is known, for that it is pepper-sharp, as pilpul. Years later, as increased my appetency towards solid doctrine, I learned to scorn this juggling of sophistries, this tossing about of the quillets and quiddities of our Law, but then I followed in wonder the prestidigitations with which my Masters halved a hair, or brought together in casuistical connexity a passage out of the treatise *Betrothals* with a passage in the treatise *Stripes*, or elenchized into verity a palpable absurd.

My teacher Samuel Archevolto was particularly agile in the formulation of such amazements. Again and again he would take, for my pleasure and the honing of his wit, four far-flung ordinances, each hidden either in a piece of commentary or a Tosfoth, and would found them, like four cornerstones, for the erection of some ingenious syllogistical structure; then he would build, with forced parallels and subtle divagations, story upon specious story, the last topped with two towers of dilemma, and the whole tipped, triangled, and crowned with some conclusion, earlier announced, and now rendered irrefutable: in wonder would I gape at this perfection: then would my teacher, adding virtuosity to virtuosity, point out the fallacy, Here lies a fallacy: with a twist of reason he would withdraw, then, one of the buttresses of our palace of logic: down would it tumble, myself astonished again; whereupon he would add, smiling: But here is the flaw which pronounced our argument fallacious: and back flew the buttress; the structure once more stood. Invariably these illusions of rationality wrung a tribute from me; they also succeeded in sowing in my mind, then unaware of the bursting seed, what was later to grow both thorn and rose, a scepticism of the speculations of reason itself.

It was at this time that there came into my father's service a Jew from Trani, one Isaac Conchico by name. My father, whilst going about on his weekly circuit of charity – my father was syndic of alms – found Conchico in a ward of our public lazaret where, being poor and having fallen sick in our midst, he was being given meat and medicine. To my father he told his tale of woe. He had been a practised weaver, both in his natal city and at Bari; his silk trade, both as to quality and as to profits, had surpassed that of all his competitors; rich, he had himself established foundations for the poor; it had been, in fact, because he had caused to be erected at Trani a synagogue higher than Trani's church that he had brought down upon himself the wrath of the clerics who, having under one pretext or another, amerced away his fortune, had at length incited his expulsion from the Kingdom of Naples. These things were false; the truth was that Conchico had consorted at Bari with persons of low repute, the rabble of its harbour, and that it had been under charge of clipping the coin that he had had to fly the domain. But Conchico's tongue was smooth, his devices cunning, and he easily won my father's sympathy. Trani, moreover, was far away; not until the following year could we test his truth. Recovered from his illness, Conchico was taken into our employ.

I disliked the man. It was not that in the fulness of my eighteen years I was shrewder than my father, but that I thought that my father had succumbed to the man's flattery. Conchico was the flatterer complete. He smiled compliment; it was suavity he sweated; he never thought acquaintance accomplished until he had curled himself beneath your very fingernail. Did my father say that it was pleasant weather, Conchico would drop his jaw, and gape, and look admiration, as if my father, and only my father, and he only in moments of crystalline discernment, ever could have made such a discovery. It was, I suppose, because the flatteries were not directed at me that I was able to sense the harsh musk behind the subtle fume.

It was also apparent to me that Conchico envied my father, envied his skill, his command, his wealth, and, above all, the happiness of his household. His fellow weavers, indeed, reported that he spoke often of my father's good fortune, and spoke so deep from the heart, they said, that it stuck in his throat; he gulped, and it was felt that he could have downed my father, too, with that self-same gulp. Even Conchico's brown copper-coloured beard, the way he plucked at it as he analyzed some matter, the way he held his head askew, disgusted me; the man did not have to speak, he simply struck an attitude, and he was sycophant.

He could not thieve from us, for no money passed through his hands; he contented himself with stealing my father's gestures. This angered me even more, for I did not care to acknowledge two fathers. I decided to speak up, then, against the fawning creature. My father, self-assured, waved me aside. 'He doesn't fool me,' he said, 'the man who will fool me will have to get up early indeed; but he *does* know his business.'

'What business is that?'

My father regarded me, not without pride, much as the apple-tree looks pridefully upon its fallen apple. His son was learning to test all things. But he did not reply.

'Can't you see,' I continued, 'that far from being grateful for what you have done for him, he is eaten up with envy of you?'

'Let him envy. It goes with his wages. Envy is the wealth of the poor.'

'Then he's very rich. And those riches he tries to conceal with his flattery ... He crawls. Nobody crawls unless to some end.'

'He's a silkworm,' said my father, smiling. 'And I do with him as I do with them. Take the silk, and ignore the worm.'

I tried an argument of trade. 'But our commercial secrets – he'll learn them. You are establishing a competitor.'

'What secrets?' My father laughed. 'Where I get my silk? He knows that as well as I. To whom I sell? He can't touch me there. We have dealt with the same silk-merchants, in the same cities, for years. The only secret left to search out is that of the silkworm. That I'd like to know, too.'

Conchico remained, therefore, privy to our affairs. My father, moreover, seemed to have been justified in his trust, qualified though it was. Our business increased, prosperity attended all our ways, my father drove forward as if drawn by a vast moving host of leashed silkworms. We were now trading southward with the cities of the littoral and northwards at the fairs of the Slavs, and when the *Serenissima* made a peace with the Sultan Murad, our merchandise reached also the bazaars of Constantinople. We so moved from strength to strength that my father was now doubling and re-doubling his ventures. With the accomplishment of his next stroke, he stood high in expectation of becoming a magnate of the magnates of Jewry.

I was now eighteen years of age, my city and its custom an open book, the routes of commerce no less familiar than the ocean of the Talmud, and my father thought that I should learn now about the wider world. I was sent, accordingly, abroad to the merchants with whom we traded – there was in especial a saltpetre undertaking which my father desired to set up as a joint adventure – and everywhere I went my father's name – he had not exaggerated – was like a writ current, like a writ sealed with the seal of the mulberry.

At this time, at my father's behest, I began a study of languages, a lore by him held to be as precious as a safe-conduct, and one, moreover, which would serve usefully in our correspondence with foreign parts. Under linguists of experience I perfected my Italian, gathering by the way – since these tongues are kindred – a smattering of the elements of French; Latin I could not speak, but learned to parse; and, little knowing how they would one day serve a holy purpose, I quite disciplined myself to German, a speech altogether unrelated to my own; from a weaver in our employ I picked up some rudiments of Slavic.

I cannot say that I acquired a mastery over these languages; it was only in Hebrew that I was proficient; as for the others, their nouns and verbs and copulae were as the twigs and branches of strange trees which I gathered carefully together, and slowly made into faggots of sentence, and kindled from them in the end some fire and meaning. My studies, moreover, bore yet other fruit, for it was through them that I fell in and became fast friends with Leon da Modena, that sweet plant now grown to a wry culture. We attended upon the same learned instructors and our companionship left upon my mind, whether for good or for evil, indelible imprints. To-day tidings come of him and of his quarrels with the rabbis of Venice, he is proclaimed and damned a heathenish gambler and cardplayer; his enemies descant upon his many vocations; to earn his daily bread, they say, he has already followed twenty-six callings; he is scoffed at, and reviled, and some there are who for his doctrine and his port would outright excommunicate him. I remember him otherwise; I remember him as a youth, the proud grandson of a sire knighted to the Order of the Golden Fleece, gay he was, curious, eager, of swelling appetite; hazard, whether of forbidden learning or of games of chance, ever excited him; a poet, but expert in the mathematic; an orator, but one who rode rhetoric as it were the steed of poetry; both with sword and epigram, a fencer; a literatus; a critic; even (but herein of the grace of King David) a dancer; an expert in chess; an astrologer; a wit – he was then, not the ne'erdowell, but the nonesuch of twenty-six talents. I much admired him.

My admiration of him was so great, in fact, that though I have learned to reject his manner of life as a whole, many of his notions, I fear, still ofttimes trouble me. He it was who introduced me to the erotic poetry of Immanuel of Rome; through him I made acquaintance with many gentiles and their ways; we exchanged confidence one with the other; we clinked canakins together; poetry, the world, wine – these were ours, and, over all, that intoxicating foam, Doubt, wherein the imps of enzyme are always at their revels. To-day, because of what I learned at Prague, I repudiate, I renounce, I abjure those empty and arrogant delights; they were wind, they were vanity; they were shadows that feign to have colour but are only darkness. Still, often when I suspect them least, when I nod, when I slide back to juvenescence, up they come, here they are, the fatuities of my youth. They set an ambush for righteousness, they hang chainlets on the tongue, they crop out in the very midst of piety.

The curiosity and pride of youth – they are vices to make miserable old age. What subjects did we not descant upon in those palmy days – the wicked theories propounded by Machiavelli for the governance of polity and people; the lecherous writings of Pietro Aretino; what makes for beauty in a woman; why the circle is the ideal form; how the people of the earth, when their tongues were confounded, continued the construction of the Tower of Babel with gesture; of concoctions to be made out of manna; of how King Solomon remembered the names and persons of his concubines; of the devices Samson used to reduce his potency, seeing, as the Talmud avers, that his every issue floated both bed and bride away; of the moon and of how it effects neap and high tide in the inlets of the heart; of these matters and of a thousand other themes biblic, talmudic, midrashic; and always, but in especial when our spirits were exalted with wine, would we return to youth's major and most orgulous preoccupation, the search for perfection.

Modena recked not wherein he found this perfection, so long he found it. Alas, we had not yet learned the virtue, the beauty, that may lie in a flaw. We sought then in the worlds of nature and of art our examples of consummate excellence; the stars in their courses, we agreed, afforded model in the highest of perfection impeccable; here were precision, impersonality, scope. Among sublunary things, however, the quest proved ever elusive. The rose, he said, were a perfection, were it not for the thorn. Of animals he held the horse, perhaps because in Venice we seldom saw one, to be, both for grace and symmetry, pattern of its kind. Man was adduced only to be dismissed. His prowess, his virtue, his genius, here possibly perfection might open a gambit.

What, then, was Man's most puissant property – his intelligence? his capacity for good? his capacity for evil? Did not the votaries of the Zohar assert that the *Sitra Achra*, that Other Prompter, old Satan himself, was – he, too! – a servant of the Lord, God's jactitated puppet who misdeemed the strings which held him for a net to cast upon mankind?

At this point Modena would launch upon an inquiry into the pejorative perfections. Ugliness – where could one find its completion, its extremest manifestation? In the lizard? The toad? Or in that inamorata whom Immanuel of Rome described as so unsurpassingly repulsive? I advanced the name of Conchico, who had lately left our service to return to Bari, and whom Modena disliked, but more wittily than I. Modena feigned seriously to entertain this candidacy but in the end dismissed it, for the perfection of Conchico's ugliness, he held, had been marred by the handsome fact of his departure. We returned to pleasanter subjects: what was the supreme vice? what – whose the perfect crime? O, life was for us at its burgeoning best, and all things, the virtues and the vices, were objects for our inquiry, toys for the mind, trifles to be juggled on air, while we stood by, ourselves abiding firm.

There came a day, however, when Evil, which to me had hitherto been but a rumour bruited out of a book, was transformed real and present. A week earlier, my father, Modena's father, Conchico, and myself had overseen the lading of a vessel, fraught with our merchandise and bound for the Levant. To this venture my father's entire fortune had been consigned; he was casting his bread upon the waters, as enjoins Qoheleth, and awaited, after not many days, to have its return ten-fold. Modena's father, too, was of the vessel's enterprise; so much of his wealth, indeed, had been stowed beneath its hatches that he decided to board ship and accompany his cargo to its destination. That was a high-flown and dithering day for us, checking weights and sorts, my father in discourse with the captain, Leon and myself busied with the stevedores, the old Modena at dawn escorted to his quarters there, in prayershawl, phylacteries and frontal, to linger over his morning service, Conchico showing himself learned in bills of lading, wise touching maritime roads, and the Venetian sun glossing our silks with benedictive rays. That was Conchico's last service to us, for on that day it was that he picked some reasonless quarrel with my father – it began with the customary flatteries and before one could repudiate them, they had all changed to recrimination – had received his wage, had pacified his spirit and begged pardon, wished us good fortune, and departed.

We did not work the week thereafter but, eased of the labour of the season, rejoiced our souls. My father attended every day in the synagogue where, after prayers, he joined sumptuously in the debates of the Talmudists. Modena and I spent much time together, he was to repair shortly to Padua where he intended to pursue further studies, and we cherished the hours still remaining to us. Then was ushered in the day of calamity. It was a Friday, late in the afternoon, when, returning home from a convivial rencounter with Modena – it was the last time I was ever to see him – I found my mother sitting on the balcony of our house – on a Friday! – dazed and silent, staring fixedly into the distance. To my greeting, to my inquiries, to my distracted pleadings, she made no answer, she seemed not even to be aware of my presence.

At last she turned to me, murmuring; she sought to move her tongue, noises came from her throat. My mother had lost her speech! The voice that had taught me my first syllables now gurgled and dribbled incoherency! I rushed through the house, seeking the servants. All were gone, except the maid who, too, sat in the kitchen, as if stunned, mumbling: Bad news!... Bad news!... The lady is smitten dumb!...

What bad news?... Where was my father?... Where were the servants?... What had happened?... Had a doctor been called?... The questions stayed not for their answer, and, in truth, it was only with the greatest difficulty and against many torrents of tears that I at last was able to surmise an inkling of what had occurred. A courier had arrived with despatches for my father, my father had hurried out of his study as if mad, had shouted something to my mother, my mother had cried out incredulous *What?... What?...*, my father had answered with a loud and tragic *Yes*, and when my mother wanted to reply, she could not find her tongue, but in an hysteria, babbled and frothed at the mouth. My father had then dashed out of doors, none knew whither. The servants had scattered to look for him.

Leaving my mother with the girl, I joined the search. He was not at the synagogue, he was not to be found at the lazaret, at the harbour we inquired but none had seen him. I bethought me of the peasants on the mainland and their mulberry orchards, and, summoning a gondolier, crossed over. I mounted one of the terraces to the orchards of *il Piccolo*, the little breeder of silkworms who supplied us our greatest weaving, and descried, in the setting sun, his olive-trees that ran as an enclosure about his mulberries.

Knagged and gnarled they stood there, the gouty olives, the knuckles and knobs of their branches rounded smooth, as if calcified, in angular agony stooped over the landscape – figures of hobbled eld, knurred and kinched. And there among them, as if he, too, had become one of them, stood my father, looking out towards the sea.

We returned home where, as my father brought himself by degrees to speak of the courier's tidings, I learned of the catastrophe which had befallen our house. The ship, in whose bottom lay all our fortune, had been seized by pirates!... The old Modena, resisting, had been made, hands free, to walk the plank, the pirates mimicking his Jewish gestures as he floundered in the waters. Those of the crew who had survived the cutlasses had been put in irons. When last seen the black flag was heading south for some corsair's cove, ill-famed for its spewing forth of slaves for the African market. Only one sailor, left for dead under the davits, and there forgotten, had devised escape, lowering, as the watch lay sodden, a boat off the stern, and making his way to Bari.

'To Bari!'

'Yes. The instructions of the captain had been to hug the coast, and this of purpose to avoid such sea-robbers. Yet it was just off the roadstead of Bari that their prize was taken.'

'Bold men!'

'Not so bold, as well-informed. They seemed to know, the man reports, they seemed to know to the last swatch what we carried aboard.'

'Conchico!'

'It could not have happened otherwise.'

'Well,' I said, forsaking that festering name, 'we will begin over again. There are always silkworms.'

'That was my first thought, too. That was why I ran to *il Piccolo* – to save, to salvage, to start over again. But he extends no further credit. And ready monies we have not. We have been ruined ... Your poor mother!...'

We had, in truth, been whelmed and overthrown. My mother dwindled for a while and passed away. (Be an angel's speech her reward in heaven who in her life found knotted up her tongue!) My father, early old, found employment with a dyer, and there eked out his daily needs and the white bread of his Sabbath; and myself, I now leaned upon my writing hand and entered apprentice to a printer in whose establishment I read proofs and for his elect patrons served scrivener and calligraphist.

We had indeed fallen to low estate. Were it not for the holy texts in which I had daily to immerse myself and from which my faltering spirit drew some sustenance, my faith had been altogether unhinged. From my friend Modena, whose loss had been surely as great as mine, I heard nothing, he was now of parts unknown. One day, however, there was brought to the shop a manuscript for setting, it was the property, the messenger said, of a Venetian senator who wished it printed for private circulation among his friends. Its authorship was unknown though some said it was from the quill of Leon da Modena. It was titled *The Perfect Crime*. I read, and as I read, I recognized the turns of his Italian.

> ... The prospect of what he was now about to do exalted him. The mere thought of it was accomplishment. Never before, he knew, had anyone dared such conception and on such a scale; and he, he was now plotting its performance: the perfect crime, the crime to be of scope unprecedented, faultless in act, defying detection.
>
> Already he lingered over the particularities of the grand unparal-

lelled plan. From no one, he reflected with pride, had he copied it; no one had inspired a single of its felicities. Sinister flash and fiat of his own phantasy, it had sprung into being, an essence complete. Nonpareil: down the generations men would marvel at the audacity of the design, at its thoroughness of vastation, at the skill and subtlety with which it would be compassed.

He considered his plan, its style and novelties. It was to be – this was paramount – a crime sans motive; search, pry, investigate, theorize, one would seek in vain to divine its intent, the purpose behind its perpetration. Malice, perhaps, one would suspect; but malice was not a motive; malice might be the consequence of a motive; it could not be a motive, sole and alone. At last – he saw it as the prophet sees the end of days – at last the magistrates and the police, the sages laic and cleric, all who have to do with the maintenance of good order and the suppression of misdeeds, all would find themselves having to hide their nescience behind that sorry fiction: the crime for crime's sake ... A *petitio principii*, a pitiable begging of the question.

And this – afflatus thrilled him, the ichor coursed through his veins – this was itself a prosperity of the first magnitude. How could one ever begin to set the wheels of justice in motion against the unspeakable outrage, when one stood, at its very discovery, nonplussed for the want of wherefore and why? Even before one commenced inquest, one would be baffled, foiled, left twitching at a foxed unravellable skein.

Thus, for certain, was jeopardy forestalled. Yet (he was not without scruples) completely to conceal the crime, to leave no trace thereof, to cover it with a darkness thick and impenetrable and thus ungallantly to deprive contenders of even the first onset of battle, such was a course, after all, which would minish, not magnify, his triumph. Not for him, then, such manoeuvres. No; purposely would he leave, in the wake of the overt act, clews numberless, clews everywhere, footprints, signs manual, a myriad tell-tales of his habitude. The landscape would be full of clews, overflowing with clews, clews clamant, ubiquitous – yet not a soul would read a one of them aright! Helpless would they be to deduce the meaning of these signs and ostents, helpless to name his name and establish his identity!

Nor would he resort to the easy stratagems of the bungling ruffian, the wretched coward who rushed to hide away the corpus delicti, to fling it into a water, or down a limepit, or into a fiery burning furnace. The victims of *his* handiwork would remain there, though prostrate, though prone, there for all to see. There would, in fact, be more than one victim, more than one relicted corpse; there would be dozens, scores, hundreds, heap upon heap, to which he would add on, aye, thousands, thousands. His reputation could not content itself with less. The doing of this thing would take time, it was true, but time was the cheapest of all commodities, the clocks were full of it, they dripped time. Let the drippings mingle.

Nor would all his quarry, he determined, perish at the same instant. He was no slaughterer, no butcher. A perfection was what he was contriving, not a shambles. Right properly spaced would they be, the fates which awaited his victims, each man watching his fellow dying and smugly thinking himself safe, until, without caveat or warning, he, too, was snatched away from life. Let them know, the survivors, let them know that here was order and process logical, and not a madman's dalliance; that it was by a master's authority that these disasters fell, and not by chance; and that what they witnessed, though by piecemeal increment, was of a vast and inscrutable design. Rapturous and short were the pleasures of felony, but here, here in prolonged crime, as to incidence indefinite but as to pattern controlled, here there was added to the gust of every accomplished enormity the delectable savor which lay in watching the terrors of anticipation. This was very good.

Yet, as a matter of charted fact, at no time, not ever would the prey suspect the snare, nor conjecture their ordained doom, nor surmise, not even remotely surmise, that *he* at last was stalking them. The survivors, it might be, might at moments sense themselves disquieted by something amiss, something out of joint, in the manner of the passing of the inexplicable defunct; but more than a disquietude, suffered only to be sighed away, it would not be. The survivors in all likelihood – this was a foreseeable aftermath – would be of the two estates: those who would suspect murder but would possess, in despite of cadavers, clews, irresistible intuition, no proof of their suspicions; and those – sequel most gratifying! – those who would be moved even to applaud his workmanship.

In his mind's eye, he saw it all, from his own first inaugurative homicide down to the last tentative gropings which they would everywhere undertake to discover his person. In anticipation he gloated over the bewilderment, the confusion, the despair, that his acts would evoke: first, the terror; then, the laughable efforts at self-preservation into which he would goad them; and finally, the many complicated devices which they would devise, presumably to appease him, but really to draw him out into the open. He smiled at the prospect. How madden'd, how mortified they would be to know, to have account and register of his every atrocity, and yet not know, not ever know – *who* had perpetrated them.

With pride, with an amused pride he previsioned the chronicling

> of his exploits; a lengthy writ would it be, detailing the stages of his career, giving the canon and tally of his destructions, speaking to his power and even to his glory. Its opening sentence – he could see it plain – its opening sentence would read:
>
> *In the beginning He created the heaven and the earth ...*

Blasphemy! We ought at the encounter of such blasphemy to have rent our garments, but, as says the sage in *Sanhedrin*, were this ordinance binding for every blasphemy heard, it were in tatters that we would go arrayed. In a printing-shop, one would perforce go naked. This pasquil, I was certain, was not, could not be from the hand of Leon da Modena. Great as must have been his bitterness over the mutations and traverses of fortune, not he, not my friend, was the one to take the counsel of Job's wife and bring himself to such a desecrating of the Name. Myself, I reproduce it, even as the chronicler reproduces the arrogant blasphemy of Rab-shakeh, only that it be the better rebuked and reprehended, as did Isaiah, saying, *Be not afraid of these words which thou hast heard.* We, however, were afraid, for we feared a trick of our enemies, a trap set to catch the Jew in a gross and shuddering impiety. We sent the messenger, therefore, to go get us the imprimatur of the Venetian censor. He never returned.

My mind then turned away from the world and its deceptions to consider the hortatives of the mystics, men of piety and scholars of our time who, quaeritating the significance of every coronated iota, studied Holy Writ in hope thus to foretell and hasten the End of Days. They sought to compute the coming of the Messiah; they hearkened attent for the tread of his foot, the sound of his trumpet; their prayers and fastings were aimed to one effect: to roll up the ages, like a carpet, and welcome the Bringer of Comfort. With their doxologies, it was reported, they assaulted the very Throne of Heaven.

Under the patronage of that prince in Israel, Don Solomon Abenaish, Duke of Mytilene (may his glory grow!) and before him of that greater, Don Joseph, Duke of Naxos (be macarized his memory!) there had lately come to be established again the holy communities of Safed and Tiberias. Here, in their sacred quorums, our Cabbalists, putting the world aside, pursued their studies and devotions. Report avouched that it was as if they had been transported out of this world, transcending it.

Beneath their fig-trees they sat, contemplative, and in the clefts of the rocks; rid of the tart taste of earthly things, they meditated heavenly. It was as if the Urim and Thummim had been found again, and were about to disclose their secrets. Emissaries sent to the forlorn corners of the Dispersion brought their message: 'Let the foxes, let the little civets spoil the vines, – soon, soon, it would flourish again, that vineyard in a very fruitful hill, that requires neither pruning, nor digging, nor fencing about. To-day our lot is difficult and full of obstruction, but that day is not far off when at last the procrastinator of quickenance will bestir him, and the Messiah-ben-Joseph will usher in the Messiah-ben-David, through whom will be builded a world of righteousness and justice. Then will the good have wild manna for their meat, and for the wicked there will be stewed a broth will burn their very gizzards. Only alms and prayers can bring this thing to pass.'

*

For its sins that were many (so is it received of our ancestors), for its sins that were many the stock of Israel, banished its land, goes vagrant over the world. Flung and dispersed, as from the hand of the sower, our scattering lies in the farthest corners of the continents. We are chaff driven before the wind which even when fallen to the ground, no growing grows from it. Therefore, in the mid watches of the night and at high noon's blaze, we dream Jerusalem. We would return. We would fare back. We would return, but we know not the highways, we are lost among the paths, we seek to come there by the straight road or by the roundabout, but always are we turned off wandering, or herded back, or, caught between gates, held.

Yet do I hold firm to the belief that our journeyings, which are under Providence, even when they run circuitous and in directions away from our purpose and hope, are journeyings which tend ever and always toward Zion.

Such passage, to what may it be likened? It may be likened to the flight of the pigeon which, though buffeted by storms and far from its dove-cote, by an inner sense, in an inscrutable course over the trackless skies, wings it, homing. To the contentions of that fish called salmon which, struggling against currents and leaping over weirs, through devious channels makes ever toward its hatching place. To the bee, buzzing zigzag among flowers that after many honeyless sallies at last sips sweetness [ ]

In contrast to the two opening chapters, the rest of the 'Golem' material consists of an extremely miscellaneous collection of notes, ranging from lists of words and phrases to passages of continuous prose. Some of these items have no apparent connection to the golem story, but, in most cases, their relevance is clear.

Some notes consist of records of Klein's extensive readings in and around the golem legend. These cover a very wide range of topics: titles of books consulted or to be consulted; information on such subjects as the golem legend, the Kabbalah, Jewish history, the history and geography of Prague, and heraldry; biographical information on some of the major figures associated with the golem legend, such as Rabbi Löw, Mordecai Meisel (a philanthropist and close friend of Rabbi Löw), and Emperor Rudolph II; and lists of words and phrases. Some of the lists of words and phrases are organized according to source (mostly the Bible or English literature contemporaneous with the events of the golem legend), some according to topic (for example, coinage, travel, food, drunkenness, sex, torture, pigs), and some according to language of origin (for example, Dutch, French, Hebrew, Indian, Italian, Slavonic, Spanish); others apparently are not organized according to any principle at all. Among the latter is a vertiginous fourteen-page list [MS 3032–45] containing hundreds of words (with definitions) such as quob, phaenigmus, elumbated, vilipend, cucupha, ganch, fleak, weanel, tuel, pults, gargol, spawl, fleam, hulver, cynegetics, trethings, epenthesis, spraints, festucous, triblet, lunt, spagyrist, collow, flix.

The rest of the 'Golem' notes consists of work at various stages of completion. There are, for example, lists of aphorisms; sketches of characters and episodes; passages of descriptive prose; poems and drafts of poems; and, most importantly, several sets of notes relating to the overall conception of the novel. Among the latter, a set of notes headed 'The Golem' [MS 3254] sketches out most of the basic themes and characters of the novel, without indicating in any detail how Klein planned to develop them:

1. Created with letters – see Sefer Yetziroh
   Created in shape from mud of Moldau
   Words – draw up list
2. Fashioned to forfend calamity.
3. Freethinker appropriates thing to himself
4. It brings salvation
5. People begin to worship it – a whole new religion established
6. It develops desires of its own. A woman it seeks
7. It speaks without vowels or consonants (?)
8. Sent to do good deeds – does them, turns evil
9. Golem turns against *atheist*.

Characters

Rabbi Jacob Löw – Deus ex machina
Scholar next to the Duke.
His daughter – Esther.
His shamash.

Shall it be written by his scribe

In another set of notes [MS 3229], Klein's plans are worked out in greater detail:

1. Description of the *matter* out of which the golem is formed
2. Make decision re chapter 2. Is it not preferable to continue right into story, using present material of chapter 2 interspersed throughout book?
3. Golem's desire for a helpmeet. Rabbi's refusal.
   Golem's contemplation of death & his notes. His attempts at suicide which lead one to believe it can't be achieved. How – at end – R. Löw achieves it.
4. Describe city of Prague in biography of Sinai or on night of going out to create golem? Preferably latter, or maybe half at one time, half at another: consider selection of social & geographic details
5. In front of Hradčany Castle, the zoo. Develop idea of golem, in one of early tests, going there & proving his affinity with animals. Near the street of the Alchemists
6. Compose a song for the alchemists, with refrain establishing equality of gold and dirt.
7. Find way to attribute death of Rabbi to his making of golem.

The most extensive and coherent of the sets of notes relating to the overall conception of the novel is a plot outline on sixteen sheets [MS 3209–24] torn out of a small pocket notebook (probably 'Notebook [9]' [MS 7385–90] in the Klein Papers, which contains a list of books relevant to 'The Golem'). The outline begins with a description of the conditions in the Prague ghetto leading to Rabbi Löw's decision to create the golem [MS 3209–10]:

The Prague Ghetto

Description – see folder (Geography of Prague)
Menaces threatening it.

a) Economic menace.
   Mordecai Meisel intervenes
b) Menace religious. Averted by a scholar with influence at Vatican. Communication by pigeons

Debate by students re coming of Messiah (see folder re Good & Evil)

Fire in Prague synagogue – preserved by doves.

Describe an intervention by Rabbi Löw.
Rabbi Löw in tallis & tfillin & other appurtenances in heraldic terms
In discussing Rabbi Löw discuss his cures, e.g., ailment cured with mould
Sermon delivered week before on 'Lowly Things' re spider & attercop

Klein's numerous notes on Prague's history, geography, and architecture suggest that he meant to place considerable emphasis on the physical setting of the story. A description of 'View of city' as it first appears to the narrator [MS 3241] indicates the symbolic weight this setting is meant to bear:

Prague – sloping huddled roofs
[.....] the first as it were a city wearing alchemist's hats
a city besotted and staggering, with drunken gables, gasping dormers, and roofs awry.
loutish, indifferent, smugly hunched, roofs tilted as though they were hats worn to shut out the world

Klein also sketched two maps, one of Prague as a whole [MS 3290], and one of the Jewish ghetto [MS 3291], identifying such key locations as the River Moldau, on the banks of which the golem is created; the Altneuschule, Rabbi Löw's synagogue and the golem's final resting place; Hradčany Castle; the Zoo; and the Street of the Alchemists.

The 'menaces threatening' the Prague ghetto are described in more detail in MS 3115, where a third menace, 'plagues,' is added to the economic and religious menaces mentioned in the plot outline, and all three are described as 'a visitation for sin and luxury.' An upsurge of messianism is noted as one response to the 'menaces' threatening the Prague ghetto: 'Darkness – The messianic hopes. Retrospective glance over past counterfeit messiahs.' One expression of these messianic hopes is the 'debate by students re coming of Messiah' referred to in the plot outline [MS 3209]. A folder labelled 'Good & Evil' contains a draft of this debate [MS 3284–5], an example of pilpul, the 'juggling of sophistries' which the narrator describes in chapter 2 [p. 151]:

Debate re Coming of Messiah in Yeshiva

That all must be good before the Messiah comes.
- Then to what purpose the Messiah since his end is achieved even before he arrives?
- Because, as it is written, He is the reward for goodness.
- Then if all, save one, are good, is the Messiah delayed?
- In truth.
- A single knave wrestles against the Messiah, and conquers?
- How is it, then, with your thesis: All must be evil before the Messiah comes. Imagine all evil, save one solitary good man. Does this good man stay off the Messiah? Is this not an absurdity?
- Touching the coming of the Messiah, there are no rules of logic.
- That then is the answer I make to your objection.

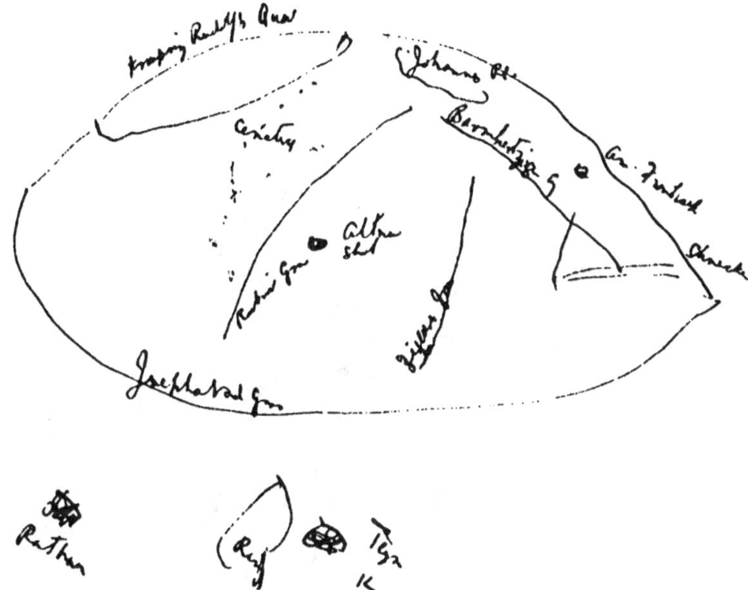

Klein's hand-drawn maps of the Jewish ghetto of Prague and (over) the city of Prague, National Archives of Canada, A.M. Klein Papers, MG30 D167, vol. 7, pp. 3290–1.

In front of Hradschin Castle. The Hirschgraben. You will reach [illegible] Defenestration [illegible]. Near here the street of Alchemists. Couldn't go out except through you

Prague

Belvedere 1536

Hirschgraben

Heights

Hradschin

Dom 1344
S. Veit

Capuchin cloister

Waldstein Pal.

Brückengasse

Left bank

Kronprinz Rudolf's Anlage

Moldau

Judengasse

Rudolfinum

Kettenbrücke

Karlsbrücke

Little Lyfe

Clementinum

Teyn K.
(1360)

Rathaus
(clock 1490)

Pulverturm
(1475)

Ferdinand S.

Altstadt

K. Franz Brück

Hauptstrasse

Wassergasse

Insel

Moldau

Palacky Brück

Wenzels Platz

National Museum

Smichov

All must be evil, comes the Messiah.

- From a total evil a supreme good? Is this conceivable?
- As conceivable is the race of mankind from the hand of God: a supreme good leading to a total evil.
- Do then the laws of crime & punishment cease with the coming of the Messiah?
- How so?
- The Messiah is the greatest of rewards. Is he to be accorded to total evil?
- Crime is punishable only in that it is singular. If evil is total, it is no longer singular; ergo, no longer punishable.
- Not punishable; but to be rewarded?
- Not rewarded; only to be corrected.
- Then why must the Messiah wait until all are evil?
- Because until all are evil there is a chance that the course may be reversed, and all may yet be good.

Proofs from scripture

1. From the strong comes forth sweetness.
2. Until all are evil, the goodness of one man may conquer the evil of another. All evil, it is Satan who rules. Satan ruling, only the Messiah can lead the rebellion.
3. All evil is the opening of a door to God. For if good reigns, God's governance of the world is minished. Men do His labour. Evil reigning, [.....] on the [..... .....] for God to set his world right again.
4. The coming of the Messiah is the day of self-fulfilment. What is good? Always a diminution of self-fulfilment. Evil is indulgence – ergo, evil is the proper prelude for the day of the Messiah.

References in the plot outline to Rabbi Löw's 'cures, e.g., ailment cured with mould' and his 'sermon ... on "Lowly Things" re spider & attercop' suggest that Klein intended to incorporate into 'The Golem' some version of his essay 'Of Lowly Things' [Canadian Jewish Chronicle, *23 June 1944, p. 4; reprinted in* Beyond Sambation, *pp. 222–4]. Taking as its starting point a traditional tale of how King David's life was saved by a spider, the essay presents the healing power of penicillin as a symbol of the value to be found in 'lowly things':*

The green mould that gathers upon bread, the feculent fur of cheese, the mushrooms of rot – this, is our *physic nonpareil*! The pus of food! This is what stays disease, and brings wholeness to gangrened limb, brings resurrection. This is resurrection's scum!

Is there not here a homily from which all may learn King David's lesson? Out of the lowly cometh exaltation, and out of the rejected healing.

[*Beyond Sambation*, p. 223]

In contrast to Rabbi Löw and his pious celebration of even the lowliest, least attractive aspects of creation is the evil Rumphaeus, the Emperor Rudolph's chamberlain and counsellor. Rumphaeus has two obsessions: sex ('a lecher and a smellsmock') and the Jews ('Jew hater – They smell gabardine & ghetto') [MS 3292]. Rumphaeus's hatred of the Jews is expressed in a passage in MS 2990:

That no-good spawn of a menstruate adultery, aborted in a gutter, suckled in a sewer, bred in a privy! That walking compost of ordure! That breathing filth! That abomination and monster! He makes my skin to crawl, my gall curdle, my nethermost stomach retch! He dares to come here to fill my presence with the garlic of his advice! Why, if my brains were reduced to a cinder – as be his! – and my judgment to a delirium – as be his! – I would still prefer the wisdom of my quietest fart to that of his loudest [....]

Although the character of Rumphaeus ultimately derives from the anti-Semitic priest Thaddeus in Rosenberg's version of the golem story (see p. xvi above), he is an atheist, inspired by the love of power rather than by religious fanaticism [MS 3113]:

King's Counsellor exploiting difficulties between himself, brother. Reader of Machiavelli's Prince. Seeking power.
The Turkish War. [ ] – A freethinker. Names of God.
Wishes to rob Jews.

Rumphaeus is something of a philosopher, the author of various aphorisms and of two philosophical treatises, 'The Rationale of Pure Murder' (also referred to as 'The Responsa') and 'The Primal Itch,' which deal with his two obsessions, Jews and sex respectively, as described in the following passages from the plot outline [MS 3211–13]:

The King's Counsellor

Protagonist of evil.
Author of *Responsa* (use other title) & similar cynicism
Intends Jews as objects of his philosophy in Responsa

There is no ecstasy without loss
Sum total of ecstasy of life of 70 = 6 hrs. if it come all at once.

He could not be flattered. To all flattery he had but one reply, I have already thought it myself.

Development of love equation

$$(a + b)^2 = a^2 + 2ab + b^2$$

What are the most beautiful objects in the world. Flowers. And they are all genitalia

The Primal Itch – causa causans
All history an itch degratinated, another substituted
Paradise: ineffable itchlessness
Hell – the itch unreachable
The creative gesture – a scratch
An itch aesthetic – pink, polka-red, suffused

Greek statuary – depilated pudenda, no appreciation of the fierceness of desire.

Love is an awareness of a sense of disproportion

We hate the perversions we love

Heard the vibration of ovaries

after the manner of beasts, belly to belly,
the manner of serpents, coil, recoil,
the manner of bees, tongue to calyx,
the manner of flowers, petal about pistil,
the manner of the mantis, gut about gizzard,
after the manner of swine, rooting, manner of scorpions.

At some point, 'Rabbi Löw suspects [Rumphaeus]. Sends golem to ransack his papers' [MS 3113]. Among these papers is 'The Rationale of Pure Murder' [MS 3573–81], a 'catechism' [MS 3109, MS 3570] consisting of '39 articles' [MS 3570] (for anachronisms in 'Rationale,' see textual note [p. 206]):

1. **Of the manifold and diverse phenomena of the cosmos, which is the most deeply to be cherished?**
   The phenomenon of life.

2. **And of the offices of civilization, which?**
The creative act.
3. **What, then, in the economy of human behaviour, social, functional, cultural, merits to be designated its *summum bonum*?**
The creation of life.
4. **Is this a consummation within human competence?**
By simple biological process, yes.
5. **Is it also otherwise of human instrumentality?**
It is otherwise of the divine only.
6. **Justify the exclusion of mere growth consequent upon insemination from the paradigm of creativity.**
Its possibility, being open to all members of mankind, can confer no special distinction; its consummation, requiring but an erect (not always) expellent and a receptive (always) continent, is vulgarly accomplished; its performance, marked invariably by indecorous gesture, lacks dignity; its authorship, dual, negates singularity; and its impulse, shared by the lowest orders of creation, precludes it from consideration among achievements uniquely human.
7. **What, then, is man's highest possible accomplishment, human, unilateral, eclectic?**
The taking of life.
8. **Articulate the nexus of equation between the creation of life and the extinction of life.**
Mastery over life.
9. **Define murder.**
Murder is a human operation, entailing both intention and act, executed by one upon the body of another, to the end that that other cease to be.
10. **What are the corollaries that follow from the foregoing definition?**
That there are excluded therefrom, as not being operations human, as being grossly pragmatic (desire for food, fear of injury), killings by animals; excluded, as entailing only act and not intention, manslaughter, which is but murder stumbled upon by accident; as entailing intention without act is excluded mere malice; as not involving the body of an other, in the parasynthetic significance of that term, the slaughter of animals is excluded, even that accomplished while in the exercise of the art of venery; and is excluded, for deficiency, as frustrate and *non-avenu*, all non-lethal assault, even that resulting in mayhem.
11. **The practise of murder as an art, what are its criteria?**
Mode of performance; choice of victim; scope of carnage; anonymity of execution.
12. **Catalogue the modes of homicide.**

By fusillade, as from bows, guns, catapults, membra, cannon; by butchery, as with knives, swords, scissors, scythes, cleavers, pens, hatchets, lancets; by battery, as through repeated contusion effected by blunt instruments; by hanging; by means toxic; by hunger; by suffocation, accomplished either after the manner of Burke or by simple garrotting; by lapidation; by *noyade*; by asphyxiation; by flaying (extensive); by amputation (piecemeal); by decapitation; from high places by jaculation; in low or hollow places by entombment; by multifarious, repetitive fracture, as on the rack; by exsanguination; by aeronation, as of the blood stream; by burning, whether through flagration of the body quick, or through incineration of the body quick and dead; by induced exhaustion; by means of cultures of virulence; by deadly radiation.

13. **Is the sequence of the foregoing catalogue hierarchic or random?**
Random. For the modes of murder acknowledge no protocol of precedence; preference is accorded only to that mode which, in the given circumstances, militates towards the perfection of those other excellences postulated in paragraph eleven.

14. **And torture?**
It is against humanity.

15. **May murder be performed by agency?**
To commit murder by agency is the sign of the craftsman; to have it committed by agency ignorant of its agency is the sign of the virtuoso.

16. **Name the motives which, lest they detract from the murderer's integrity, ought to be ignored, or if not ignored, suppressed, in making choice of victim.**
Passion, since it deprives the praxis of that impersonality without which it is no art but an indulgence; greed, since that corrupts.

17. **What, then, is a murder's basic justifiable motive?**
The victim's innocence.

18. **Justify this motive.**
Because in such case, and in such case only, is the act of murder not the mere effect of a cause (greed, passion), but itself a First Cause.

19. **Tabulate in descending order, with comment, the categories of murder.**
Deicide: save as hereinafter to be provided for (Responsum [ ]), impossible of execution.
Parricide: artistically suspect as being almost invariably tainted by self-interest.
Fratricide: largest as to scope, since all men are brothers.

20. **Establishing the termini of the vocation of murder from its earliest beginnings to the present day, outline the graph of its progress.**

Let x mark the spot where Cain killed, and let y stand for the area of contemporary genocide; then, the line drawn from x the spot to y the area must be a line increasing triangularly in thickness, with acceleration rising in height, with intensity in colour darkening.

21. **Seeing the advances, hitherto unimaginable, already achieved, is further progress to be considered impossible?**
By no means. The prospects are sanguine for, given the total population of the globe as [ ],000,000,000, more or less, multiplying this sum by the factor, variable as to generations and fractions of generations, of natural increase, the said factor the mean between arithmetic and geometric progression, and subtracting from the multiplic[ ] such losses, actuarially calculated, as must inevitably ensue from the intrusions of hazard, flood, fire, famine, fever, and excepting from computation the one irremoveable (by definition) unit calculating, not calculated, one must necessarily arrive at a field of potentiality numbering [ ],999,999,999, more or less.

22. **The potential progressively actualized, would not such exercitation, augmentatively deprivative of audience increasingly diminishing, defeat itself?**
There are other planets, some of which are reputed to be inhabited by living creatures, humanoid if not human.

23. **Failing all further object, would not suicide, – the homologation of murderer with murderee, – afford instance of the art seen in its highest?**
No.

24. **Why?**
Because it is inefficient, since the actuality of achievement eliminates the potentiality of repetition; because it is not of sportsmanship since the victim must necessarily consent and the author not ever jeopardized easily escape; because it is wasteful since it attains distinction only to lose it.

25. **Ascribe to society its true motivations impelling it to organize to seek to repress, under the penalties of the law, said criminal, the pursuit and exercise of the vocation.**
On the part of the weak – fear, lest they be used as the media of art; on the part of the strong – chagrin, for that they have been anticipated; and on the part of Authority – appetence, secretly, with impunity, indeed with honour, to perpetrate the proscribed.

26. **In what manner does the Artist, uncertain *pro tanto* in his act, allay qualms of conscience?**
In the knowledge that life is difficult and that it is he who brings reprieve; that Death is beautiful and that it is he who has hastened its coming.

27. **Death beautiful?**
So described by the theologians, so sung by the poets: as the greatest of all goods, the jewel of the just, the folding of the hands to sleep, the abode of the blessed, the necessary end, the crossed bar, the golden exit, the panacea, the devoutly to be wished, the prospect of liberty, the long way home, as amiable and lovely Death, Death lovely and soothing.

28. **Establish, in accordance with the rationale of the philosophers, the character of murder, not antinomian, at worst adiaphoric.**
This is self-evident. What philosopher's superfluous proof is it that is demanded?

29. **By syllogism (Aristotelian).**
To prove a truth is commendable;
That all men are mortal is a truth;
∴ To prove all men mortal is commendable.

30. **From subjective idealism (Berkeleyan).**
Affirmatively: Since to be is to be perceived, and only that is which is perceived, murder, a mode of perception, must necessarily be an act creative, bringing into perception and thus into being, what, before murder perceived it, was not.
Negatively: Since no object exists except as it exists in the mind of its beholder, no man exists except as another man's idea; consequently murder is but the transformation of an idea and, as such, not felonious.

31. **By the dialectic (Platonic).**
[ ]

32. **By the dialectic (materialist).**
Since all that is in the world, including man, is matter; and since the law of the world is continuous change of matter; murder, being but a change in the matter of man, runs in conformity with the law of the world.

33. **From doctrines theological (western).**
To every man there is given past, present, and future, the sum of which, being eternity, is constant.
Murder is an act interruptive of the present in the act of presenting an increasing past with portions of a diminishing future.
What murder effects, therefore, by its decurtation of a growing past it compensates for by its preservation of an intact futurity.

34. **From doctrines theosophical (eastern).**
The whole of life, being made up of incarnation plus a number of re-incarnations in a set series, all moving towards final consummation, murder, an incarnating instance, far from destroying, accelerates the apocatastatic process.

35. **By dilemma.**
The victim of murder is either dead or alive.

If alive, murder has not been accomplished, and hence the wrong (sic) has not been perpetrated.
If dead, the victim, deprived of consciousness, cannot be said to suffer any wrong whatsoever.
By principle of rational consistency (eclectic) how can the non-existent exist, and the existing be non-existent?

36. **Express, with quadrilateral asseverativeness and octuple iteration, in form affirmative, interrogative, and responsive, the truth which renders murder [ ]**
Shall we all die?
We shall die all.
All die shall we?
Die all we shall.

37. **By the categorical imperative (Kantian).**
Always treat humanity in others, not as a means, but as an end.

38. **By the hedonistic calculus (Benthamite).**
Combining Responsum 21 and Responsum 27: the greatest good of the greatest number.

39. **The proofs having been made, with what feelings are they to be regarded?**
With incredulity, at the wisdom of philosophers; with disdain, as having been supererogatory.

According to MS *3113, Rumphaeus is a 'freethinker' with an interest in the 'names of God.' A list headed '70 names of God' [*MS *3012] is flippant, even blasphemous, in tone:*

Glory of God		כבוד
Presence, Divine Abiding	D.A.	שכינה
Word of God		מימרא
Endless-All		אין סוף
Ancient of Days		
Tetragrammaton	The four-letter word	יהוה
Ineffable Name	Unspeakable	שם המפורש
The Place	Locusfocus	המקום
	Mummimpotent[?]	
The Absolute	That which is free from all necessary relation	
The Oversoul		
The Only One	The Hego	

MS *3015 adds 'bastard' after 'The Absolute' and 'oversob' after 'The Oversoul.'*

Finally, Rumphaeus 'plans ritual murder accusation' [MS 3113]. The only one at court with the power to stop Rumphaeus is the emperor himself, Rudolph II, but as Klein portrays him, he has neither the will nor the desire to do so. Klein notes Rudolph's enlightened patronage of the famous astronomers Tycho Brahe and Kepler, but he also attributes to him a superstitious fascination with astrology and alchemy [MS 3059]:

What was going on under Rudolph – astrologers
Tycho Brahe
Kepler
Studied the stars. Thought one day he would discover a new one. In the meantime a pleasure to look at them.
Dross into gold.

A further note on Rudolph [MS 3293] suggests that his attitude to the Jews is ambiguous at best and, if he is not an evil figure, he is at least susceptible to the evil blandishments of Rumphaeus:

Rudolph
Art collector – Jews antiques
The trouble with the Jews is they belong to human race
Didn't know whether he was sane or merely feigning sanity

Rabbi Löw is inspired to create the golem by the prophet Elijah, whose appearance is briefly sketched in the plot outline [MS 3214]:

The Advent of Elijah
Peddler from far-off. Vendor of pots and pans.
Leaves mandrake in one pot.

This vision of Elijah is expanded upon in MS 3101:

Vision of Elijah seen by Löw (2 Kings 2:11)
Incognito – a peddler,* with horse & waggon גילוי אליהו Seen against sunset.
One of the thirty six. Tried to sell him & finally left with him mandragora – shape of a man.
This to instruct him to make golem

* The peddler tells story of the cataleptic congregation; frozen in prayer. [*Klein's note*]

God reveals thru dreams – Job 33:14, 15

The page of the plot outline preceding the creation of the golem is headed 'The Alchemists' [MS 3215] and consists of only one note: 'Their song – Gold is merds.' There are several references to alchemy elsewhere in the 'Golem' material, but since they are all quite brief it is impossible to draw any detailed conclusions about Klein's plans. However, it seems likely that Klein intended to suggest an analogy between the creation of gold out of 'merds' and of the golem out of mud.

The golem itself is dealt with at substantial length in the 'Golem' material. One set of notes headed 'Rabbi Löw' [MS 3230] deals in broad outline with the nature of the golem and the act of its creation:

1. After custom of Talmudists, inquires from little children their text of the day.
2. In making the golem, considers the faces of mankind.
3. The golem and his original humility, subsequent arrogance.
4. The golem in times of calm, his idleness
5. The golem implores the rabbi for the creation of another golem to be a helpmeet to him.
6. The difficulty of the golem's voice. All things sculptural created, but the voice, the sign of distinction between man and animal.
   How resolved. (a) by elementary sounds
   (b) by pantomime
   (c) by stopping his interlocutors at appropriate syllables
7. In what lay golem's strength –

In another set of notes [MS 3244], Klein considers various ways of presenting the act of creation:

1. In paragraphs before chapter of creation of golem, evoke rules of the scribe. Build chap. on basis of emanations
   (Preliminary discussion re improvements on man) (Elaborate on Bezalel)
2. Re ten commandments & morality, attribute section to King's chamberlain
3. The purity of approach to task of creating golem to be written in terms hortatory
4. Phylacteries for secret messages
5. Colophon – Blessing & curse

6. When golem is made, he is average – mixture of all animals – vulpine, canine, leonine, psittaceous, simian

*The 'rules of the scribe' were alluded to by Rabbi Löw in the opening chapter of the novel, when he was enjoining his scribe Sinai to record the story of the golem [p. 000]. By elaborating on those rules at this crucial point in the narrative, Klein emphasizes the parallel between the narrative act and the act of creating the golem. According to the plot outline [MS 3222], Klein intended to make use of a section of his essay 'The Bible Manuscripts' in which 'the rules of the scribe' are discussed [*Canadian Jewish Chronicle*, 5 October 1951, p. 10; reprinted in* Beyond Sambation*, pp. 136–7].*

The 'preliminary discussion re improvements on man' referred to in the plot outline is elaborated in MS 3047:

I would prepare a memorandum to be submitted to the Heavenly Throne, with recommendations for the better creation of man.

1. Divisibility and adjustability of limbs. It is suggested that the human body would be much increased in efficiency, and the human soul (quare) much increased in its happiness if the varied limbs and members of the human frame were [.........] removable, and therefore adjustable, at will. Such a consummation would add greatly to our ubiquity – the head from body removable does multiply life by two – dexterity is amplified, etc.
2. Alternativeness in sex. One half of the world does not know how the other half feels. Would social order be too greatly upset if at given or willed periods in life, male should have the privilege of changing into female, and vice versa. The complete life.
3. The transference of the procreative capacity to any given part of the physical areas. Why should not fertilization ensue, if so desired, at the juncture of fingertips, the union of brows, the kissing of kneecaps. Or at all simultaneously! Aye, there were a life to be lived!
4. Vision in the dark.
5. Versatility of methods of locomotion. In this, man is still most primitive, the machine's aborigine. He knows only motion pedestrian; of [.......] progression rotary, or sliding, or flying, he knows nothing at all.
6. Aging – (vetus – [ ]). Why not all at once? Youth continuous to the day of death.
7. The abolition of the natural disgraces. (See above)
8. The privilege of wilful transparency of thought. It is a grave failing not to be able to communicate one's thought without verbalization, without utterance; greater still, that even when uttered, the one communicated-

to is never certain of the authenticity of the thing-communicated. Would it not be better if, by an act of will, thought could glow on the forehead like a neon – or better, thought, like a secret air-wave communicated to the receptive ear. Weep, hypocrisy – your death is near[?].

A note in MS 3128 – 'Conspires a race of humans against the human race' – which probably refers to Rumphaeus, suggests a parallel with Rabbi Löw's pride in his ability to better God's creation.

The actual creation of the golem is described in the plot outline [MS 3216–19] as follows:

Creation of Golem

Ablutions before creation
With letters – see Sefer Yetziroh
    from mud of Moldau

Inquiry into Urim & Thummim
Ezekiel's chariot

Animation by slip of paper & emeth on forehead. אמת מארץ תצמח

When destroyed, aleph taken out of his forehead. אמת-מת

Holy earth – 1 ingredient. Also sand, he coruscates, shines, dazzles, blinds.

(Excursus on Bezalel – in shadow of God) as artist, sculptor of golem.
Aholiab, son of Ahisamach to help Bezalel

The Golem: homunculus, mannikin (See O.E.D.)
    Has no faculty of speech.
    Rabbi Löw understands his gestures

Legal questions re golem:
    Can golem be added to a minyan
    Whether golem's dead body pollutes
Before making golem, recite ps. 91
No trace of either good or evil intentions in golem
G. exempt from laws, both commands and prohibitions
Gets verbal instruction from Heaven
    אתה ברא גלם דבוק החמר ותגזור זדים חבל טורפי ישראל

179 'The Golem'

By moonlight. At midnight. Chanted חצות, lament for Jerusalem.
Invoke constellations to hasten embryonic period

At first used as intelligencer

Four elements in golem: fire, air, water, earth

Walked seven times around clay figure
Show piecemeal construction of golem רמ"ח אברים
Name for golem?

Golem at first water-carrier. Not to arouse suspicion.

Golem provided with amulet which made him invisible. Heard conversation. Reported in pantomime ...

MS 3231, headed 'The Making of the Golem,' elaborates on the rituals leading up to the act of creation:

Time: Adar
Full moon – incantation
Purim (time of masks, appearances)

Preliminaries:
Ablutions
Fasting
Study of Maaseh Breshith
Sefer Yetziroh, by whose help R. Oshaiah & R. Chaninah created a 3 year old calf (San. 65b, 67b)
Maimonides
R. Joshua b. Chananyah in the same way produced deers and fawns from cucumbers and pumpkins (T.J. San. vii, 154)

Attendance for בת-קול ob & yidonim Is. 8.19
pitkas – tablets from heaven

Disciples: A Cohen
A Levite – Bezalel – shadow of God
The Rabbi
Scribe

Appearance of Prague at midnight. Preliminary reading of Chatzoth.

MS 3232, headed 'Israel earth,' elaborates on the act of creation itself:

Procedure re Adam Kadmon

1. The elements 4 – correspond to 4 fabrics in sacred tent, 12 precious stones, 12 signs of zodiac, 12 tribes of Israel – gloss
2. The mystic circle. – walked seven times around it
3. Anathema – Shedim
   Asmodai
   Lilith – Adam's first wife
   Dumah – angel of stillness of death
   shabriri – causes blindness
   tezazeth – insanity
   Ben Nefilim – epilepsy

Rabbi's appearance as he performs rite:

Tfillin the cubes of piety
Describe like heraldry
with tfillin attired, with tallis mantling fimbriated azure cucullated or capoched upon the head

The note in the plot outline, 'Invoke constellations to hasten embryonic period' [MS 3217], is developed in two fragmentary passages [MS 2989, 3235]:

As he scanned the heavens glimmering above like some arachnid web shimmering with dew, he descried amidst the maidenhair confusion and tentativeness of the skies the twin symbols of Jewish history: first the scapegoat Azazel sent fletched, ramm'd, and dogg'd into depths inhospitable and up unscaleable heights, the bullying and crabbish gentiles all about it, against its bleatings roaring; and then, as further he probed and fished among the constellations, mobile like water, like fire capering, ambivalence resolved itself, and he beheld a new shape in backward motion arched, then librated, and at last in virginal outline clear – the lion of Judah, rampant, supporting Torahs: it was like the very homeopathics of the scorpion whose venom is its own balm.

It would neither grow nor open except with incantation.
It central, it fixed,
The satellite constellations made their tournies about it,
Nine times.

Nine times the moon circled about it
(Lisping of lunes, planetary labials, the abracadabra of birth)
And then, on the two hundred and seventieth day,
The exhausted stars paused in their dance, the moon was breathless.

After the episode of the golem's creation, the plot outline moves directly to the golem's downfall. MS *3220, headed 'Cult of Golem,' describes the first stages in this process:*

Salvations achieved by him so miraculous many, Jew & gentile, begin to worship him

He develops desires of his own. Seeks a woman. The rabbi's daughter

MS *3105 adds one detail: 'Describe rites (Sanhedrin 65b – conjure by means of membrum virile).'*

*The plot outline concludes with a brief sketch of the golem's destruction [*MS *3221, 3224]:*

Rumphaeus plans to kidnap Golem
Succeeds, but golem eventually turns against him.
Ultimately golem goes mad.

Conclusion:
Go to the attic of the synagogue at Prague. Mount etc. & there behold dust, ash, etc.

Destruction of golem: Creation, stood at feet, looking towards head. Reverse.
Book of Creation read backwards
Candles.

Selected Notes and Fragments

Modigliani tours the ghetto

1. Purple cheeks.
2. Beggar – green face, and white eyes, like mouldy bread.
3. Girl sitting on top of fellow's neck reading book in his hand.
4. Jew hanging on by his nose to hooks near window of a fish shop.
5. Dog led by leash of bitch's tail.
6. Barber shop with red-white candy post; sun licking it.
7. Women charioteers with hump in front and back, the dromedaries of the pack.
8. Cafeteria – smoked meat sandwiches, fried udders, roasted briskets.
9. Philosophers stirring tea the livelong day.
10. Trees, men with wooden legs in need of a haircut.
11. Beneath million million watts of sun, a Jew walks with umbrella.
12. Reading letters out of Assyria.
13. Midget with formidable weapon of rubber, swatting giant flies.
14. Arms with bodies attached.
15. Man with tzitzith dangling from his fly selling miracles of Rabbi.
16. Herring hanging like fruit from trees.

*

Bon Mots

Flattery is the utterance of compliments incredible to the flattered. It is practically impossible to achieve.

When a gentile is in misery, he is sorry he was born; when one of us is in such case, he is sorry he was born a Jew.

Greed is a kind of intelligence.

Impatient with the merely capable poet. Second-story man, rises above the pedestrian but still lives in flats like a hundred million others. The basement poet – Villon. The penthouse poet – Rilke!

A scientist is one who in a matter-of-fact voice imagines.

For women the medical approach – inspection, palpation, percussion.

He's so orthodox he's now thinking of having his nose circumcised.

Jews of the Mosaic Persuasion. Sign of the persuasion: the coronated member.

75% of world novels built on principle Penis erectus.

The books you were going to write – table of contents and index all ready.

Husbands deep

the ramrod prophets of the stiffnecked race.

The radio on the mizrach wall.

The chevalier, the marquis, and the hyphenated fabulist.

Our glory swims away in contraceptives.

The gutturals of constipation.

The arch of Titus – alliterate the gnat of troubled titus ticking[?] testa, testa, testiamb.

Menu: [ ] saignant
Crochenez à confiture
Youpin à l'arlésienne
Bonne bouche bordé
Rabbin en brochettes
Pucelle fouettée[?]

*

If individuality exists at all, it exists secretly, like a file concealed in a bread.

Talk to me, she had said, talk to me dirty. It was one of the best.

God's itching powder — sex.

Re escape – Really no alternative. The Jewish nightmare.
Man with defect, corrects it, no good, never any good, ineradicable. His defect is that he lives. A nightmare.

Violin – wonderful instrument – a human voice, to no human attached.
The radio, a little cantor at my mizrach wall.

A scientist is one who imagines in a matter-of-fact voice.

Will-to-live – a practical joke, like someone trying to get off chair, but his suspenders have been tied to it; he wants to go; can't; everybody laughs.

Mountains get lonely. Have only each to each to speak to. Get tired; look about for others. Sometimes will speak even to hills; after all, a hill is a mountain lying down.

Weather is making poetry for next week. Meteorologist proof-reads in advance. Satirize this [....].

Can't write to-day. No cigarettes. I must have incense.

*

Is this our Canadian poet, they say, this fellow with the foreign name? Presumption indeed! What does he know of fir-trees? Has ever a local flower sprouted in his song? Is he the one to sing Canadian weather, or Canuck dew, or flora and fauna made confederate? Can he track our forests without guide?

We must beware of him, and his Semitic subtleties. One day we shall find, if we let him off his Asian reservation, that he has accented our speech, and circumcised our hearts. He will have made Galilee out of the open Yukon; and in the dark of night, as we sleep a saxon sleep, he will plaster the walls of our public buildings with slogans from the prophets. It must not be.

For what is K to Hecuba or Hecuba to K. The kike, he has no sense of the fitness of things. Isaiah on Sunday going to church – we are men of tolerance, and do not object. But Isaiah read to factory-hands, Isaiah made a member of a union, Isaiah come with the burden against private initiative and public enterprise?

No, I am not, as they understand it, a Canadian poet. No politician will ever quote a line of mine. If ever my verses are made the topic of a sermon, it will be as warning to the unwary. No, I am not a Canadian poet. I have not stolen a single line of British poesy. All that has happened has been that the

Good Lord has seen fit to put me in this particular corner of his garden; I am not so vain as to imagine that because I am here it is best, or so blasphemous as to imagine that the Lord has not better to show.

*

At the Turkish bath. Prepare the pail of water, and the broom. The poet Ravitch is here who on the highest hottest plank would dream of mermaids, while seaweeds flagellate his froward behind.

Morning shave – substitute for shachris. Toothbrush – חללים חללים. Meditation – shave. Benediction – hair on face שלא עשני אשה. Powder: Latin קטרת.

Man, vegetable, animal, mineral? A rational vegetable. Fat Slavic cabbagephiz; carrotpoll Scandinavian; darknegromelon, red within; olive Italian; forgetmenotsinflax the Dane; languedoïl leek; gold Indian maize; and Jew, Jew – the vegetable stew.

Along the ghetto street shuffled my Unclejew etc. See Black Book.

*

Before the riesenrising giganticograndogmentative sierrasoaring golgoliatha, before the himmelayan aukrockrocrococolassal, this mistodawn mountain brood – little menshevik man, diminiscute, pettikin, nit! Not! Herewas and aeons uralter before began this gnotorious gnat, bisbisbuzzing his shmug and prickly way, these grandours and alpephants stood. Felsenful! In the balls of the urth fullcanic, glassial in the wallow of welkin, eisberg fought firestone. Ructions! Regorgitations! Granites and canyonades! And man was not homo. Adamic the stone, the roc primeval.

As from God's first petrifiat, they hoar, they have ben. We stutter and stimmer, balputiant. Mummount! Herrenhorn! Towerturtor! Babelbrick! Rising regardant from vale to hill to cliff to crag to scarp at las to peakpicpicolo, glorhea in excelsis, we cry Ap-hoch-ellipse!

*

Yerushalayim

When in those days of one's childhood when the great cities of the earth enter into one's life not as cities but as sounds – London, two slow drumbeats; Paris, the drawing of a bow over a violin; Bagdad, a flute of assonance; Rome, the single cello string plucked vibrating – the name Jerusalem always called to me, short long, short long, like the blast of a silver trumpet.

*

The clamour and brouhaha raised by these grager-grinding grinning youngsters he would ordinarily have considered an aggression upon his peace; how in a place of worship was one to tolerate such clangabang and brekekex, such pandemoniac hullabaloo and stridency – in its deafening clack-clackoustics, filippic ratatat and kickeronian sonorosnore, cymbal and racket and gourd, how in the world reconcile such utterant-mutterant fracas and hellodeon with synagogal sweet decorum! But tonight it was music, in all its raucous intensity music and melos, a symphony in which the poor little improvised instruments made a joyful noise, overwhelming with incantations hoarse and shrill, with pharophonics and babble and gragerogrex and torquemadatumps, with chmelnizicattos and nazinoisidom all who in the reverberant ages rose up to destroy us.

*

1. He's not convinced!
2. Then, the other two.
3. (A. Priori, midwife A. Posteriori, autopsist)
4. The pig that re-swines itself.
5. Hospital in Germany. (May 16, 1948) Eye focussed on huge nerved chart of the brain. Cerebellum, cerebrum, cere – brum.
6. The flaying of the shadow. Peter Shlemiehl.
7. Intermarriage urged. A procession of Villon's daughters – the fat Margot, [ ]. He shakes his shiksa-spear.
8. Dair arr no Zhermans heer.
9. Treatment with insulin etc.
10. The constellations circle into view, in the various shapes of citron, unleavened bread & grager.
11. The article on the grager instruments for Purim.
12. His father appears in vision. Warns him against apostasy. Threatens to tear his garment, dons sackcloth and ash. His mother laments, breaks her hands backward.
13. Situation parallelled by casting out a demon, a dibbuk.
14. The Responsa of Rabbi Gentile.
    Include reference to 613.
    Identify that of the world which is of the greatest value.
    Life.
    Identify the activity which is of the highest worth.
    Creation.
    Compose a maximum.
    The creation of life.
    Is this maximum achievable?

No; it is the prerogative of God. Nor does biological creation meet the requirement.

*

He translated aurea mediocritas – golden mediocrity.

Yiddish yidiom.

after the manner of beasts – belly to back; the manner of serpents, six to nine; the manner of bees, tongue to calyx; the manner of flowers, petals about pistil; etc. the manner of mantis, gut and gizzard; after the manner of swine, rooting; manner of scorpion.

What are the most beautiful objects in the world?
Flowers. And they are all genitalia.

He was skilful in the creation of types; he had the advantage of a hackneyed mind.

More! More! More!
You talk like a bride!

A difficult author – could be understood only by a sharp head and flat ass.

Proof that language made for prostitution
 gutter-holes
 labials
 con-sonant
 voyelles (from voyou).

Ponce (E) pimp, ponce the lion.

The trouble with the Jews is that they belong to the human race.

The lavish McTavish?

Envy is the wealth of the poor.

Love is an awareness of a sense of disproportion.

I wake up to find myself – drowsy.

Put a man and woman in one room – the results may be love. Put man and man: hate.

We hate the perversion we love.

The homo is a comic character – His activity is so unsymmetrical.

A variation of [..........]

the flat nosebridge and hollow eyesockets (no image is returned) of the Angel of Death.

The pot of gold at the end of the rainbow.
But I'm interested only in the rainbow.

flotsam on the seacoast of Bohemia.

prodigally beautiful.

so alive, yet so old the cobwebs clung between testicles and crotch.

St. Francis of the mezuzah.

henna of gehenna.

God invented Adam and has lived since on the royalties.

Assimilated in all ways save by epispasm.

The broken cracknels of the matzo-square.

A dossier for God: fathoming His aliases.

The opposite of posterity is hostility.

Kaplan et al. The father-in-law, the son-in-law, the ghost-in-law.

Worships her this side adultery.

In the desert nothing grows, except religions.

Holy m'rachamim.

The old lech: he feigned he was a homo to put women off their guard.

Praying mantis.

Jewry's aeolian drifts.

And then the ham writer couldn't write any more. He suffered from literary tenesmus.

Quote A.H. Clough on Decalogue, in connection with Churchill's poem to Roosevelt.

Churchill's gesture – that of the man who used his wife as a bowling ball.

The marxists' two discoveries: the stomach's peristalsis and the motion of the pendulum.

All great poets are contemporaries out of time.

*

The blouse was stitched, point by point and dot by dot, in greens and blues and reds, the greens in change of hues, now like rush, now like reed, now like grass, the blue like the sky in its times, sky of dawn, sky of dusk, sky of high noon, and the reds like rose, sheath on sheath, all twirl'd and sloped, in straight lines or curves, through criss, through cross, to shape the gay Slav shapes; thus the sleeves were bright of cuff, as if to lift, to make to shine, to crown the arms; and the braid about the throat was a round of spring, sprig, leaf, and bloom; those dots were, in truth, like the motes and scents, the sweet dust of field and farm and woods; and when she walked, yes, as she breathed that blouse swelled taut with its full plump lines, and you had to watch her, you had to steal looks at her, you could not keep your eyes off her, the thought of the shine of sun on fields of hay so strong in you, so strong the thought of fresh cool barns, birds in the eaves, all else in the world still, while a hand groped and made to stir that blouse of spring and summer's unfastening releasing season.

... the Chinese character, small lattice of vermilion, twig-tied, bamboo-slivered

He resented, as if they were memorials of his own degradation, Europe's proud crests and scutcheons that seemed to deride him and jeer at him, as he moved through Europe's capitals. Blazoning, on public monument, over sculptured gate, even on tapestry of antique chair, the aristocracy of its founders, their every curling line curled, as it were, a fastidious nose at him. He walked amidst a taunting of scrolls, a heckling of banners. Yet how upstart, how unworthily won, this aristocracy.

*

Poetry – heavenly labials in a world of gutturals.

*

And, cornucopic, the unfathomable horn
Its musk of plenty toxic on the air.

The nulls and zeros of the day long hours
The wild laocoön cauchemar of the night.

ABBREVIATIONS
TEXTUAL NOTES
EXPLANATORY NOTES
APPENDIX

Abbreviations

WORKS BY KLEIN

BS	*Beyond Sambation: Selected Essays and Editorials 1928–1955*. Ed. M.W. Steinberg and Usher Caplan. Toronto: University of Toronto Press 1982
CP	*Complete Poems*. 2 vols. Ed. Zailig Pollock. Toronto: University of Toronto Press 1990
LER	*Literary Essays and Reviews*. Ed. Usher Caplan and M.W. Steinberg. Toronto: University of Toronto Press 1987
SS	*The Second Scroll*. New York: Alfred Knopf 1951
Stories	*Short Stories*. Ed. M.W. Steinberg. Toronto: University of Toronto Press 1983

REFERENCE WORKS

Gordon	Hirsch Loeb Gordon. *The Maggid of Caro*. New York: Pardes 1949
JE	*The Jewish Encyclopedia*. New York and London: Funk and Wagnalls Co. 1906
LOTD	Usher Caplan. *Like One That Dreamed: A Portrait of A.M. Klein*. Toronto: McGraw Hill Ryerson Ltd 1982
Lowenthal	Marvin Lowenthal. *A World Passed By: Scenes and Memories of Jewish Civilization in Europe and North Africa*. New York and London: Harper & Brothers 1933
Müller	Ernst Müller. *History of Jewish Mysticism*. Oxford: East and West Library 1946
OED	*The Oxford English Dictionary*. Oxford: Oxford University Press 1928
Roth	Cecil Roth. *A Short History of the Jewish People*. London: East and West Library 1948
Waxman	Meyer Waxman. *A History of Jewish Literature*. 6 vols. 2d ed. Cranbury, N.J.: Thomas Yosellof 1938

Textual Notes

FROM THE 'RAW MATERIAL' FILE

This edition prints most of Klein's 'Raw Material' file [MS 3454–558], which contains a number of items, in no discernible order, ranging from rough notes to more than twenty pages of continuous prose. The following items from the file have not been printed: fragmentary notes and rough drafts [MS 3456–8, 3460–3, 3479, 3481, 3488, 3490, 3505, 3509, 3550–3, 3557–8]; two versions of material which appears elsewhere in the file, recast as memories of a prison convict [MS 3516–20, 3522–3]; and an unfinished sketch, entitled 'Uncle Nachman' [MS 3524–5], which has no apparent relation with the other items in the 'Raw Material' file.

In addition to material which Klein kept in the 'Raw Material' file, there are several sets of related notes elsewhere in the Klein Papers [MS 7425, 7428, 7519, 7561, 7567, 7593, 7594]. MS 7594 has been printed in this edition.

The following is a list of all of the texts printed in the 'Raw Material' section of this edition. They have been arranged in what the editors consider to be the most likely chronological order, with the exception of item 1, whose date of composition is unclear:

1. MS 3521 ('Whatever I think, or imagine ...').

MS 3521 consists of a single sheet in the same ink throughout, with some minor revisions in that ink, as well as in a second one, and in pencil.

2. MS 3465–94 ('No thing happens but it is autobiographical ...') and MS 3464 ('Man: vegetable, animal, mineral ...').

MS 3465–94 consist of twenty-five sheets in one ink up to MS 3485, and in a second ink, beginning at 'Neumann did a sketch of me ...,' to the end. The sheets are numbered in pencil. There are some marginal markings in pencil, and a few revisions in ink. MS 3467, the verso of MS 3466, contains a passage ('What is fragrance ... tides.') which has been incorporated into the text at the appropriate point, determined by comparison with the revised version of the text in MS 3498. MS 3488, the verso of MS 3487, contains notes for Klein's review of *Person, Place and Thing* by Karl Shapiro ['Jewish Self-Hatred,' *Canadian Jewish Chronicle*, 14 January 1944]. They have not been printed in this edition; nor have other notes in MS 3479, 3488, and 3490. MS 3464 consists of a single sheet on the same paper and in the same ink as MS 3465–85, with a few revisions in that ink. It contains two entries which were evidently written later, and these have been inserted at the appropriate point.

3. MS 3554–6 ('Expatiate on conversion ...').

MS 3554–6 consist of three sheets in the same ink throughout, with no revisions. Items 2, 7, and 11 are cancelled in that ink, and there are check marks in pencil in the left margin opposite items 2–4, 6, 9, and 23–5. Klein has left out number 17.

4. MS 3495–513 ('I feel like one ...') and MS 3514–15 ('The doctor's waiting-room ...').

MS 3514–15, an earlier draft of MS 3504, contain additional material, which has been inserted at the appropriate point.

MS 3495–513 consist of eighteen sheets in two different inks, changing to the second in mid-word in MS 3498 ('In/dian'), and back to the first in mid-sentence in MS 3510 ('was /the true door'). The sheets are numbered (1–10, 14–21) in the first ink, and MS 3505, the verso of MS 3504, contains a note in pencil: '10–14 empty.' There are a few revisions, in the first ink. The letter 'A' has been added in ink at the top of MS 3500 ('I am at my oldest sister's funeral ...'). MS 3514–15 consist of two sheets in a single ink, heavily revised in that ink. The phrase 'etc. etc.' is added in pencil at the end.

5. MS 7594 ('The world diminished by the contents ...').

MS 7594 contains notes, not printed in this edition, for the second version of 'The Inverted Tree.'

MS 7594 consists of a single sheet in the same ink throughout. A partially illegible phrase has been added in pencil to the outline over the words 'Vanity, mimesis, afflatus.'

6. MS 3526–49 ('I feel like one who lives ...').

MS 3526–49 consist of twenty-three sheets in the same ink throughout. All but the first sheet are numbered, in that ink. There are several revisions, some quite substantial, in that ink and in pencil. MS 3546, the verso of MS 3545, contains a passage ('I had ... one's mouth.') which has been inserted into the text at the appropriate point, which Klein indicated with an asterisk.

7. MS 3454–6 ('A Documentary, with Commentary') and MS 3459 ('*Newspaper clipping*. Report of death ...'). Klein has left out numbers 6, 23–6, and 41–9.

MS 3454–6 and MS 3459 consist of four sheets in the same ink throughout, with a few revisions in that ink. Several items are checked off in pencil. Notes and drafts in MS 3456–8 and MS 3460–2 have not been printed.

The physical appearance of these items suggests that they all date from a similar period, and their contents suggest a date of composition of c. 1942–c. 1944.

There is not enough evidence to establish the date of composition of item 1, but the date of composition of item 2, the diary, can be placed with some confidence between the end of 1942 and the beginning of 1944. The 28 September entry in the diary [MS 3474] refers to a letter from Peter Devries of *Poetry* magazine; Klein's reply to this letter, dated 29 September 1942, has survived. The sketch by Ernst Neumann referred to in MS 3485 is, in all likelihood, the one reproduced on the jacket of the present volume: it is dated 1943. The fact that the ink changes at this point suggests that some time may have passed between the previous entry and this one. Finally, the notes for the Shapiro review (see p. 196), which appear to be a late addition to the manuscript, point to a date of composition before 14 January 1944, the date of publication of the review.

Items 3–6, consisting of notes for and drafts of 'The Inverted Tree,' probably date from between late 1943 and 1944. Item 5 contains a reference to the novelist Hans Natonek, whose *In Search of Myself* is the subject of a set of notes by Klein (not printed in this edition) dated 5 December 1943 [MS 3557]. June 1945, the date of publication of 'Portrait of the Poet as Landscape,' would seem to be the latest possible date for 'The Inverted Tree,' since items 5 and 6 contain material which was later incorporated into the poem (see pp. 32 and 44). The probable date of composition of 'The Inverted Tree' can be narrowed even further. On the assumption that Klein began work on the first draft not long after 5 December 1943 (the date of the notes to Natonek), he almost certainly completed the two drafts before the end of 1944 since they consist of fewer than thirty-five pages of text, much of it in the form of notes or of slightly revised versions of earlier texts. And there was probably a considerable gap between the completion of 'Raw Material' and the writing of 'Portrait,' during which Klein worked on 'Stranger and Afraid' (see textual notes to 'Stranger and Afraid'). Two autobiographical references support a date of composition not later than 1944 for 'The Inverted Tree': (1) In the second version of 'The Inverted Tree' Kay is described as being thirty-five (later changed to thirty), which was Klein's age in 1944. (2) In the same version, Klein describes a negative review which appears four years after the publication of Kay's book of poems, citing a review of *Hath Not a Jew ...* by Allen Lesser (see explanatory note to '*Current Jewish Affairs*' [p. 216]). Since *Hath Not a Jew* ... was published in 1940, the probable date of this episode is 1944. (Lesser's review actually appeared in 1942.)

A range of c. 1942–c. 1944 for 'Raw Material' as a whole is consistent with item 7, 'A Documentary, with Commentary,' which refers to several works dating from this period. (It also contains possible references to two works which were first published in 1945, 'Sonnet Unrhymed' ['Poem on contraceptives'] and 'One More Utopia' ['utopia'], but which were probably written earlier.) This range is also consistent with the date of a grant application which Klein submitted to the Guggenheim Foundation in October 1943 (see Harold Heft, 'The Lost A.M. Klein Guggenheim Application,' *Canadian Poetry* 32 [Spring/Summer 1993], 73–81) and which is closely related to 'A Documentary, with Commentary.' Under 'Plans for Work' the application refers to two items listed in 'A Documentary, with Commentary': 'Ashkenazate Anthology' and 'Elegy – James Joyce' (the latter included in an earlier version not printed in this edition).

7 dye-mounds] *eds.*; dye-mounds (glass) *MS 3471*
14 paragraph 4] *eds.*; paragraph 3 *MS 3484*
21 *heading supplied by eds.*
25 that upon the passing] *eds.*; to that upon the passing *MS 3503*
26–7 The oath ... time, perhaps] *inserted by eds. from MS 3514–15*
27 odour of cloth] *eds.*; odour cloth *MS 3514*
waiting-room] *eds.*; waiting *MS 3515*
to afford him] *eds.*; to afford me *MS 3515*
forget about it] *eds.*; forget it about *MS 3515*
31 earth!//Or] *line space supplied by eds. (The section following the line space was added by Klein to the verso of MS 3512.)*
32 [Version 2]] *supplied by eds.*
35 she was spoken to] *eds.*; she was spoken, too, *MS 3530*
38 This to me ... when encased] *Klein went on to revise this passage in MS 3535, but the revisions are incomplete and do not provide a coherent text.*

'STRANGER AND AFRAID'

The manuscript of 'Stranger and Afraid' [MS 3726–79] consists of fifty-two sheets (with notes on MS 3733 and MS 3759, the versos of MS 3732 and MS 3758) in the same ink throughout. They are numbered in that ink. From MS 3749 on, beginning with 'We are ...' [p. 66], Klein adopted a new format for the beginnings of sections, using small capitals for the initial word or phrase; and he revised the earlier sheets for the sake of consistency. There appear to have been several later stages of revision, in at least three different inks and in pencil. MS 3777–9, beginning with 'Nothing to do ...' [p. 87], appear to have been added later, since there is a gap at the bottom of the previous sheet, MS 3776. There are a few very minor revisions on these final sheets.

Several sheets of preparatory material are filed at the National Archives in a folder labelled 'Stranger and Afraid: Notes' [MS 3715–25]. MS 3715–17 consist of notes dealing with the structure of the novel, and MS 3718–25 of drafts for MS 3768 and MS 3777. In addition to these, several related items [MS 3156, 7425, 7430] are filed elsewhere in the Klein Papers.

Appearance and content suggest a date of composition of c. 1944, soon after the completion of 'Raw Material' (c. 1942–c. 1944). Two sections of 'Stranger and Afraid' are closely based on passages in 'Raw Material': MS 3735–7 ('For she has a talent ... in a person's face''') is based on MS 3529–30; and MS 3756 ('These are the charms ... brekekex') on MS 3465 and MS 3496–7. Since one of the passages from 'Raw Material,' MS 3529–30, occurs near the end of the file chronologically (in the second version of the 'Inverted Tree'), Klein must have written 'Stranger and Afraid' after completing all or most of 'Raw Material'; and he probably did so very soon after, since the paper and ink used in 'Stranger and Afraid' are the same as those used in the second version of 'The Inverted Tree.'

51 act of God.)/At last *Klein replaced the original section heading* April 1 *with* I. *The number has not been retained, since none of the other sections is numbered.*

67 walls./[ ]/I] *There is a gap at the bottom of* MS *3749, where Klein has added the note* (Get the list?) *in a later ink.*

73 in actual participation] *eds.*; to actual participation *MS 3758*

76 not only ... the non-readers] *Klein went on to revise this passage in* MS *3762, but the revisions are incomplete and do not provide a coherent text.*

77 also flashy] *Klein went on to revise this passage in* MS *3764, but the revisions are incomplete and do not provide a coherent text.*

78 (Get that? ... Class, eh?)] *Klein added the interjected comments to the original passage in* MS *3765, and wrote* insert comments *in the left margin. He did not, however, indicate how he intended to distinguish the comments from the main text.*

82 a ball] *eds.*; ball *MS 3770*

87 like [ ]. Their] *eds. In* MS *3776,* like *is followed by* (Mexican) *and space for one word.*

think about except time] *eds. (reading in* MS *3723 and* MS *3724, earlier drafts of* MS *3777);* think about time *MS 3777*

88 marmor [ ]. Their] *eds. In* MS *3778,* marmor *is followed by* (blind) *and space for one word.*

DIARIES (1944 AND 1945)

The manuscript of the 1944 diary [MS 1292–9] consists of the first eight leaves of a bound notebook. The manuscript is in two different inks, the first for 2–5 April and 9–10 April, the second for 6–8 April. There are a few minor revisions.

The manuscript for the 1945 diary [MS 1300–3] consists of four sheets in the same ink throughout. The handwriting is less careful than in the 1944 diary and there are more revisions.

Both manuscripts probably date from a period soon after the events recorded, but it is likely that they are worked-up versions of the events, rather than immediate, daily records. The rougher 1945 manuscript probably represents an earlier state of revision than the manuscript from 1944, which is very similar to the fictionalized diary section of 'Raw Material' [MS 3464–94] in its ink, paper, and format.

95 (lesser) Reich] *eds.*; (lesser Reich) *MS 1300*

'THE CONTEMPORARY POET'

The manuscript of 'The Contemporary Poet' [MS 6569–71] consists of two sheets (MS 6570 is the verso of MS 6569), in the same ink throughout, with a few minor revisions. MS 6570–1 are numbered '2' and '3' respectively.

The manuscript is dated 'April 10, 1946.'

Some notes on further reading at the bottom of MS 6571 have been omitted.

101 Tests ... Auden: *Klein's intended arrangement of these lines is not entirely clear from the manuscript.*

'MARGINALIA'

The manuscript of 'Marginalia' [MS 5196–249] consists of three groups of texts:

I. Five longer essays, each on several sheets [MS 5196–216]:
1. '*Project*: To discover ...' [MS 5196–9]
2. 'The Man with the Hoe' [MS 5200–2]
3. 'Shakespeare's Dog' [MS 5203–8]
4. 'Previsions' [MS 5209–10]
5. 'My dear A.J.M. ...' [MS 5211–16]

II. Eight shorter essays, each on two or more half sheets [MS 5217–39]:
1. 'The classical simile' [MS 5217–18]
2. '"I don't know much about poetry ..."' [MS 5219–20]
3. '– This poem has no form? ...' [MS 5221–3]
4. '$x^2 + 2xy + y^2$' [MS 5224–5]
5. 'Towards an aesthetic' [MS 5226–7]
6. 'The poem as circular force' [MS 5228–30]
7. 'The Ballad of Sir Patrick Spens: A Scenario' [MS 5231–4]
8. 'Is it really a part of speech ...' [MS 5235–9]

III. Ten sets of aphorisms or brief observations, each on a single half sheet [MS 5240–9]:
1. 'Prose is concerned with denotations ...' [MS 5240]
2. 'Of the imitators of Eliot ...' [MS 5241]
3. 'The lunatic, the lover ...' [MS 5242]
4. 'To what purpose ...' [MS 5243]
5. 'Fiat of metaphor ...' [MS 5244]
6. 'In the writing of poetry ...' [MS 5245]
7. 'Sonnets ...' [MS 5246]
8. 'Even Milton ...' [MS 5247]
9. 'The purpose of rhyme ...' [MS 5248]
10. 'The Proper Eating' [MS 5249]

In the first group, item 1 is in the same ink throughout, with a few revisions. Items 2–4 are in a second ink throughout, with numerous revisions in that ink and some later additions in pencil. Item 5 is in a third ink throughout, with a few revisions. The sheets of each item are numbered. The sheets of the first two items were originally stapled together, as were the sheets of each of the other items.

In the second group, the items are in the same ink throughout, with a few revisions in that ink. The poem consisting of punctuation marks in item 8 was revised in a second ink. The sheets of items 2 and 4 are numbered. The sheets of each item were originally stapled together.

In the third group, the items are in the same ink throughout with the exception of an addition to MS 5241 ('No one ...'). There are very few revisions.

The following items have not been printed in this edition because they were published by Klein, and are included in *LER*: item 5 of the first group [*LER*, pp. 166–9; revised as 'Queen Mab and Mickey Mouse']; and items 3, 5, and 6 of the second group [*LER*, pp. 189–90, 182–3, 183–4].

The Klein Papers also contain a set of notes for 'Marginalia' [MS 5173–95], which have not been printed in this edition.

'Marginalia' appears to date from the late forties. Several items clearly grew out of Klein's teaching at McGill, especially items 2 and 3 of the first group; and the items which Klein published all appeared between 1946 and 1948, in the *Canadian Jewish Chronicle.*

The word 'or' is used to separate most of the examples cited in MS 5196–8. Where 'or' is missing, the editors have supplied it for the sake of consistency [pp. 103–5].

105 total of these] *eds.*; total is these *MS 5198*
107 the poet ... felicities] *Klein went on to revise this passage in* MS *5202, but the revisions are incomplete and do not provide a coherent text.*
113 lighter in sailing] *reading in the original restored by eds.*; light in sailing *MS 5208*
114 paganism./[ ]/There] Quote here from Waste Land *added in* MS *5210*
115 lintel':/[ ]/'Six] (Milton Ode on the Nativity) *added in* MS *5210*
was created hugest] *eds.*; created hugest *MS 5217*
117 a guid sailor] *reading in the original restored by eds.*; guid sailor *MS 5231*
118 signed it] *reading in the original restored by eds.*; signed *MS 5231*
120 religions] *reading in the original restored by eds.*; the religions *MS 5237*

'TOWARDS A PSYCHOANALYSIS OF G.M. HOPKINS: THE ART OF THE RORSCHACH'

The manuscript of 'Towards a Psychoanalysis of G.M. Hopkins' [MS 5090–5] consists of five sheets: MS 5090–2 and MS 5094–5 are numbered, and MS 5093 is the unnumbered verso of MS 5092. The manuscript is in red ink up to '*inscape,* and *sake*' on MS 5092, and completed and revised throughout in black ink. The revisions consist of minor verbal changes, rearrangement of some of the quotations, and incomplete additions to MS 5093 ['The notebooks ... The drawings:']. No notes or drafts have survived.

In October of 1956, Klein made use of substantial portions of 'Towards a Psychoanalysis' in a lecture on Hopkins, the last lecture of his career, which he gave at Assumption College in Windsor, Ontario [*LOTD*, p. 207]. The Klein Papers contain three sets of notes for this lecture: a first draft [MS 6947–57], a fair copy dated 6 February 1956 [MS 6939–46], and a typescript [MS 6958–65]. After the first draft, Klein deleted all references to psychoanalysis and to the Rorschach blot.

The manuscript appears to date from c. 1948/1949. Evidence for the later date is an interview which Alan Heuser gave to Usher Caplan in 1974, in which he stated that in July of 1949 Klein showed him the manuscript of an essay on 'schizoid tendencies in Hopkins' which made use of the image of the Rorschach blot. The earliest possible date for the manuscript is 1944, the year in which Austin Warren's 'Instress of Inscape,' from which Klein quotes, appeared in the *Kenyon Review* 6 (1944), 369–82. (The essay was reprinted several years later in a revised version as 'Gerard Manley Hopkins,' in *Rage for Order: Essays in Criticism* [Ann Arbor, Mich.: University of Michigan Press 1948], pp. 52–65, but it is from the earlier version that Klein quotes.) However, it is unlikely that the manuscript dates from much before 1948, since the lecture notes on Hopkins from the course on modern poetry which Klein gave at McGill from 1945 to 1948 contain no hint of the argument which he develops in the essay.

Klein misspells 'Rorschach,' either as 'Rohrschach' or as 'Rohrshach.' These misspellings have been corrected. Klein sometimes misquotes Hopkins: the misquotations have been allowed to stand, but the correct versions are cited, in parentheses, in the explanatory notes.

126 instances of this] *eds.*; instances this *MS 5093*
128 lesser] *eds. (reading in MS 6954, the first draft of the 1956 lecture)*; less *MS 5095*

UNTITLED NOVEL

The manuscript of the first chapter of Klein's untitled novel [MS 4458–72] consists of fourteen numbered sheets (with a note on MS 4471, the verso of MS 4470), in the same ink throughout. There are numerous revisions in that ink, as well as a few in a second ink and in pencil. The manuscript of the second chapter [MS 4473–8] consists of six sheets, numbered except for the first. They are of different paper than that used for the first chapter, but in the same ink, with numerous revisions in that ink. The sheets were originally stapled together in two separate groups corresponding to the two chapters.

Several sheets of preparatory material [MS 4443–57] are filed in one of Klein's folders, labelled 'The Plot' [MS 4442]. These consist of a plot summary [MS 4443–4] and notes and drafts for various episodes. In addition to these, several related items [MS 7263–7, 7539, 7558] are filed elsewhere in the Klein Papers.

Klein seems to have been undecided about the place of the chapters in the novel. The chapters are headed 'CHAPTER ONE' and 'Chapter Two: *Adloyada*'; but the first heading appears to be a later addition, and, in the plot summary, 'Hapaxlegomenon' and 'Adloyada' are identified as chapters 2 and 3 respectively. At some point, Klein separated the two chapters, for they were not filed together when his papers were deposited in the National Archives; and in Klein's own inventory of his literary manuscripts, 'Adloyada' is listed as item 3, while 'Hapaxlegomenon' is listed under item 13, 'Sundry writing.'

The novel appears to be set in 1948: there is a reference in MS 7263 to the date of Purim as 24 March, which was the date on which Purim began in that year; and the events of the novel correspond to the period immediately leading up to the foundation of the State of Israel. However, there is one piece of evidence which suggests a later date of composition, at least for 'Adloyada.' In that chapter [p. 140] one character comments on a newspaper report that Ernest Bevin suffers from haemorrhoids and he cites 1 Samuel 5.6. In 'Mr. Bevin's Ailment,' *Canadian Jewish Chronicle*, 21 April 1950, p. 3, Klein comments on the same newspaper report and cites the same biblical passage.

129 CHAPTER ONE: HAPAXLEGOMENON] *eds.*; CHAPTER ONE *MS 4458*
130 personage!] *followed by* Quote Landor *added in pencil in* MS *4460*
131 written:] *followed by* Quote Noah? *added in pencil in* MS *4461*
136 would have to] *eds.*; would to *MS 4468*
to be bad] *eds.*; be bad *MS 4469*

'THE GOLEM'

The manuscript of chapters 1 and 2 [MS 3296–331] consists of thirty-two numbered and two unnumbered sheets. The unnumbered sheets contain two separate texts, on MS 3328 and its verso MS 3329, and on MS 3330 (there are some irrelevant markings on MS 3331, the verso of MS 3330). The manuscript is in the same ink throughout, with many minor revisions in that ink. There is a smaller number of revisions and notes for revisions in a different ink on the first five sheets and in pencil throughout; some of these, in chapter 1, are quite substantial (see notes below).

The 'Golem' notes [MS 2986–3295] are extremely diverse physically. Klein used several different kinds of ink as well as pencil, and he seems to have written on anything that was available – in addition to sheets of looseleaf of various kinds, there are sheets torn out of notebooks and desk calendars, index cards, tearsheets, odd scraps of paper and cardboard, even cigarette packages.

Except for some fragmentary items [MS 7271–82, 7338, 7390] and the drafts for 'The Rationale of Pure Murder' (see below), the notes were kept by Klein in eight folders, labelled by him as follows:

40	Golem: vocabulary. [ink]	MS 2986–3126
40a	Character & Colour [pencil]	MS 3127–52
40b	Phrasing, Prosody [pencil] Golem [ink]	MS 3153–207
40c	Geography of Prague [pencil]	MS 3208–27
40d	The Golem. 1. [ink]	MS 3228–45
40e	Separate subjects – Cabbala, Mould [pencil]	MS 3246–79
41a	Good & Evil [pencil] (Golem) [ink]	MS 3280–8
41b	Rumphaeus [pencil]	MS 3289–95

Some, but not all, of these folders seem to correspond to those listed at the end of Klein's inventory of his literary manuscripts [pp. 255–60]. Each contains material which we would expect from its label, but most contain other material as well: for example, maps of Prague and the Prague ghetto [MS 3290–1] are in the 'Rumphaeus' folder rather than in 'Geography of Prague.'

Except for an outline [MS 3166], material related to 'The Rationale of Pure Murder' is not filed with the 'Golem' notes. This material consists of three drafts [MS 3559–69; MS 3570–2, 3576–81; MS 3573–5] as well as two sheets of related notes [MS 3585–6]. Drafts 1 and 2 are in the same ink throughout and there are many minor revisions to them in that ink. Draft 2 also contains revisions in two other inks on its first sheet, and in pencil throughout. Draft 3, which is in the same ink throughout, and contains some minor revisions in that ink, incorporates most of the revisions to the first sheet of Draft 2. Draft 1 ('The Responsa') contains twenty-two numbered items, corresponding to items 1–25 in Draft 2. Draft 2 ('The Responsa') contains items 1–39. Draft 3 ('The Rationale of Pure Murder') is a fair copy of the first three sheets of the revised version of Draft 2, consisting of items 1–16, with some minor changes. Draft 2 has been chosen as copy-text for items 17–39, but for items 1–16, which are incompletely revised at several points in Draft 2, the copy-text is Draft 3.

There is an early version of Modena's essay 'The Perfect Crime,' entitled 'Detective Story, or A Likely Story' [MS 3582–4], in the same

National Archives folder as the drafts for 'Rationale of Pure Murder.' (It is included in *Stories*, pp. 210–12.) The manuscript is in the same ink throughout, and there are a few minor revisions to it in that ink.

Some of the material in the 'Golem' folders appears to date from the mid-forties or even earlier, but evidence of style, handwriting, ink, and paper suggests a date in the early to mid-fifties for most it. Conclusive evidence for a *post quem* date in the early fifties for some of the material is of two sorts: (1) Klein's references to the 5 October 1951 issue of the *Canadian Jewish Chronicle* [MS 3222] and to his translation of the 'Kaddish' (c. 1951/1952) [MS 3303]; and (2) his use of sheets from a 1950 desk calendar [MS 3014–15, 3266–72] and from a copy of the 20 February 1953 issue of the *Canadian Jewish Chronicle* [MS 3168] for note paper.

Chapters 1 and 2 probably predate many of the 'Golem' notes: there is no preliminary material for these chapters in any of the notes, and some notes [MS 3222, MS 3229] refer to them as already completed.

'The Rationale of Pure Murder' probably dates from before 'The Golem' since it contains a number of historical references which are inconsistent with the period in which the novel is set. This suggests that sometime after completing 'The Rationale,' Klein decided to incorporate it into 'The Golem' but had not yet made the necessary revisions.

'Detective Story, or A Likely Story' dates from the early to mid-forties. It is identical in handwriting, ink, and paper to 'Stranger and Afraid' and to the second version of 'The Inverted Tree,' and one of Klein's notes [MS 7425] indicates that he considered working it into the first version of 'The Inverted Tree.'

144 delivers the funeral oration] delivers *altered to* delivered *in MS 3299 as part of an incomplete revision*

145 too,/[ ]/Without] *The bottom third of MS 3301 is blank.*

146 wings!/Yesterday] *Notes in MS 3303 indicate that Klein considered dividing chapter 1 into two new chapters at this point, and ending the new chapter 1 with a translation of the 'Kaddish,' presumably after the necessary revisions had been made.*

do not speak like that] like that *deleted in MS 3304 as part of an incomplete revision*

149 CHAPTER TWO] *eds.*; II *MS 3308*

158 having to hide] *eds.*; to hide *MS 3324*

160 My mind ... sweetness] *corresponds to the unnumbered sheets at the end of the manuscript [MS 3328–30]*

164 shut out the world] *ed.*; shut out the world (?) *MS 3241*

170 cultural] *may be* cultured *MS 3573*

172 let y stand for] y *altered to* yz/2 *in* MS *3576 as part of an incomplete revision*

174 40–50 *is added at the end of Draft 2 [*MS *3581], but there are no corresponding items.*

SELECTED NOTES AND FRAGMENTS

The following is a list of all of the texts printed in the 'Selected Notes and Fragments' section of this edition. They have been arranged in what the editors consider to be the most likely chronological order:

1. MS 3156 ('Modigliani tours the ghetto').

MS 3156 consists of a single sheet in the same ink throughout.

The sheet is filed with the 'Golem' material, but handwriting and content suggest a date in the late thirties. The text is, in any case, no later than 1945 since some passages have been incorporated from it into 'Stranger and Afraid' (see explanatory note to 'Modigliani tours the ghetto' [pp. 252–3]).

2. MS 3169–71 ('Bon Mots').

MS 3169–71 consist of two sheets (MS 3170 is the verso of MS 3169) in the same ink throughout.

The sheets are filed with the 'Golem' material, but handwriting and verbal parallels with 'Raw Material' suggest a date in the early forties (see explanatory note to 'Flattery ... imagines' [p. 253]).

3. MS 7427–8 ('If individuality exists ...').

MS 7427–8 consist of two sheets in the same ink throughout.

Handwriting and verbal parallels with 'Raw Material' suggest a date in the early forties (see explanatory notes to 'mizrach wall' and 'Violin ... in advance' [p. 253]).

4. MS 7440 ('Is this our Canadian poet ...').

MS 7440 consists of a single sheet in the same ink throughout with some revisions in that ink and in pencil.

Handwriting and verbal parallels with 'Raw Material' suggest a date in the early forties.

5. MS 3463 ('At the Turkish bath').

MS 3463 consists of a single sheet in the same ink throughout.

It is on the same kind of paper as MS 3169 in 'Raw Material,' with which it is filed. This and verbal parallels suggest a date in the early forties (see explanatory notes to 'Man ... stew' and 'Along ... Unclejew' [p. 253]).

6. MS 7446 ('Before the riesenrising ...').

MS 7446 consists of a single sheet in the same ink throughout, with revisions in that ink.

Handwriting and stylistic parallels with the end of 'Stranger and Afraid' suggest a date in the mid-forties.

7. MS 4456 ('Yerushalayim').

MS 4456 consists of a single sheet in pencil throughout with revisions in pencil.

Handwriting and its close relationship with the untitled novel, with which it is filed, suggest a date in the late forties.

8. MS 4457 ('The clamour ...').

MS 4457 consists of a single sheet in pencil throughout with revisions in the same ink.

Handwriting and its close relationship with the untitled novel, with which it is filed, suggest a date in the late forties.

9. MS 3165–6 ('He's not convinced ...').

MS 3165–6 consist of two sheets in the same ink throughout.

Handwriting and verbal parallels with 'The Golem,' with which they are filed, suggest a date in the late forties or early fifties (see explanatory note to 'Responsa ... requirement' [p. 254]).

10. MS 3191–5 ('He translated ...').

MS 3191–5 consist of five sheets in the same ink throughout, with the exception of one brief passage at the top of MS 3194 ('God invented ... royalties.').

The sheets are of the same paper as that used for MS 3165–6 in 'The Golem,' with which they are filed. This and verbal parallels suggest a date in the late forties or early fifties (see explanatory notes to 'After ... genitalia,' 'The trouble ... race,' and 'Envy ... disproportion' [p. 254]).

11. MS 7443–4 ('The blouse ...').

MS 7443–4 consist of two sheets in the same ink throughout. 'BLOUSE,' 'CHINESE,' and 'OF ARMORIAL BEARINGS' are pencilled into the left margin of each of the three paragraphs respectively.

Handwriting and the relationship of the third paragraph to passages dealing with heraldry in the 'Golem' notes [MS 3201–5, 3209, and 3232] suggest a date in the late forties or early fifties.

12. MS 7421 ('Poetry ...').

MS 7421 consists of a single sheet in the same ink throughout.

Handwriting and verbal parallel with MS 3192 suggest a date in the late forties or early fifties.

13. MS 7393 ('And, cornucopic ...').

MS 7393 consists of a single sheet in the same ink throughout.

Dated 'June 1st 1955.'

185 seen fit] *eds.*; seen *MS 7440*

Explanatory Notes

FROM THE 'RAW MATERIAL' FILE

toothache ... weltanschauung: Compare 'Dentist' [pp. 16–17].

Ich dien: (Ger.) 'I serve'; motto of the Prince of Wales

mute inglorious: Compare 'mute inglorious Milton' [Thomas Gray, 'Elegy Written in a Country Churchyard,' 59].

cunniform: Compare 'Freud's cunniform writ' [MS 7269]. Elsewhere [pp. 22 and 78] Klein uses the spelling 'cunneiform.'

Non omnis moriar: (Lat.) 'I will not entirely die' [Horace, *Odes* 3.30.6]

froggish ... brekekex: a reference to Aesop's fable of the frog which burst in attempting to inflate itself to the size of a bull. 'Brekekex' is from the chorus of Aristophanes' *The Frogs*. The chorus is quoted in James Joyce's *Finnegans Wake* (New York: Viking Press 1939), p. 4, which Klein had recently been reading.

Lady Pertelote: the hen in Chaucer's 'Nun's Priest's Tale'

Li Tai Po, drunk ... love: Li Tai Po (c. 700–62) was a Chinese poet of the T'ang dynasty. Many of his poems deal with love and wine.

Succoth: A palm branch (along with a willow branch and myrtle branch) and a citron are shaken as part of the ritual of the Jewish holiday of Succoth, the Feast of Tabernacles.

ease in Zion: Compare 'Woe to them that are at ease in Zion' [Amos 6.1].

lore in Babylon: Babylon was noted for its eminent academies in the Talmudic and post-Talmudic periods.

citeron-proteron: a pun on 'hysteron proteron,' 'a figure of speech in which the word or phrase which should properly come last is put first' [*OED*]

comforted apples: Compare 'Stay me with flagons, comfort me with apples: for I am sick of love' [Song of Solomon 2.5].

how ... nations: Lamentations 1.1

Blastart Duelord: Compare 'Blessed art Thou, O Lord,' the standard opening of Jewish benedictions.

burden of Klein: A number of biblical prophecies, most frequently in the Book of Isaiah, begin with the phrase 'the burden of ...'

Rabinovitch: Israel Rabinovitch, editor of the *Keneder Adler* ('Canadian Eagle'), Montreal's Yiddish-language daily, for which Klein wrote a column in English at about this time. Klein later translated Rabinovitch's *Of Jewish Music, Ancient and Modern* (Montreal: Book Centre 1952).

The library: the Jewish Public Library of Montreal

Am Ha-Sepher: (Heb.) 'the people of the Book'

Talmud: usually refers to the Bablyonian Talmud (which differs from the Jerusalem Talmud), a compendium of commentaries on the Mishnah by generations of scholars and jurists in many academies beginning in the third century and ending with its redaction at the end of the fifth century. Together with the Bible, it constitutes the basis of traditional Jewish law and culture.

Maimonides: Moses ben Maimon (1135–1204), Spanish-born Jewish religious philosopher, legal scholar, and physician

Halevi: Yehuda Halevi (before 1075–1141), philosopher and the major poet of the golden age of medieval Jewish culture in Spain

Bialik: Chaim Nachman Bialik (1873–1934), the major modern Hebrew poet

Argumentum ad vulgum: (Lat.) 'argument addressed to the mob'

jargon: Yiddish writers in the nineteenth and twentieth centuries had to defend Yiddish against the charge that it was not a real language; a common Yiddish term for the language was *zhargon*, that is, 'jargon' in the sense of a debased, hybrid speech. Compare 'Merchants, or in Slav or jargon, / Driving each his petty bargain' ['Ballad of the Dancing Bear,' 19–20 (*CP*, 1.157)].

Peretz: Isaac Leib Peretz (1852–1915), the central figure in modern Yiddish literature and an important figure in modern Hebrew literature

Mendele: Mendele Mokher Sforim (Shalom Jacob Abramovitsch) (1835–1917), generally considered the founder of modern literary Yiddish as well as of a new realism in modern Hebrew literature

Kaddish: that is, the mourner's *Kaddish*, a prayer traditionally recited by the nearest male kin of the deceased, especially a son

of what avail ... souls: Compare 'For what is a man profited, if he shall gain the whole world, and lose his own soul?' [Matthew 16.26].

Rabbi Yochanan ben Zakkai: Rabbi Yoḥanan ben Zakkai (1st century AD) was the leading scholar in the period following the destruction of the Temple. He received permission from Vespasian to go to Jabneh, where he established a centre of learning, thus ensuring the survival of Judaism.

sellers ... mess: Compare the proverbial phrase 'to sell one's birthright for a mess of pottage.' This phrase, which refers to Esau's selling his birthright to Jacob [Genesis 25.29–34], does not actually occur in the King James Version.

pneumothorax: 'the presence of air or gas in the cavity of the thorax, i.e. in the pleura, usually caused by a wound or by perforation of the lung' [*OED*]

sard: 'a variety of cornelian, varying in colour from pale golden yellow to reddish orange' [*OED*]

Regrating: To regrate is 'to buy up (market commodities, esp. victuals) in order to sell again at a profit in the same or a neighbouring market' [OED].

Lombard: 'a native of Lombardy engaged as a banker, money-changer, or pawnbroker; hence applied *gen.* to a person carrying on any of these businesses' [OED]. Compare 'lombard schemes' ['Pawnshop,' 31 (CP, 2.576)].

Colman: Klein's first son, born in 1937

Aristotle ... rational vegetable: The reference is to Seneca's definition of man as a rational animal: 'Rationale animal est homo' [*Epistulae ad Lucilium*, 41, section 8]. Aristotle defined man not as a rational but as a political animal [*Politics*, Book 1, chapter 2].

Et ... livres: Compare 'La chair est triste, hélas, et j'ai lu tous les livres' [Mallarmé, 'Brise marine,' 1]; quoted in 'Diary of Abraham Segal, Poet,' 176 [CP, 1.237].

minette: (Fr.) fashionable, sophisticated young woman

'Come two, like shadows': The poem was submitted to *Poetry* (Chicago) on 31 August 1942, and appeared in number 61 (February 1943), 595.

Plato ... screen: a reference to Plato's myth of the cave in the seventh book of the *Republic*

the maestro: Klein is referring to Samuel Bronfman, the prominent Montreal industrialist and philanthropist, head of Seagram's, and president of the Canadian Jewish Congress, 1939–62. Bronfman employed Klein as a writer and public relations counsel.

called for in the premises: Klein uses this phrase, in the sense of 'whatever is customarily required,' in a letter to Alfred A. Knopf Inc., 9 Oct. 1951.

baksheesh: 'Oriental term for: A gratuity, present of money, "tip"' [OED]

maka: (Yid.) 'plague' or 'scourge'; from the Hebrew word for 'blow' or 'wound' or 'plague'

zdaka: (Yid.) 'charity,' 'alms.' In the Bible, the Hebrew word *ẓdaka* means primarily 'righteousness,' 'justice.'

Chait: Sam Chait, Klein's law partner at this time

Eloise and Abie: a reference to the medieval lovers Eloise and Abelard

at her back ... near: Compare 'But at my back I always hear / Time's wingèd chariot hurrying near' [Andrew Marvell, 'To His Coy Mistress,' 21–2].

Aroint ... runion: Compare '"Aroint thee, witch!" the rump-fed ronyon cries' [*Macbeth* 1.3.6].

Quousque tandem: (Lat.) 'How long.' Compare 'Quousque tandem abutere, Catilina, patientia nostra' ('How long will you abuse our patience, Catiline') [Cicero, *In Catilinam* 1.1.1].

The Lay of the Fast Minstrel: Compare *The Lay of the Last Minstrel* by Sir Walter Scott.

Ode to Nightingale ... sun: The Ode which Klein is parodying is, in fact, 'To Autumn.' Compare 'Season of mists and mellow fruitfulness, / Close bosom-friend of the maturing sun' ['To Autumn,' 1–2].

à toutes fins que de droit: (Fr.) 'for all legal purposes'

prays act of admission: To pray act of admission is to acknowledge an admission with a view to making it irreversible.

Nuptias ... nuptias Although the passage is partially illegible, the reference is clearly to the principle of marriage law, *Nuptias non concubitus sed consensus facit*: 'It is consent not cohabitation, which makes a marriage' [Earl Jowitt, *The Dictionary of English Law* (London: Sweet & Maxwell Limited 1959)].

sans ... everything: Compare 'Sans teeth, sans eyes, sans taste, sans everything' [*As You Like It*, 2.7.166].

Neumann ... sketch: Ernst Neumann (1907–55) was a Montreal artist and a friend of Klein's. The sketch is reproduced on the jacket of the present volume.

that ... minds: Compare John Milton's description of fame as 'that last infirmity of noble mind' [*Lycidas*, 71].

Sholem Asch ... Nazarene: Sholem Asch (1880–1957) was a popular Yiddish novelist. His works were translated into many languages, and he was the first Yiddish writer to enjoy an international reputation. *The Nazarene* was a novel on the life of Christ, the first of a trilogy on the founders of Christianity. Asch's interest in Christianity caused a furore in some Jewish circles, which Klein dismissed as 'this donning of sackloth over the supposedly imminent sprinkling of Asch. Finally, the entire affair seems to us to be no more than a tempest in a baptismal font' ['The Thirteenth Apostle?' (*LER*, p. 37)].

Maurice Samuel: (1895–1972), American author and translator from Yiddish and Hebrew, born in Romania. He was an influential and popular exponent of Zionist ideology and a great admirer of Klein's work, especially *The Second Scroll*.

Villon: François Villon (1431–63?), French poet whose experiences in the criminal underworld are reflected in his poems

Rilke: Rainer Maria Rilke (1875–1926), German lyric poet, a major influence on Klein's work in the forties

may one ... ache: In 'The Yiddish Proverb,' Klein cites 'the oath full-mouthed breathing execration ... "May all his teeth fall out, except one – for toothache!"' [*LER*, p. 121].

Girlie Show: The first two lines are a quotation from Keats's 'Ode on a Grecian Urn,' 8–9 (with 'feigning' in place of 'struggle'). Klein imitates the stanzaic structure of the Ode.

Pan: Pan, the son of Hermes, was the goat-footed pastoral god of fertility. He was associated with Dionysus and Dionysian rites.

omphalos: (Gr.) 'navel'; the navel-shaped stone used in the rites of many Greek and Roman cults. The most famous was at the oracle of Delphi.

razed ... salted ground: After their final victory over Carthage in the third Punic War, the Romans razed the city and sowed its site with salt.

Adam Smith ... stealth: a reference to Adam Smith (1723–90), the Scottish economist whose *Inquiry into the Nature and Causes of the Wealth of Nations* (1776) argued that in a laissez-faire economy the impulse of self-interest would bring about the public welfare

conversion ... vibrations: Compare 'Numbers it is. All music when you come to think ... Vibrations ... Musemathematics' [*Ulysses*, pp. 273–4].

A noir etc: Compare 'A noir, E blanc, I rouge, U vert, O bleu: voyelles, / Je dirai quelque jour vos naissances latentes' [Arthur Rimbaud, 'Voyelles'].

cantor ... mizrach wall: *Mizraḥ* is Hebrew for 'east.' In places west of Jerusalem (e.g., Europe), Jews traditionally face eastward during prayers. The cantor, leading the worshippers, normally stands at the front, close to the east wall.

inverted tree: the lungs. Aristotle compared the human body to an inverted tree [*De Partibus Animalium* 4.10], and the comparison was adopted by a number of Jewish writers, as noted in a passage in the article on 'Botany' in JE. Klein may also have had in mind the Kabbalistic 'tree of the *Sefirot*,' a diagram of the ten *sefirot* or stages of divine emanation in the form of a 'reversed tree' [Gershom Scholem, *Kabbalah* (New York: New American Library 1974), p. 106].

no birds sing: Compare 'The sedge has wither'd from the lake, / And no birds sing' [Keats, 'La Belle Dame Sans Merci,' 3–4].

Rilke poem on air: probably the first sonnet from Book 2 of *Sonnets to Orpheus*. See note to 'Rilke' [p. 212].

Bevel in the ear: Compare 'having lost the bevel in the ear' ['Portrait of the Poet as Landscape,' 67 (CP, 2.636)].

salon ... beasts: Compare

... As if the books were boards,
and, at a button, had slid away, revealing
bars, and behind, cement – his secret – where wild beasts
yawned, and waved paw, circled, ran forward, roared
for the week's meat.

['The Library,' 23–7 (CP, 2.620)]

S. attempt: that is, suicide attempt

S. – Dante ... trees: 'S.' is 'suicide,' as in 'S. attempt' in Klein's item 16. The Dante reference is to Canto 13 of the *Inferno*, where suicides are punished by being transformed into trees. When Dante arrives at the Forest of Suicides, he breaks off a branch from one of the trees, and it bleeds.

pares his nails: Compare 'The artist, like the God of creation, remains within or behind or beyond or above his handiwork, invisible, refined out of existence, indifferent, paring his fingernails' [James Joyce, *A Portrait of the Artist as a Young Man* (Harmondsworth: Penguin 1960), p. 215].

cunneiform: See note to 'cunniform' [p. 209].

my oldest sister: Ida (Chaya) Rachel Katz, Klein's half-sister (eldest child of Kalman and his first wife, Miriam), died at the age of fifty-eight on 5 December 1943 and was buried the following day.

Applebaum's funeral chapel: a fictional name. The funeral of Klein's sister was held at Paperman's.

my other sisters: Bessie (Woolf) and Dora (Weinstein), children of the marriage of Kalman and Yetta

my brother: Klein had two half-brothers, Jack and Velvel, children of Kalman and Yetta.

Colman ... Samuel: See note to 'Colman' [p. 211]. Klein's second son, Samuel (he later changed his name to Sandor), was born in 1941.

Elizabeth: Klein's wife was named Bessie.

I am a garden ... sing: See note to 'no birds sing' [p. 213].

as my numbered senses flowered: Compare 'the first flowering of senses five' ['Autobiographical,' 69 (CP, 2.566)].

deodand: 'a personal chattel which, having been the immediate occasion of the death of a human being, was given to God as an expiatory offering' [OED]

Levite ... bread: Compare 'Bakers most priestly, in your robes of flour, / White Levites at your altar'd ovens' ['Bread,' 17–18 (CP, 2.618)].

Nero ... bath: The Emperor Nero committed suicide after the Roman fashion by slitting his wrists while immersed in a warm bath.

wine-pale: a reference to the Homeric epithet for the sea, 'wine-dark'

world ... paid back: Compare 'O, somehow pay back the daily larcenies of the lung!' ['Portrait of the Poet as Landscape,' 157 (CP, 2.639)].

Cursed ... pentameter: Compare 'and he will curse his quintuplet senses' ['Portrait of the Poet as Landscape,' 39 (CP, 2.635)].

Vanity, mimesis, afflatus: Compare Section V of 'Portrait of the Poet as Landscape' [119–32 (CP, 2.638)].

unpraised ... unlabelled: Compare 'naming, praising' ['Portrait of the Poet as Landscape,' 135 (CP, 2.639)].

My inventory ... taken: Compare 'taking a green inventory' ['Portrait of the Poet as Landscape,' 134 (CP, 2.638)].

photographer ... glimpse: Compare

> And now in imagination he has climbed
> another planet, the better to look
> with single camera view upon this earth –
>
> ['Portrait of the Poet as Landscape,' 146–8 (CP, 2.639)]

kohled: Kohl is 'a powder used in the East to darken the eyelids, etc.' [OED].

fast-days ... Thursdays: There are numerous fast-days in the Jewish calendar, most of which are observed only by very pious Jews. 'Some pious Jews also fast every Monday and Thursday in commemoration of the destruction of the Temple, of the burning of the Torah, and of the desecration of God's name' ['Fasting and Fast-Days,' JE].

Sabbath ... New Moon: The Blessing of the New Moon is recited in the synagogue on the Sabbath before the new moon appears. The ceremony is traditionally a joyous one.

siddur: (Heb.) 'prayerbook'

old-fashioned Yiddish ... prayerbooks: Because most women in the Jewish communities of eastern Europe could not read Hebrew, prayerbooks were composed for them in Yiddish.

Rebono shel Olam: (Heb.) 'Lord of the Universe'

meaning of idle tears: Compare 'Tears, idle tears, I know what they mean' [Tennyson, 'Tears, Idle Tears,' 1].

perruqueless: 'Jewesses (married and pious) wear perruques. The custom has died out in America; but not for my mother' [letter to A.J.M. Smith, 21 January 1943].

her little kaddish: See note to 'Kaddish' [p. 210]. The phrase is often used to mean 'son.'

demons ... go away: Jewish parents often publicly denigrated their children to protect them from the evil eye (*ayin haraah*).

morphine: Compare

> Juice of the poppy, conjuror of timeless twilights,
> Eternities of peace in which the fretful world
> Like a tame tiger at the feet lies curled.
>
> ['Grace before Poison,' 28–30 (CP, 2.506)]

In a letter to the Jewish Publication Society, 1 July 1943, Klein comments on these lines that 'morphine is spoken of in flattering terms, – but note, it is morphine for medicinal purposes. I myself have on several occasions received the blessing of its effects, and they are precisely as described in the last lines of the poem.'

Medical Arts Building: located at 1538 Sherbrooke West

Urim and Thummim: (Heb.) a priestly device in ancient Israel for obtaining oracles, kept in the breastplate of the high priest [Exodus 28.30]

Belshazzar ... wall: Daniel 5.25 recounts how, while King Belshazzar of Babylonia was feasting, a hand appeared which wrote the words *mene, mene, tekel, ufarsin* on a wall. Daniel correctly interpreted these words as predicting Belshazzar's defeat by the Persians.

three-leaved ... sheathes: Compare

> And all my Aprils there are marked and spotted
> upon the adder's tongue, darting in light,
> upon the easy threes of trilliums, dark green, green, and white.
>
> ['The Mountain,' 23–5 (CP, 2.690)]

Baba: (Yid.) 'grandmother'

Shmulikl: Yiddish diminutive for Shmuel, that is, Samuel

he wrapped ... flag: Compare 'We find that all of the advertisers, for one reason or another, have wrapped themselves in the flag' ['Advertising Declares War' (BS, p. 164)].

pink-brush ... menace: Compare 'these tattle-tale menaces, these pink-brush phobias' [BS, p. 163].

Every time ... pay: Compare 'Is there a statesman who has uttered some colloquialism which has entered the popular parlance? It is ore for the copy-writer; in a week he will dish it up as the punchline of an ad, advancing the interests of some very pedestrian article' [BS, p. 163].

While Rome ... fiddle: Compare 'These fiddlers fiddle even while Rome burns' [BS, p. 164].

tobacco ads ... morale: Compare 'Did you know that tobacco increases the war-effort? So it is, indeed; tobacco, says the ingenious copy-writer, steadies nerves. In war and in industry steady nerves are an asset. Ergo, tobacco is our secret weapon!' [BS, p. 164].

shoe-manufacturer ... Boots: Compare 'Here, for example, is a shoe-manufacturer. He looks for a war-angle in which to perch his shoes. At last, he has it! In essential industry, he announces in capital letters, shoes are essential! Apparently before Pearl Harbour, everybody went barefoot' [BS, p. 164].

soap account ... enchanting: Compare 'Women are being employed more and more in war-industry. They still, however, wish to remain feminine. After the grime and the oil of ammunition labour, do working wives still wish to keep their hands enchanting? Use so-and-so's Soap' [BS, p. 165].

Secret Service ... agency: Compare 'Another advertising genius, aware of the fact that the public is war-conscious, heads his ad with the ominous words, in bold black letters: Secret Service. You would imagine that here you were going to be made privy to some hair-raising revelations. You read. The secret service is a matrimonial agency!' [BS, p. 164].

But ... silver: Compare the deleted section of 'Portrait of the Poet as Landscape' [CP, 2.640].

Current Jewish Affairs: The account of Allen Little's review of Kay's book in *Current Jewish Affairs* is based on a review by Allen Lesser of *Hath Not a Jew* ... in the *Contemporary Jewish Record* 5 (June 1942), 333. Kay's letter to Nachtigal is a slightly revised version of one Klein wrote to Abraham G. Duker, editor of the *Contemporary Jewish Record*, on 26 June 1942 [MS 156–8].

distinguished writer: Ludwig Lewisohn (1882–1955), an American novelist, essayist, and translator. He was a great admirer of Klein's poetry, and his essay on Klein, 'Concerning a Jewish Poet,' *Jewish Standard* (September 1936), 8, 39, from which Klein quotes, was reprinted as the foreword to *Hath Not a Jew* ...

mottling ... yclept: Compare 'All week his figure mottles / The city lanes' ('Portraits of a Minyan,' 115–16 [CP 1.138]) and 'Of yore yclept in old Judaea Zvi' ('Childe Harold's Pilgrimage,' 1 [CP, 2.475]).

assimilationist ... swastika: In 'Portrait, and Commentary,' a satirical attack on *Commentary*, the successor to the *Contemporary Jewish Record*, Klein claims that its editor 'finds it hard to distinguish / The four-shanked aleph from the swastika' [15–16, (*CP*, 2.667)].

he did not like me, Dr. Fell: Compare

I do not love you, Dr. Fell,
But why I cannot tell;
But this I know full well,
I do not love you, Dr. Fell.

[Thomas Brown (1663–1704), trans. of Martial's Epigram 1.32]

stercoraceous ... merdivore: 'dung-like dung-eater, wormy dung-eater'

little breeds: 'lesser breeds' in the letter to Duker

King Frederick of Prussia: Frederick William I (1688–1740), King of Prussia (1713–40), had an obsession with tall soldiers; all the soldiers in his Grenadier Guards were at least six feet tall.

veldt: See pp. 21–2 and 32–3.

reconstructionist: the *Reconstructionist*, journal of the Reconstructionist movement, whose aim is to shift the concerns of Judaism away from the afterlife to the attainment of salvation in this world

On ... Angel: See 'Les Vespasiennes,' 17–18 [*CP*, 2.627]: '... we are not God. Not God. Why, not, / not even angels ...'

we ... born: See 'We Who Are About to Be Born: A Parable' [*Stories*, pp. 213–16].

utopia: See 'One More Utopia' [*Stories*, pp. 217–23].

Ghetto poem: See 'Autobiographical,' 1 [*CP*, 2.564]: 'Out of the ghetto streets ...'

Montreal poem: See 'Montreal' [*CP*, 2.621–3].

Poem on old age: See 'The Green Old Age' [*CP*, 2.619].

Poem on bread: See 'Bread' [*CP*, 2.617–18].

Inverted Tree: See pp. 21–31 and 32–47.

Section on Lomza: See pp. 36–8.

Letter to Nachtigal: See pp. 44–7.

Playlet re Colman: See pp. 7–8 and 23–4.

Poem on contraceptives: See 'Sonnet Unrhymed' [*CP*, 2.645].

Poem on poisons: See 'Grace before Poison' [*CP*, 505–6].

Ashkenazate anthology: In his 1943 application to the Guggenheim Foundation (see textual note to 'A Documentary, with Commentary' [p. 196]), Klein lists, under 'Plans for Work,' 'An Ashkenazate Anthology – a series of poems, portraits of anonymous Jews – a cross-section of Jewish life.' 'Ashkenazi' (from the Heb. for Germany, 'Ashkenaz') refers to the Jews of Germany and their descendants in other countries, especially eastern Europe. Klein perhaps uses 'Ashkenazate' rather than 'Ashkenazi' to avoid 'nazi.'

Epitaph for Shakespeare: See 'Epitaph' [*CP*, 2.626].

Poem on father: See 'Petition For That My Father's Soul Should Enter into Heaven' [*CP*, 1.315–17].

Bread: See 'Bread' [CP, 2.617–18].
Advertising: See pp. 41–4.
Autobiographical: See 'Autobiographical' [CP, 2.564–7].
Badchan: (Heb.) jester or merrymaker, particularly at traditional Jewish weddings, in eastern Europe
Dentist: See 'Dentist' [CP, 2.568–9].
always after: See 'Love,' 22 [CP, 2.573–4]: 'And after, always, every man is sad.'

'STRANGER AND AFRAID'

Title: 'I, a stranger and afraid / In a world I never made' [A.E. Housman, *Last Poems*, 12.17–18]
souffleur: (Fr.) 'prompter'
obsession ... craves: Compare 'Bread' [CP, 2.617–18].
planetary ... revolutions: Compare

> The planetary motion of the blood
> Also the peregrinations of routine,
> And the bright pendulum of dialectic,
> All go awry,
> Lose their direction and their polarhood
> Before the keen
> Weltschmerz residing in a cavity!
>
> ['Dentist,' 1–7 (CP, 2.568)]

A little touch ... kin: Compare 'One touch of nature makes the whole world kin' [*Troilus and Cressida*, 3.3.175].
Turcotte: Edmond Turcotte was editor of *Le Canada* at this time, but it is highly unlikely that Klein has him in mind, since, according to Klein, he was a 'liberal-minded' opponent of anti-Semitism ['*Le Canada* and "This Hatred"' (BS, p. 251)].
Drizen: from the Yiddish *draytsen*, meaning 'thirteen'
No doubt ... map: See notes to pp. 34–5.
her crown: a reference to the Yiddish term of endearment, *mayn kroyn*, 'my crown.' Compare 'My fallen crown!' [SS, p. 13].
as who should say: a common phrase in Shakespeare
sub specie aeternitatis: (Lat.) 'under the aspect of eternity,' Spinoza's term for the view of the world as contained in God
Bordeaux Jail: a fortress-like men's prison, built in 1912, situated in the north-central section of Montreal Island, close to the river, near Gouin Boulevard. Administered by the Province of Quebec, Bordeaux was used for prisoners awaiting sentence and for those whose sentences were two years or less. Its cells were intended to hold no more than one occupant, but there could have been two to a cell at times when the prison was overpopulated.

Elizabeth: Klein's wife was named Bessie.

Turrets: a popular brand of cigarettes

notebook ... addresses, appointments, poems in germination: Nine such notebooks are to be found in the Klein Papers [MS 7178—390].

caducean: 'Caducean' means 'of or pertaining to a caduceus' [OED], the wand, with two serpents twined round it, carried by Hermes, messenger of the gods. This meaning, however, does not seem relevant to the passage. Klein may have had in mind 'caduciary,' meaning 'subject, relating to, or by way of escheat or lapse,' that is, 'confiscated' [OED].

impedimenta: 'things which impede or encumber progress; baggage; travelling equipment (of an army, etc.)' [OED]. Klein generally uses it to mean the baggage of civilization. For examples, see explanatory note to 'Childe Harold's Pilgrimage,' 28 [CP, 2.958].

cynosure ... eyes: Compare 'The cynosure of neighbouring eyes' [John Milton, 'L'Allegro,' 80]. 'Cynosure' means the pole-star, hence 'something that serves for guidance or direction; a "guiding star"' [OED].

ding an sich: (Ger.) 'thing in itself,' a term from Kantian philosophy referring to realities which exist irrespective of our ability to perceive them

black year: the Yiddish curse, *a shvarts yor*

Bishop Berkeley ... mind: a reference to the philosophy of Bishop George Berkeley (1685–1753) which holds that physical objects exist only in being perceived

Le Chameau: an anti-Semitic journal edited in the thirties in Montreal by the fascist Adrien Arcand

Nor ... Sabbath: Labour of any sort is forbidden on the Sabbath.

Let the heathen rage: Compare 'Why do the heathen rage, and the people imagine a vain thing?' [Psalms 2.1].

Camillien Houde: mayor of Montreal. For Klein's attitude to Houde, see introductory explanatory note to 'Political Meeting' [CP, 2.1010].

imprecations of Deuteronomy: Deuteronomy 28.15–68 contains a list of terrible curses that are to befall the Jewish nation if it fails to observe God's laws.

numerus clausus: quota of Jews admitted to institutes of higher learning, professions, etc. The policy was officially implemented in pre-Revolutionary Russia and eastern Europe and unofficially elsewhere.

ghetto bench: Beginning in the mid-thirties, Jewish students in some Polish universities were required to attend lectures in segregated areas of the classroom.

ten lamps: the ten commandments. Klein is paraphrasing 'The Jew' by Isaac Rosenberg, which he quotes in 'Shevuoth,' *Canadian Jewish Chronicle*, 8 June 1951, p. 3 [BS, p. 404]:

> Moses, from whose loins I sprung,
> Lit by a lamp in his blood
> Ten immutable rules ...

saintly Hillel: Hillel the elder, greatest of the sages of the Second Temple period, renowned for his tolerance and gentle nature

Maimonides: Moses ben Maimon (1135–1204), Spanish-born Jewish religious philosopher, legal scholar, and physician

body ... loaves: Compare 'Elegy,' 86–7 [CP, 2.675]: 'the slabs and ovens ... / The manshaped loaves of sacrifice.'

golgotha sums: Golgotha, the site of the crucifixion, is from the Aramaic for skull, *gulgulta*.

first volume ... Shylock's famous speech: The speech is from *The Merchant of Venice*, 3.1.53–73. The title of Klein's volume is *Hath Not a Jew ...*

thirteen ... Maimonides: In his commentary on the Mishnah, Maimonides formulated thirteen articles of faith, which have been widely accepted and have been incorporated into the prayerbook.

six hundred and thirteen: according to rabbinic teaching, the total number of commandments and prohibitions

auto-da-fés: *Auto-da-fé* is Portuguese for 'act of faith,' referring to a ceremony at which the Inquisition pronounced sentence on its victims, generally death by fire.

winds of April ... cup: The festival of Passover generally falls in April. As part of the ritual of the Passover meal or *seder*, a glass of wine is set for the prophet Elijah and a door is left ajar for him. Compare 'small schemes that an April wind doth scheme' ['Haggadah,' 85 (CP, 1.130)].

sad music ... synagogue: Compare 'sadness sweet of synagogal hum' ['Autobiographical,' 9 (CP, 2.564)].

Feast of Tabernacles ... citron: During the Feast of Tabernacles, or Succoth, a *succah*, or branch-covered booth, is built in which one is required to sleep and eat for the duration of the festival. As part of the Succoth ritual, a blessing is made over a citron, and branches of the palm, willow, and myrtle.

Purim ... mask: Purim celebrates the defeat of Haman, who plotted the destruction of the Jews of Persia, as recounted in the biblical Book of Esther. As part of the celebrations children wear costumes and masks.

Fifteenth of Shvat ... Trees: *Tu bishvat* (Heb., 'the fifteenth of Shvat') is the festival of New Year for trees, a holiday celebrated especially by children.

Oak of Mamre: Mamre, near Hebron, was one of the dwelling places of Abraham. See, in particular, Genesis 18. The Hebrew *elonei Mamre*, 'terebinths of Mamre,' is rendered as 'plains of Mamre' in the King James Version. Josephus, in *The Jewish War* (4.537), speaks of an immense terebinth near Hebron 'said to be as old as creation.'

Resh Lakish ... scholar: Simeon ben Lakish, one of the sages of the Talmud, who was reputed to have been a gladiator in his early years. See explanatory note to 'Ave Atque Vale,' 29–30 [CP, 1.391].

Rabbi Akiva ... academy: Rabbi Akiva, one of the most celebrated sages of the Mishnaic period. According to legend, he was a poor shepherd until he was forty;

at first, unable to pay for his lessons, he sat outside a window where he could hear them without being noticed.

Rabbi bar bar Hunah: probably an error for Rabbah Bar Bar Ḥana, a famous storyteller of the Talmudic period. See explanatory note to 'Ave Atque Vale,' 33–4 [CP, 1.392], where he is referred to as Bar Huna.

grains one by one: Compare 'the grain picked up, like tic-tacs out of time: / first one; an other; singly; one by one' ['Grain Elevator,' 18–19 (CP, 2.650)].

message to Garcia: This phrase is usually used in the sense of a manly exploit. It is based on an episode in the Spanish Civil War in which Lieutenant Andrew Rowan risked his life to deliver a message to General Calixto Garcia. The phrase was popularized as the title of a lay sermon by Elbert Hubbard.

These ... brekekex: See notes to p. 4.

ballad ... names: a reference to 'Ballade des dames du temps jadi' by François Villon

tzitzith: (Heb.) the eight-threaded tassels or fringes on the four corners of prayer shawls or other special four-cornered garments worn by religiously observant Jewish males. See Numbers 15.37–41 and Deuteronomy 22.12.

miracles ... Baal Shem Tov: The Baal Shem Tov (Israel ben Eliezer, c. 1700–60) was the founder of Chassidism. His followers attributed many miracles to him.

kishkas: (Yid.) 'guts'

truckdrivers: The Yiddish equivalent of 'truckdriver' is *baal agolah* (literally, 'coachman,' 'carter'), used to refer to coarse, uneducated individuals.

Chevra Thillim Linath Hatzedek: the name of a synagogue which stood at 4299 Clark; Kalman Klein was a founding member. *Chevra Thillim* and *Linath Hatzedek* are, respectively, Hebrew for 'association of the psalms' (i.e., reciters of the psalms) and 'charitable lodging.'

niftar: (Heb.) 'the deceased'

exonerated: in the original Latin sense of 'being relieved of a burden'

Rabbi Simcha Garber: the teacher under whom Klein studied the Talmud. See explanatory note to 'Sophist' [CP, 1.377].

Mizraim: (Heb.) Egypt

press-machine: Klein's father worked as a presser.

rigour of labour ... embittered: Compare Exodus 1.14: 'And they made their lives bitter with hard bondage.'

pagan dance ... holy, holy, holy: Compare 'Holy, holy, holy, is the Lord of hosts: the whole earth is full of his glory' [Isaiah 6.3]. When reciting these words, which form part of the Jewish liturgy, worshippers raise their bodies on the tips of their toes three times.

rameses ... pithom: treasury cities built by the enslaved Israelites in Egypt [Exodus 1.11]

Tomarkin: Mendel Tomarkin, whose Marble Works, 3778 St Lawrence Boulevard, were in operation at the time of Kalman Klein's death

Shrine ... dome: St Joseph's Oratory, a massive domed structure constructed on the site of a small chapel built by Brother André (Alfred Bessette, 1845–1937), a porter at Notre Dame College, famed for his piety and healing powers

Fletcher's field: a park on the eastern slope of Mount Royal

we sat ... tree: Compare 'By the rivers of Babylon, there we sat down, yea, we wept, when we remembered Zion. We hanged our harps upon the willows in the midst thereof' [Psalms 137.1–2].

Art Gallery ... Basilicoria: a reference to Samuel Butler's poem 'A Psalm of Montreal,' described by Klein as 'a cry of ironic distaste evoked from him by the spectacle of Greek statuary standing in a local museum, pantaloon'd or brassiered to spare a possible outraged modesty' ['O God! O Montreal!' *Canadian Jewish Chronicle*, 10 April 1947, p. 3] The relevant passage is:

> Stowed away in a Montreal lumber room
> The Discobolus standeth and turneth his face to the wall;
> Dusty, cobweb-covered, maimed and set at naught,
> Beauty crieth in an attic and no man regardeth.
> O God! O Montreal!

Compare 'O God! O Montreal!' 4 [CP, 2.700]: 'discoboli jockstrapped and brassiered nymphs.'

Technicon: 'Technic' means 'pertaining to art' [OED].

eocene: 'the epithet applied to the lowest division of the Tertiary strata, and to the geological period which they represent' [OED]

glyptics: 'Glyptic' means 'the art of carving or engraving, esp. on precious stones' [OED].

agamic: 'characterized by the absence of sexual action' [OED]

non-ithyphallic: 'Ithyphallic' means 'pertaining to or associated with the phallus carried in procession at the Bacchic festivals; grossly indecent, obscene' [OED].

Basilicoria: (from Gr.) 'royal mountain'; that is, Montreal

aulic: 'of or pertaining to a court; courtly' [OED]

megacenotaph: (from Gr.) 'large empty tomb'

etesian: 'the distinctive epithet of certain winds in the region of the Mediterranean blowing from the NW. for about 40 days annually in the summer' [OED]; that is, 'windy'

ethnarchs: 'Ethnarch' means 'a governor of a nation or people' [OED].

lalagate: (from Gr.) 'babble'

enchiridion: 'a handbook or manual' [OED]

hypostyle: (from Gr.) 'the lowest course of a building'

ioxantholeucomelachlorose: (from Gr.) 'violet-yellow-white-black-green'

Pragma & Gasteropragma: (from Gr.) 'business and stomach-business'

Kalla: (from Gr.) 'beautiful'

Agatha: (from Gr.) 'good'

Gemmadactylate: (from Lat. and Gr.) 'with rings on their fingers'

callipyginous: 'Callipygian' means 'of, pertaining to, or having well-shaped or finely developed buttocks' [OED].

anemonate: 'Anemonal' means 'of or pertaining to the wind' [OED].
brontapoplect: (from Gr.) 'thunderstruck'
archon: 'a ruler or president generally' [OED]
Kappa Pi Rho: the Greek equivalent of CPR (Canadian Pacific Railway)
psilaformal: (from Gr. and Lat.) 'barely formal'
sarcocarp: 'the fleshy part of a drupaceous fruit lying between the epicarp and the endocarp, being the part usually eaten' [OED]
dolytrichose: (from Gr.) 'longhair'
proctoscopists: 'Proctoscope,' means 'a rectal speculum' [OED]; therefore, 'someone who examines rectums.' Compare the episode in *Ulysses* in which Leopold Bloom fantasizes about examining the statues of the 'naked goddesses' at the 'library museum' to see if they have rectums [p. 174].

DIARY (1944)

Dave: David Lewis, socialist politician and close friend of Klein's. Lewis had a life-long involvement with the CCF and NDP (of which he was leader during 1971–4), and at the time of this diary he was national secretary of the CCF.
W. Circle: Workmen's Circle ('Arbeiter Ring'), a Jewish fraternal order with a socialist cultural orientation. The Workmen's Circle Centre was located at 4848 St Lawrence.
kibbudim: (Yid.) 'honours'
Bundists: members of the Bund (Yid., 'Union'), an international Jewish socialist party founded in Russia in 1897. Bundists opposed Jewish nationalism, in particular Zionism.
Poalei Zionists: Labour Zionists. 'Poalei Zion' (Heb., 'Labourers of Zion') was a worldwide socialist Zionist movement founded in Russia in 1906.
Rubinstein: Michael Rubinstein, a lawyer active in Jewish labour circles, and a member of the Provincial Council Executive of the CCF
Albert Eaton: an administrator and leader in the labour movement in Quebec and a Labour Zionist
Jacques Casgrain: a young lawyer whom the CCF employed as a Quebec organizer in 1943 and 1944, in hopes of making inroads into the French-Canadian community
Cartier: Cartier, the federal riding where Klein lived, had a predominantly Jewish population and had been represented by Jewish members since 1917.
his defeat last August: In 1940 Lewis had run unsuccessfully in Cartier against the Liberal incumbent Peter Bercovitch. When a by-election was called in August 1943, after Bercovitch's death, he was defeated again, this time by Fred Rose of the communist Labour Progressive Party.
differences of opinion: During the 1943 campaign, Klein had evidently warned Lewis, who was not a Zionist, against alienating the Zionist element in Cartier.
my father's membership ... unemployment: Klein's father, Kalman, was a presser and

a member of the Amalgamated Clothing Workers of America. 'It became almost a legend in the family that because of his religious principles he had once remained unemployed for over a year' [*LOTD*, p. 29].

pluck a rose: that is, Fred Rose. See note to 'his defeat last August' [p. 223].

with ... bed: translation of a Yiddish expression, *mit a gezunten kop in a kranken bet*

Eagle: the *Keneder Adler* ('Canadian Eagle'), Montreal's Yiddish-language daily, for which Klein wrote a column in English at about this time

Medres: Israel Medres, journalist and author, on the staff of the *Keneder Adler*. Medres was a communist; hence 'Russian wolfhound.'

Wolofsky: Hirsch Wolofsky, publisher of the *Keneder Adler* and the *Canadian Jewish Chronicle*, of which Klein was editor at this time

Star: the *Montreal Star*, a daily newspaper

Gazette: the *Montreal Gazette*, a daily newspaper

C.P.: Canadian Press, Canada's principal news agency, inaugurated in 1917

B.: Samuel Bronfman. See note to 'the maestro' [p. 211].

Neumanesque: See note to 'Neumann ... sketch' [p. 212].

Tynkoff, Fogul: Lazarus Tinkoff, and H.B. Fogul, lawyers with offices at 276 St James West, near Klein's own

Ruddick: Bruce Ruddick, member of the editorial board of *Preview* magazine (see following note)

Pegi ... Patrick: Peggy Anderson (née Doernbach) was the wife of Patrick Anderson, poet and founder and leading editor of *Preview* magazine, which published a number of poems by Klein, and whose editorial board Klein joined in March 1944. Patrick Anderson was born in England and came to Montreal in 1941, where he taught at Selwyn House, a private school. He was a Marxist at this time.

L.P. ... capitalists: the Labour Progressive Party, the name adopted by the Canadian Communist Party in 1942 in response to its banning by the federal government. At this time, Communist parties around the world were urging cooperation with the capitalists in a common front against Fascism.

Michoels & Feffer: Shloime Mikhoels was the leading Soviet Yiddish actor, head of the Moscow State Jewish Theatre. He was chairman of the Jewish Anti-Fascist League, which, in 1943, travelled throughout Canada, the United States, Mexico, and England to encourage support for the Soviet war effort. The Soviet Jewish poet Itzik Feffer was also a member of the League. The murder of Mikhoels, in 1948, by agents of Stalin, marked the beginning of a campaign to destroy all Jewish cultural leaders and institutions in the Soviet Union, which lasted until Stalin's death. In 1952, as part of this campaign, Feffer was murdered, along with many other Yiddish writers.

J.F.: Joseph N. Frank, a businessman active in Zionist organizations and a friend of Klein's

Willkie: Wendell Lewis Willkie led a fight between 1942 and 1944 to liberalize the Republican Party and to oppose isolationism.

Ben Caplan: an old friend of Klein's

Klein & the 400: an allusion to 'the four hundred,' a late-nineteenth-century term for the social élite of New York, which came into more general use as a designation of social exclusiveness

H.M.C.S. Donnacona: Royal Canadian Navy Volunteer Reserve, Montreal Division, at the time located in the former Winter Club, on Drummond between St Catherine and Sherbrooke

A. Levine: a prominent Montreal Zionist, one of the founders of the Zionist Organization of Canada, and a communist sympathizer

Nat Gaisin: Nathan Gaisin, businessman and member of various Zionist organizations

Rosenstein: A.J. Rosenstein, a lawyer. He shared an office with Klein for a short while in the late thirties.

Harold Freeman: Harold S. Freeman, a lawyer

Batshaw: Harry Batshaw, lawyer, and, from 1950, justice of the Quebec Supreme Court

disagreed ... war: During the thirties, the CCF opposed Canadian involvement in a European war, a policy which it did not entirely abandon until the fall of France and the Battle of Britain in 1940. In 1939 Klein wrote an article in the *Keneder Adler*, entitled 'Mr. Woodsworth and Peace,' attacking this policy [*Keneder Adler*, 12 April 1939, p. 6].

R.B. Bennett: Richard Bedford Bennett, Conservative prime minister of Canada from 1930 to 1935

Tarshises: The Tarshises were in-laws of Batshaw.

Temple ... Shaar Hashomayim: Batshaw was a trustee of the Shaar Hashomayim Synagogue from 1939 to 1942.

Sophie: Sophie Lewis, wife of David Lewis

Man's heart ... know it: 'The heart is deceitful above all things, and desperately wicked: who can know it?' [Jeremiah 17.9]

Federation: the Federation of Jewish Philanthropies, established in 1914 to unite the various competing Jewish charitable organizations in Montreal

Colman: Klein's first son, born in 1937

Hitleriad: published by New Directions in 1944

poems in Preview: 'Commercial Bank' and 'Bread,' which appeared in the March 1944 issue of *Preview*

DIARY (1945)

Dr. James: F. Cyril James, principal and vice-chancellor of McGill University

Ibn Saud: the founder of Saudi Arabia and its first king

bloody picturesqueness of the Arabs: Compare Klein's discussion of the appeal to

Westerners of the 'romance' of the Arabs in 'The Changing Middle East' [BS, pp. 441–4].

Golden Bough: a monumental study of comparative folklore, magic, and religion by Sir James George Frazer, originally published in 1890. It had an enormous impact in the early twentieth century, especially on anthropology, psychology, and literature.

Akhnaton, and Tutankhamen: Akhnaton, or Ikhnaton, was an Egyptian pharaoh of the eighteenth dynasty who abandoned polytheism for a monotheism based on the worship of the sun. Polytheism was restored under his son-in-law and successor Tutankhamen.

Mussolini's death: In April 1945, Mussolini was tried in a summary court martial and shot, along with his mistress Clara Petacci. Their bodies were hung in a public square in Milan.

In Effigo Dei: (Lat.) 'in the likeness of God'; a quotation from Genesis 5.1, in the Vulgate. *Effigo* should be *Effigie*.

Dr. MacMillan: Cyrus MacMillan, chairman of the English Department at McGill

Bess: Klein's wife, Bessie (née Kozlov)

Rosenstein: See note to 'Rosenstein' [p. 225].

Central Cadillac ... up five points: Central Cadillac Mines Ltd, a Montreal company, whose stock went from thirteen to seventeen points on the day in question

Jacob Glatstein: a leading Yiddish poet. Glatstein's review of Klein's *Poems*, 'The English-Jewish Poet A.M. Klein' (in Yiddish), appeared in *Yiddisher Kemfer* [New York], 4 May 1945, pp. 15–17.

Sir Ronald: probably Sir Ronald Storrs (1881–1955), British military governor (1917–20) and district commissioner (1920–6) of Jerusalem. In 'Sir Ronald Storrs to the Rescue,' *Canadian Jewish Chronicle*, 11 August 1944, p. 3, Klein attacks Storrs for being hostile to Zionism and for finding 'the Arabs infinitely more picturesque.' Compare Klein's comment on 'the bloody picturesqueness of the Arabs' [p. 96].

Disney films: For Klein's interest in Walt Disney, see 'Queen Mab and Mickey Mouse' [*LER*, p. 166].

father ... inheritance: 'Kalman had left his wife and children no financial inheritance. In the forties Klein would sometimes joke about this, with a touch of bitterness, as the great misfortune of his life' [LOTD, p. 67]. Compare 'My father bequeathed me no wide estates; / No keys and ledgers were my heritage' ['Heirloom,' 1–2 (CP, 1.298)].

'THE CONTEMPORARY POET'

platitude ... understood: Compare 'How they do fear the slap of the flat of the platitude!' ['Portrait of the Poet as Landscape,' 73 (CP, 2.636)].

prophetic sadness of Eliot: In 'T.S. Eliot and the Nobel Prize,' Klein says of Eliot that he is 'the *laudator temporis acti* – the man who sings the good old days gone by ...; it is Eliot's virtue that he converts this platitudinous attitude into something vigorous and almost revolutionary' [LER, p. 272].

Radio. McLeish: The American poet Archibald MacLeish (1892–1982) wrote experimental verse dramas for radio.

I want to be alone: attributed to Greta Garbo

I would rather ... Thoreau: quoted from Henry David Thoreau (1817–62), 'Economy,' in *Walden* (Princeton: Princeton University Press 1971), p. 37

O that ... unhappy: Compare the French proverb 'Ah les bons vieux temps où nous étions si malheureux.'

Kipling ... Eliot: Eliot edited a selection of Kipling's poems. In 'T.S. Eliot and the Nobel Prize,' Klein refers to 'the pathetic effort which Eliot makes in the introduction to that book to prove Kipling is a considerable poet' [LER, p. 275].

Tennyson ... Auden ... thinker: In his introduction to *Tennyson: An Introduction and Selection* (London: Phoenix 1946), p. x, W.H. Auden characterizes Tennyson as 'undoubtedly the stupidest' of English poets.

Edmund Wilson: (1895–1972), American author and literary and social critic

R.P. Blackmur: (1904–65), American poet and literary critic, one of the founders of the New Criticism

Scientific ... experiments: See note to 'Richards' below.

Kenneth Burke: (1897–), American literary critic and philosopher, influenced by Marxism and psychoanalysis

Richards: I.A. Richards (1893–1979), founding member of the Cambridge school of literary criticism; emphasized practical criticism and studied the psychological basis of aesthetic response

Ogden: C.K. Ogden (1889–1957), originator of Basic English, which was supported by I.A. Richards. See 'Basic English' [CP, 2.615–17].

'MARGINALIA'

Palgrave's Golden Treasury: *The Golden Treasury of the Best Songs and Lyrical Poems in the English Language* (1861), edited by Francis Turner Palgrave, was the most influential Victorian anthology of poetry and was frequently reprinted. The following notes identifying the quotations cite Palgrave's numbering and, where he supplies them, titles.

Many ... be: No. 274 ('Written in the Euganean Hills, North Italy'), Percy Bysshe Shelley

Most ... eyes: No. 269 ('The Inner Vision'), William Wordsworth

The ... man: No. 57 ('Life'), Francis Bacon

The ... past: No. 162 ('To the Same [i.e., Mary Unwin]'), William Cowper

And ... true: No. 154 ('The Sailor's Wife'), William Julius Mickle
And ... stream: No. 258 ('Yarrow Visited'), William Wordsworth
And ... thus: No. 33 ('The Lover's Appeal'), Thomas Wyatt
Blow ... wind: No. 42 (untitled), William Shakespeare
Avenge ... bones: No. 64 ('On the Late Massacre in Piemont'), John Milton
Awake ... awake: No. 140 ('The Progress of Poesy'), Thomas Gray
Hence ... joys: No. 113 ('Il Penseroso'), John Milton
Doth ... move: No. 59 (untitled), William Drummond
Shall ... day: No. 18 ('To His Love'), William Shakespeare
Why ... lover: No. 101 ('Encouragements to a Lover'), John Suckling
Art ... slumbers: No. 54 ('The Happy Heart'), Thomas Dekker
How ... winning: No. 183 ('Freedom and Love'), Thomas Campbell
How ... taught: No. 72 ('Character of a Happy Life'), Henry Wotton
How ... makes: No. 185 ('Echoes'), Thomas Moore
Like ... shore: No. 30 ('Revolutions'), William Shakespeare
Like ... sphere: No. 16 ('Rosaline'), Thomas Lodge
Douglas: No. 247 ('Composed at Neidpath Castle, the Property of Lord Queensbury, 1803'), William Wordsworth
Cyriack: No. 77 ('To Cyriack Skinner'), John Milton
Milton ... hour: No. 213 ('The Same [i.e., "London, MDCCCII"]'), William Wordsworth
wee ... beastie: No. 144 ('To a Field Mouse'), Robert Burns
Quod erat sciendum: (Lat.) 'which was to be known,' on analogy with *quod erat demonstrandum* ('which was to be demonstrated')
The Man with the Hoe: 'The Man with a Hoe' (1899) by the American poet Edwin Markham (1852–1940) was one of the most popular poems of social protest in its time. Klein made a number of marginal annotations to the poem in his teaching copy of Louis Untermeyer, *Modern American Poetry* (New York: Harcourt, Brace and Company 1942), pp. 111–12.
Knights of Labour: an American labour organization, founded in 1869 and very influential towards the end of the nineteenth century
I.W.W.: the Industrial Workers of the World, a revolutionary industrial union organized in Chicago in 1905, with the aim of uniting all workers in 'one big union' for the purpose of overthrowing capitalism. It had lost most of its influence by the thirties.
trumpet and prophecy: 'Be through my lips to unawakened Earth / The trumpet of a prophecy' [Percy Bysshe Shelley, 'Ode to the West Wind,' 68–9].
Milton's 'dread shape': The phrase 'dread shape' does not actually occur in Milton's works. Klein may have in mind Milton's description of Satan as the 'dread commander ... in shape and gesture proudly eminent' [*Paradise Lost*, 1.589–90].
immedicable: 'wounds immedicable' [John Milton, 'Samson Agonistes,' 620]
Dominion ... sea: 'He shall have dominion also from sea to sea' [Psalms 72.8].

swing of Pleiades: Compare 'Canst thou bind the sweet influences of Pleiades?' [Job 38.31].

whirlwinds: 'Then the Lord answered Job out of the whirlwind' [Job 38.1].

how will it be with: probably a reference to Jeremiah 42.17: 'So it shall be with all the men that set their faces to go into Egypt to sojourn there; they shall die by the sword, by the famine, and by the pestilence: and none of them shall remain or escape from the evil that I will bring upon them.'

last judgment: The poem ends with a vision of the Last Judgment.

parallelismus membrorum: (Lat.) 'parallelism of clauses,' the use of parallel clauses in biblical verse

Millet: Jean François Millet (1814–75), French painter of scenes of peasant labour, the best known of which is the *Angelus* (1859). The epigraph of the poem states that it was 'written after seeing Millet's world-famous painting.'

Quintilian: Marcus Fabius Quintilianus (c. 35–c. 95), Roman rhetorician. His *Institutio oratoria*, a complete survey of rhetoric in twelve books, had a great influence in antiquity and in the Renaissance.

E pur muove: (Ital.) 'And yet it moves'; the words which Galileo is reputed to have said under his breath after being forced by the Inquisition to retract his claim that the earth moves

Untermeyer ... melody: Untermeyer, p. 136. Klein has underlined these words and marked them 'NB' in the margin.

Bacon, Lord Verulam: Francis Bacon (1561–1626), whom some believe to have written Shakespeare's plays

Success is Failure: '... much of Robinson's work seems a protest, a criticism by implication, of that type of standardized success which so much of the world worships. Frustration and defeat are like an organ-point heard below the varying music of his verse; failure is almost glorified in his pages' [Untermeyer, p. 136; marked by Klein].

all the years of his life was scared of a skirt: Robinson led a reclusive existence and never married.

Manningham's Diary: John Manningham was a barrister of the Middle Temple, and a contemporary of Shakespeare. The anecdote which Klein cites is from Manningham's *Diary*, which was published in 1868. Klein abridges the passage slightly.

Baby Snooks: a radio character played by the American actress Fanny Brice

having put the question ... stays to answer: Compare ' "What is truth?" said jesting Pilate; and would not stay for an answer' [Francis Bacon, 'Of Truth'].

oratio recta: (Lat.) 'direct speech'

Tophet: a location in the Valley of the Son of Hinnom, south of Jerusalem, where children were sacrificed to Baal and Moloch in the times of Isaiah and Jeremiah; by extension a name for a place of conflagration, and, specifically, for Hell

Sir Nicholas l'Estrange: (d. 1655). The anecdote which Klein cites was included in

Merry Passages and Feasts by Sir Nicholas L'Estrange, selections of which were published as *Anecdotes and Traditions* in 1839. Klein abridges the passage considerably.

myriad-minded: 'our myriad-minded Shakespeare' [Samuel Taylor Coleridge, *Biographia Literaria*, chapter 14]

had this to say: A note in MS 5207 indicates that Klein intended to insert at least part of a long passage from *Specimen of a Commentary on Shakespeare* (1794) by Walter Whiter, cited by Stanley Edgar Hyman in 'The Critical Achievement of Caroline Spurgeon,' *Kenyon Review* 10 (1948), 94–5, which discusses 'the dog-fawning-melting-candy association' [93] in Shakespeare.

Mermaid Tavern: tavern in London frequented by Jonson and Shakespeare

Drummond of Hawthornden: Scottish poet (1585–1649), who published notes of his conversations with Ben Jonson

Which ... invention: This passage is quoted from *Worthies of England* (1662) by Thomas Fuller (1608–61).

paragraph ... Timber: The source of the passage which Klein quotes is *Timber, or Discoveries* (c. 1630) by Ben Jonson (1572–1637): 'for I lov'd the man and do honour his memory (on this side idolatry) as much as any.'

régisseur: (Fr,) 'theatre manager'

Eyes ... not: 'Hear now this, O foolish people, and without understanding; which have eyes, and see not; which have ears, and hear not' [Jeremiah 5.21].

Matthew, Chapter 2: 'Now when Jesus was born in Bethlehem of Judaea in the days of Herod the king, behold, there came wise men from the east to Jerusalem, Saying, Where is he that is born of the King of the Jews?' [Matthew 2.1–2].

Matthew, Chapter 27: 'Then were there two thieves crucified with him, one on the right hand, and another on the left' [Matthew 27.38]

Matthew 27:35: 'And they crucified him, and parted his garments, casting lots.'

Thus ... delays: *Paradise Lost*, 1.192, 196–7, 201–8. The original has 'huge' rather than 'large.'

simile ... Aristotle: For Aristotle's discussion of simile, see *Rhetoric*, 1406a, 1410a.

gesturing his too too solid flesh away: Compare 'O that this too too solid [the *Riverside* edition has 'sallied'] flesh would melt, / Thaw, and resolve itself into a dew' [*Hamlet*, 1.2.129–30].

Will ... red: *Macbeth*, 2.1.56–60

ochlocratic: 'Ochlocracy' is 'government by the mob or the lowest of the people; mob-rule' [OED].

its forgotten etymology ... crimson of the flesh: The original meaning of 'incarnadine' is 'flesh-coloured.'

I ... noise: 'Immortal Autumn'

dépassant: (Fr.) the edging or frill on a garment

comma ... curled: Compare 'curl themselves in a comma' ['Portrait of the Poet as Landscape,' 69 (CP, 2.636)].

O sweet ... squeezing and: 'La Guerre,' II
the second comma: The original has a period, not a comma.
Poem 98: 'Portraits,' IV
The ... madman: *A Midsummer Night's Dream*, 5.1.7–10
that ... merit: John Milton, *Paradise Lost*, 1.197
Clausewitz: Karl von Clausewitz (1780–1831), author of *On War*
How much goodlier ... tents: Compare 'How goodly are thy tents, O Jacob, and thy tabernacles, O Israel!' [Numbers 24.5].
Th' enamel'd, ... wearing?: John Milton, 'On the Morning of Chirst's Nativity,' 143; from the versions of 1629 and 1673 respectively

'TOWARDS A PSYCHOANALYSIS OF G.M. HOPKINS: THE ART OF THE RORSCHACH'

Klein quotes from the 'Oxford Bookshelf' edition of Hopkins's poems (*Poems of Gerard Manley Hopkins*, ed. with notes by Robert Bridges, 2d edition, with an appendix of additional poems, and a critical introduction by Charles Williams [London: Oxford University Press 1930]). In the notes which identify quotations, passages marked by Klein in his copy are indicated. When Klein misquotes, the correct version is given in parentheses. Unless otherwise noted, italics in the quoted passages were added by Klein.

Rorschach: In the Rorschach test, named after the Swiss psychologist Hermann Rorschach (1884–1922), the responses of the subject to a standard series of inkblot designs are analysed and interpreted.
tatter-tassel-tangled: 'The Woodlark,' 33
skeined ... variety: 'Spelt from Sibyl's Leaves,' 11; marked
windpuff ... fawn-froth: 'Inversnaid,' 5 ('windpuff-bonnet of fáwn-fróth'); marked
dappled-with-damson: 'The Wreck of the Deutschland,' 37; marked
May ... greenery: '(Ashboughs),' a.8–9; marked
trickling increment: 'St. Alphonsus Rodriguez,' 10; marked
mazy ... water-wattled: 'Penmaen Pool,' 23 ('mazy sands all water-wattled'); marked
love-laced: 'Brothers,' 3; marked
fire-folk: 'The Starlight Night,' 2; marked
elves eyes: 'The Starlight Night,' 4 ('elves'-eyes')
flakedoves: 'The Starlight Night,' 7 ('Flake-doves')
Mankind's medley: 'The Loss of the Eurydice,' 54; marked
seared ... toil: 'God's Grandeur,' 6 ('seared with trade; bleared, smeared with toil'); marked
when ... apple: 'The May Magnificat,' 37 ('When drop-of-blood-and-foam-dapple / Bloom lights the orchard-apple'); marked

fallers ... frothpits: 'St. Winefred's Well,' c. 7; marked
selfyeast of spirit: 'I wake and feel the fell of dark, not day,' 12; marked
he puts ... jar: 'The Bugler's First Communion,' 45 ('I have put my lips on pleas / Would brandle adamantine heaven with ride and jar'); marked
all ... coil: '(Carrion Comfort),' 10; marked
ruck ... sight: 'The Habit of Perfection,' 11–12 ('This ruck and reel which you remark / Coils, keeps, and teases simple sight.'); marked
when ... lush: 'Spring,' 2; marked
wiry ... whirlwind-swivelled: 'The Wreck of the Deutschland,' 103
like ... foil: 'God's Grandeur,' 2; marked
stormflakes ... flowers: 'The Wreck of the Deutschland,' 168 ('Storm flakes were scroll-leaved flowers'); marked
his ... whirl: 'The Sea and the Skylark,' 6–7; marked
What ... came: 'As kingfishers catch fire, dragonflies dráw fláme,' 8; italics in the original; marked
like ... name: 'As kingfishers catch fire, dragonflies dráw fláme,' 3–4; marked
Feathery ... corn: quoted in 'Instress of Inscape,' 373
Inscape ... seeing into: 'Instress of Inscape,' 372–3
I mean ... abroad: *Poems*, p. 109; italics in the original; marked
two rhythms ... together: *Poems*, p. 3; marked
same and tame: *Poems*, p. 2; marked
Remark ... asunder: *Poems*, p. 4; first set of italics in the original; marked
Two licences ... itself: *Poems*, p. 4; italics in the original; marked
consternation of Dr. Bridges: In a marked passage [*Poems*, pp. 98–9], Robert Bridges criticizes some of Hopkins's rhymes as 'hideous.' However, he does not object to any of Hopkins's 'folded over' rhymes as Klein claims. On the contrary, in his notes to 'The Wreck of the Deutschland,' as evidence that the poem 'will be of interest' to 'the metrist and rhythmist,' he cites lines 105–8 as 'the first example of a rhyme which depends on running over to the next line' [*Poems*, p. 104].
She ... Knock: 'The Wreck of the Deutschland,' 105–8; marked
A bugler ... will): 'The Bugler's First Communion,' 1–4; marked
tmesis: the separation of a compound word by an intervening word or words
Saxo cere- comminuit -brum: 'He shattered his brain with a rock' (Lat.); a frequently cited example of tmesis from the epic poet Ennius. The normal form would be *Saxo cerebrum comminuit*. In a marked passage, Hopkins cites this example in his explanation of 'wind- lilylocks -laced' [*Poems*, p. 116].
brim ... ful: 'The Wreck of the Deutschland,' 62 ('Brim, in a flash, full'); marked, and 'tmesis' added in the margin
wind- lilylocks -laced: 'Harry Ploughman,' 15
aposiopesis: a sudden breaking off of a thought in the middle of a sentence
But ... she: 'The Wreck of the Deutschland,' 217–20; 'aposiopesis' added in the margin
Our ... Lord: 'The Wreck of the Deutschland,' 280; marked

UNTITLED NOVEL

Hapaxlegomenon: (Gr., 'said once') a word or form of word that occurs only once. Klein refers to 'Saadia's hapaxlegomenon' in a note on *Waxman*, 1.168 [MS 3266].

The voice ... created voice: 'He [Philo Judaeus] was the first to propound the theory that the voice of God pronouncing the Commandments was an especially created voice' [*Waxman*, 1.110]. Klein refers to this passage in a note [MS 3266].

Philo of Alexandria: Philo Judaeus (c. 20 B.C.–A.D. 50), Jewish philosopher who sought to synthesize Greek and Jewish thought

Pimontel: a variant of the Sephardic Jewish name Pimentel, which derives from the Spanish *pimienta* or Portuguese *pimenta*, meaning pepper. The name seems to have originally belonged to families of spice traders. Klein may have chosen it here to suggest that his narrator is a master of *pilpul*. See note to 'pepper-sharp, as pilpul' [p. 242].

Kerem Israel Talmud Torah: *Talmud Torah* (Heb., 'study of the Law') refers to Jewish education in general, and, in particular, to Jewish religious schools. As a child, Klein attended the Talmud Torah near his home, Kerem Israel (Heb., 'vineyard of Israel') Hebrew Free School.

Rabbi Glazer: probably based on Rabbi Simcha Garber. See explanatory note to 'Sophist' [*CP*, 1.377].

Mr. Herscovitch: Klein had a teacher of this name.

Mr. Nathan Gordon: a prominent lawyer and Jewish community figure (not to be confused with Rabbi Nathan Gordon, the spiritual leader of Temple Emanu-el at the time Klein was a child)

learned in the jots and tittles: Rabbi Akiba 'is said by later generations to have interpreted every letter in the Torah, even every superfluous dot' [*Waxman*, 1.67]. The phrase 'one jot or one tittle,' in the general sense of 'the very least or a very little part, point, or amount; a whit' [OED], occurs in Matthew 5.18. 'Jot' comes from *iota*, the name of the smallest letter of the Greek alphabet, which is the equivalent of the Hebrew *yod*, the smallest letter of the Hebrew alphabet. (See note to 'alephule ... paipetit' [p. 235].) One of the meanings of 'tittle' is 'any one of Hebrew or Arabic vowel-points and accents' [OED].

Simchas Torah: (Heb., 'the rejoicing of the Law') a holiday marking the conclusion of one annual reading of the Torah and the beginning of the next

confirmed thirteen years: The *bar mitzvah* ceremony marks the confirmation of a Jewish male, at the age of thirteen, as an adult obliged to observe the precepts of Judaism.

aliyah: (Heb., 'ascent') a 'going-up' to recite a blessing on the reading from the Torah in the synagogue during services

Wolf the son of Kalman: Klein's father was named Kalman. Kalman Klein had a son named Velvel, the Yiddish diminutive for 'wolf,' by an earlier marriage.

Yenta: Klein's mother was named Yenta in Yiddish.

Tza'ar ... tzir: 'suffering ... messenger'

Because it is written: [ ]: A note added by Klein in MS 4461 – 'Quote Noah?' – indicates that the passage he had in mind was Genesis 6.16: 'A window [*ẓohar*] shalt thou make to the ark.'

King Solomon ... Jerusalem: Song of Solomon 3.9–10. *Apiryon* is translated 'chariot' in the King James Version.

Gaon of Wilna ... Wilner Gaon: Elijah ben Solomon Zalman (1720–97); one of the most influential Jewish thinkers and spiritual leaders of modern times, a leading opponent of Chassidism. *Gaon* (Heb., 'majesty,' 'excellence') is an honorific applied to outstanding Talmudic scholars. Wilna is Vilnius, the capital of Lithuania, formerly a centre of Jewish learning.

PRDS of knowledge ... sibilant: PRDS, pronounced *pardes* (Heb., 'orchard'), is an acronym for the four methods of Bible interpretation: *pshat* (literal), *remez* (allegorical), *drash* (homiletical), and *sod* (mystical).

red heifer: (Heb., *parah adumah*) an animal whose ashes were used for ritual purification [Numbers 19]. The details of this ritual are the subject of the Talmudic treatise *Parah*.

ordeal ... adultery: Numbers 5.11–31

Jeshurun waxed fat: Compare 'But Jeshurun waxed fat, and kicked: thou art waxen fat, thou art grown thick, thou art covered with fatness; then he forsook God, which made him, and lightly esteemed the Rock of his salvation' [Deuteronomy 32.15].

bare-headed: Orthodox Jewish men are required to keep their heads covered at all times.

Liver-and-sourmilk ... trefah combination: Jewish dietary law forbids the combination of meat and milk products. Ritually forbidden food of any kind is referred to as *trefah*.

of course and of course: a translation of the Yiddish phrase *a vada un a vada*, meaning 'most certainly.' The passage as a whole is full of Yiddish turns of phrase.

Shechinah: The *shekhinah* (Heb., 'dwelling') is the numinous immanence of God in the world.

elegists ... Kairuwan: Fez and Kairouan, in Morocco and Tunisia respectively, were important centres of Jewish culture and scholarship in the Middle Ages.

rhymes of the Andalusians: Andalusia was the most important centre of Hebrew poetry in the Middle Ages. The poets of Andalusia were influenced by the rhyming verse forms of Arabic poetry.

Kalonymos clan: an eminent German family of rabbis, scholars, and poets. 'The art of composing sacred poetry became a hereditary trait in this family and for over a century and a half, they were the mouthpieces of the Jewries of France and Germany voicing their grief and hope' [*Waxman*, 1.246]. Klein frequently used the pseudonym 'Ben Kalonymos (or Kalonymus),' meaning 'the son of Kalonymos.' The name of Klein's father, Kalman, is a cognate of Kalonymos.

Toledo ... Mayence: Toledo and Rome were both important centres of Hebrew poetry in the Middle Ages, the first associated with such poets as Yehuda Halevi, a number of whose poems Klein translated [CP, 2.768–75], and Yehuda ben Solomon al-Ḥarizi, noted below; the second especially with Immanuel of Rome, whose poem 'The Prescription' Klein translated [CP, 2.765–6]. Mayence, or Mainz, in Germany, was associated especially with the Kalonymos family (see above).

Levites: the tribe of Israel responsible for various sacred functions, including Temple music

wrestling with an angel ... thigh-bone wrenched: Genesis 32.24–32 describes how Jacob wrestled with an angel who put his thigh out of joint.

Halevi ... Chaucerian English: Yehuda Halevi (before 1075–1141) was a philosopher and the major poet of the golden age of medieval Jewish culture in Spain. Klein translated a number of his poems, three of them into Chaucerian English: 'To Jerusalem the Holy' [CP, 2.768], 'Lord, Hele Me, Y-Wis I Shal Be Heled' [CP, 2.769], and 'O Heighte Sovereign, O Worldes Prys' [CP, 2.772–3]. Klein's poem 'Yehuda Halevi, His Pilgrimage' contains a translation of Halevi's 'Ode to Zion' [CP, 2.554–5].

Alharizi: Yehuda ben Solomon al-Ḥarizi (1170–1235), a Spanish-Hebrew poet and translator, especially noted for his virtuosity

no vowel letters ... pointillation: The twenty-two letters of the Hebrew alphabet represent consonants. Signs indicating vowel sounds are a later development and are frequently omitted.

Fr thr ... opn splchr: 'For there is no faithfulness in their mouth; their inward part is very wickedness; their throat is an open sepulchre' [Psalms 5.9].

alephule ... paipetit: Klein's fanciful diminutives for the Hebrew letters *aleph, bet, gimel ... yod* (the equivalent of the Greek *iota*), *tes, mem, nun, pai*

exPOUND: a reference to Ezra Pound, whose translations were extremely free and experimental

Chatterton: Thomas Chatterton (1752–70) composed imitation medieval verse which he attempted to pass off as originals. After the forgeries were discovered, he committed suicide.

Mangan: James Clarence Mangan (1803–49), an Irish poet, who published a number of his own works under the guise of translations

hard rock ... flow forth: When the Israelites were suffering from thirst in the wilderness of Sin, God commanded Moses to strike a rock with his rod, causing water to flow from it [Exodus 17.1–7].

Code Napoleon: (Fr.) the name given in 1807 to the French Civil Code; used here of the Quebec Civil Code, which derives from the French Civil Code

considérant: (Fr.) 'grounds for judgment'

sui generis: (Lat.) 'of its own kind, unique'

cause d'espèce: (Fr.; *cause* should be *cas*) 'exception'

law's glorious incertitude: The phrase dates back to at least the eighteenth century. See explanatory note to 'Of Daumiers a Portfolio,' 41/42 [CP, 2.954].

Sûreté Provinciale: (Fr.) 'Provincial Police'

building up ... Rameses: Pithom and Rameses were treasury cities built by the enslaved Israelites in Egypt [Exodus 1.11]. After Moses commanded Pharaoh to free the Israelites, Pharaoh increased their burden by forcing them to gather the straw themselves which they needed for making bricks [Exodus 5.6–7].

Nimrods: 'He was a mighty hunter before the Lord: wherefore it is said, Even as Nimrod the mighty hunter before the Lord' [Genesis 10.9].

Adloyada: The Talmud [*Megillah* 7b] states that on Purim one should drink '*until one no longer knows* (*ad d'la yada*, in Aramaic) the difference between "Cursed be Haman" and "Blessed be Mordecai."' Haman was the evil counsellor of King Ahasuerus whose plans to destroy the Jews were frustrated by Queen Esther and her uncle Mordecai. *Adloyada* became the name of the modern-day Purim street carnival and parade, first held in Tel Aviv in 1912.

Chevra Thillim: See note to *Chevra Thillim Linath Hatzedek* [p. 221].

Reading ... Esther: The Book of Esther is read in the synagogue on Purim.

High Holy Days: the Jewish New Year (Rosh Hashanah), during which people are judged and have their fate inscribed by God for the following year; and the Day of Atonement (Yom Kipur), ten days later, the day on which their destinies are sealed by God

Days of Awe and Contrition: *yamim noraim*, a term referring either to the High Holy Days or more broadly to the ten days of penitence between the Jewish New Year and the Day of Atonement

Sabbath of Sabbaths: a translation of the Hebrew phrase *shabbat shabbaton*, which appears in Exodus 31.15 and Leviticus 16.31. In the former it refers to the Sabbath, in the latter to the Day of Atonement.

casting ... purparts: The name Purim derives from *pur*, Hebrew for 'lottery,' the method used by Haman to select the day on which he intended to begin the massacre of the Jews. 'Purpart' means 'a portion, a share, esp. in an inheritance' [OED].

ten unspeakable ... decabarbaric: During the reading of the Book of Esther, it is traditional to utter in one breath the names of Haman's ten sons, who were all hanged.

purlins: A 'purlin' is 'a horizontal beam, usually one of two or more, which run along the length of a roof, resting upon the principal rafters (which they cross at right angles), and lending support to the common rafters or boards of the roof' [OED].

Purim players: One of the customs associated with Purim is the *Purim shpil* (Yid.), or Purim play, performed in elaborate costumes.

Ahasueros ... fool: King Ahasuerus was traditionally presented as a fool.

Vashti... Esther: King Ahasuerus's first wife, whom he repudiated when she refused to appear before him and his guests at a feast. Esther was chosen to replace her.

shamash: (Heb.) 'sexton, caretaker'

Blessed be the comer: a translation of the Hebrew phrase *barukh haba*, the traditional greeting for guests

yahrzeit: (Yid.) 'anniversary'; specifically, the anniversary of the death of a parent or close relative, when *Kaddish* is recited and the grave visited

Shmoneh Esreh: (Heb., 'eighteen') the core of every Jewish worship service, consisting of nineteen (originally eighteen) benedictions; also know as the *Amidah* (Heb., 'standing up'), as one stands while reciting it

upon him, peace: a literal translation of the Hebrew phrase *alav hashalom*, equivalent to 'May he rest in peace'

new light in Eden: a reference to the Yiddish phrase *zol er hoben a likhtiken gan eden*, 'May he have a bright Garden of Eden,' used out of respect for the dead

carrying a mad: a translation of the Yiddish expression *trogen a kaas*

eastern wall: See note to 'cantor ... mizrach wall' [p. 213]. The eastern wall represents the place of honour, the front of the synagogue.

Jewish Eagle: the *Keneder Adler*, ('Canadian Eagle'), Montreal's Yiddish-language daily

Megillah: (Heb.) 'scroll,' that is, the Book of Esther

fracture ... people: a translation of the Hebrew phrase *shever bat ami*, which appears in Jeremiah 8.11, 21, Lamentations 2.11, 3.48, and elsewhere in the Bible

to destroy ... children and women: Esther 4.13

remnant: a reference to the Hebrew phrase *she'erit hapeletah* ('the rest that escaped' or 'the last survivors'), which occurs in 1 Chronicles 4.43, expressing the belief that the future of the nation of Israel would be assured by a faithful remnant surviving the disasters which would befall the Jewish people. After the Second World War, the phrase was used to refer to the survivors of the Holocaust.

Bevin: Ernest Bevin, foreign minister in the British Labour government from 1945 to 1951. Favouring the establishment of a federated Arab-Israeli state, he imposed a limit on Jewish immigration to British-mandated Palestine after the Second World War.

Israel exists and persists: 'Exists and persists' is a translation of an ancient Hebrew expression *ḥai vekayam*, which in the past was usually used in reference either to God or to King David; in modern times it has come to be used in a slogan expressing Jewish national determination, *yisrael ḥai vekayam*.

Madagascar: a reference to the Madagascar Plan, first advocated in 1885 and later taken up by the Nazis, according to which the Jews of Europe would be shipped to Madagascar with the financing coming from world Jewry. The plan was eventually abandoned in favour of the 'Final Solution.'

Cyprus: Jews who were captured attempting to immigrate to Palestine were interned by the British in Cyprus.

each ... vine: 'And Judah and Israel dwelt safely, every man under his vine and under his fig tree' [1 Kings 4.25].

And the Lord ... hinderparts: 'And he smote his enemies in their hinder parts' [Psalms 78.66].

And he smote ... thereof: 'But the hand of the Lord was heavy upon them of Ashdod, and he destroyed them, and smote them with emerods, even Ashdod and the coasts thereof' [1 Samuel 5.6]. 'Emerods' is an archaic spelling of haemorrhoids.

great leviathan ... wild ox: According to Jewish tradition, with the coming of the Messiah a banquet will be given by God to all the righteous, at which the flesh of the leviathan and the behemoth ('the wild ox') will be served.

wine ... Noah's day: After the flood, Noah planted a vineyard and became drunk from the wine he produced [Genesis 9.20–1].

Nebuchadnezzar: ruler of Babylon, 605–562 B.C.; laid siege to Jerusalem and destroyed the first Temple in 586 B.C.

Seleucid: Antiochus IV Epiphanes, of the Syrian Seleucid dynasty, occupied Jerusalem in 168 B.C. His brutal rule led to the Hasmonean revolt celebrated on Chanukah.

Pobodonostyev: Konstantin Petrovich Pobedonostsev (1827–1907), Russian anti-Semitic statesman and ideologue of anti-Jewish legislation in Russia

matzo: unleavened bread eaten on Passover

auto-da-fé: (Portuguese, 'act of faith') ceremony at which the Inquisition pronounced sentence on its victims, usually death by fire

fatima: Fatima was the daughter of Mohammed. The Fatimid dynasty, which claimed descent from her, was responsible for persecution of the Jews, especially in the eleventh century.

latkes: fried potato pancakes eaten on Chanukah

Braided bread: referring to braided egg-bread (Heb., *halah*), eaten at meals on the Sabbath and holidays

Haman taschen: (Yid.) 'Haman pockets,' fruit-filled pastry in the shape of a triangle, supposedly the shape of Haman's hat, eaten on Purim

'THE GOLEM'

our own ... the Sixth Millenium: The year of Rabbi Löw's death, according to the Jewish calendar, which reckons from the creation of the world (*anno mundi*), was 5369. Elul, the last month of the Jewish year, is regarded as a month of penance, preceding Rosh Hashanah.

Sinai ... scribe: Compare 'Can it be ... that this writ we cherish is not at all the reportage of God's Sinai, but the feigning, the invention of some petty molehill of a Sinai, a scribe's secret megalomania?' ['The Bible Manuscripts' (*LER*, p. 135)]. Rabbi Löw had a younger brother named Sinai.

Hohe: The article on 'Judah Löw' in *JE* states that he was 'known also as Der Hohe

Rabbi Löw.' *Höhe* is German for 'height' or 'highness'; *heykh* in Yiddish means 'height' or 'tallness.' Compare 'that height and tallness of his' [p. 146].

Cabbalist: a student of the Kabbalah, the corpus of Jewish mystical texts

exonerated this burdened world: See note to 'exonerated' [p. 221].

slightest stumbling ... to naught: Compare 'Exorcism Vain' [CP, 1.204].

Moldau: the river which passes through Prague

aleph ... tau ... beth ... shin: the first, last, second, and second last letters of the Hebrew alphabet. There may be a reference to the Kabbalistic method of interpretation by the substitution of letters, known as 'the *At Bash* where the letters placed at the beginning of the alphabet exchange with those placed at the end, thus, the *Aleph* with the *Tau*, the *Beth* with the *Shin*, etc.' [*Waxman*, 2.345].

bereshith, in principio: Hebrew and Latin, respectively, for the first words of the Book of Genesis: 'In the beginning'

scribe out of Hibernia ... Tergesta ... daedalian: 'Hibernia' and 'Tergesta' are Latin respectively for 'Ireland' and 'Trieste.' Klein is alluding to James Joyce, who left Ireland for Trieste, where he began *Ulysses*. 'Daedalian' (lit., 'of or after the style of Daedalus; skilful, ingenious, formed with art') is an allusion to Stephen Dedalus, one of the central characters of *Ulysses*.

Sed et serpens: (Lat.) 'Now the serpent'; the opening words of Genesis 3, in the Vulgate translation of the Bible

nowed: 'knotted; tied in a knot' [OED]

minium: vermilion, used as a red pigment in manuscript illumination

Soncinos ... consonants: The Soncinos were a family of Hebrew printers in Italy, Turkey, and Egypt in the fifteenth and sixteenth centuries. The article on the Soncinos in JE reproduces the head-piece which Klein describes.

tombstones ... acre: 'In not much more than an acre, twelve thousand stones tread upon one another, and their number falls far short of their total inhabitants' [*Lowenthal*, p. 332; cited by Klein in MS 3130].

Sarmatic: Polish

two hands ... a virgin bride: 'On most of the tombstones there are symbolical signs: two hands with spread fingers for a kohen; a ewer, with or without basin, for a Levite; a grape for an ordinary Israelite. A female figure is the symbol for a virgin, and a similar figure, with a rose in the raised left hand, for a virgin bride' [JE, 'Prague'].

Cohen ... ewer: The Levites were the tribe assigned various sacred functions; ewers were used by them in the Temple service. Those who served as priests in the Temple were known as *kohanim* (Heb. 'priests'); their descendants perform a special benediction with outspread fingers.

Judenstadt: (Ger.) 'Jews' city,' that is, 'ghetto'

votive lamp: lit on the anniversary of the death of a relative

Altneuschule: (Yid.) 'Old-New Synagogue,' Rabbi Löw's synagogue in Prague

Ark of the Covenant: the receptacle in the synagogue in which the Torah scrolls are kept

Rabbi Solomon Lencyz: unidentified; but Lenchitza (Leczycza in Polish), a town in Poland, was the site of a ritual-murder accusation and the resultant torture and slaughter of many Jews in 1639.

Tablets ... broken: a reference to the tables of the Law shattered by Moses [Exodus 32.19]

Judah Leib ... Lion: The lion (*leyb* in Yiddish, *Löwe* in German) is the symbol of the tribe of Judah, and, by extension, of the Jewish people. There was a 'rampant lion (Löw – lion) carved on [the] face' of Rabbi Löw's tomb [*Lowenthal*, p. 335; cited in MS 3133]. See notes to 'Leon da Modena' [p. 243] and 'lion ... Torahs' [p. 252].

pearls of great price: See Matthew 13.46.

sod sodoth – arcana of arcana: Hebrew and Latin respectively for 'secret of secrets'

hidden there: According to legend, the remains of the golem are hidden to this day in the attic of the *Altneuschule*.

ram's horn ... dead: According to tradition, the coming of the Messiah and the resurrection of the dead will be heralded by the blowing of a ram's horn.

Curtain ... Paragud: *Gordon*, p. 159, for which there are notes in MS 3009–11, explains this concept as follows: 'The divine abode, or what is known popularly as "heaven" is in Jewish eschatology an immense auditorium where the souls of the pious are engaged continuously in interpretation of the Torah under the chairmanship of the Almighty ... A curtain, called in Hebrew *pargod* (compare the Greek *paragodes*), fenced off this auditorium from those not privileged to stay within it. But the academic proceedings could be heard from behind the *pargod* by chosen living men, who were given the privilege of sending up their spirits in quest of information.'

Mordecai Meisel: (1528–1601), Prague financier and philanthropist; a close friend of Rabbi Löw

unknown ... Cyprus: probably the prophet Elijah, who appears to Rabbi Löw as 'a peddler, with horse and waggon' [p. 175]. Elijah appears frequently in Jewish folklore as the herald of the Messiah.

Hradčany Castle: the royal residence, located at the top of Hradčany Hill in the centre of Prague

church of St. Vitus: a Gothic cathedral, containing the tombs of many kings and emperors

Then was the voice ... wings: This passage is virtually identical to one describing the funeral rites of 'Uncle Galuth' in 'In Praise of the Diaspora' [BS, p. 468].

El Moleh Rachmim: (Heb., 'O Lord, Full of Compassion') prayer for the departed recited at funeral services and memorial occasions

Shechinah: The *shekhinah* (Heb.,'dwelling,' 'abiding') is the numinous immanence of God in the world.

Babel: See Genesis 11.1–9.
Elijah: See note to 'unknown ... Cyprus' [p. 240].
Unutterable Name: the tetragrammaton, the personal name of God, which is written in the Bible with the four consonants YHWH. It is forbidden to attempt to pronounce it as written. The tetragrammaton was frequently used in magic rituals such as the creation of the golem.
death-bed ... speck invisible terrifies: According to the Talmud, 'when a sick person is about to depart, [the Angel of Death] stands above his head-pillow with his sword drawn out in his hand and a drop of gall hanging on it. As the sick person beholds it, he trembles and opens his mouth in fright' [*Avodah Zarah* 20b].
Tannaim: the sages of the period when the Mishnah, the legal codification of basic Jewish law, was compiled (c. A.D. 20–200)
In the accounting ... the intention or the act: 'In criminal cases wrongful intent must accompany the wrongful act in order to make the culprit punishable by law ... In civil cases, the law disregards the intention, and considers only the injury done by the act' [*JE*, 'Intention'].
Sweetness ... fell: a reference to the episode in Judges 14.5–20, in which Samson killed a lion and later found that bees had made their hive in its carcass
The Holy Vessels ... Scrolls: Among the works by Rabbi Löw mentioned in the article on him in *JE* is one entitled *Bi'urim 'al Dine Mezuzah, Ketibat Megillah, Kele ha-Ḳodesh, Bigde Kehunnah we-Sammane ha Ḳeṭoret*, which can be translated as *Commentaries on the Laws of the Mezuzah, the Writing of the Scroll, the Holy Vessels, the Vestments of the Priesthood, and the Perfumes of the Incense.*
eight rules ... holy writ: In 'The Bible Manuscripts' [*LER*, pp. 136–7], Klein lists ten rules to be observed by the Torah scribe.
Hear ... One: the opening words of the *Shema*, the declaration of God's unity, part of the daily liturgy and traditionally recited immediately before death
blessed ... away: Compare 'the Lord gave, and the Lord hath taken away; blessed be the name of the Lord' [Job 1.21].
Cuneo: capital of the Italian province of that name, with a Jewish community dating back to the fourteenth century
blown glass: Venice was famous for its glass.
Giudecca: an island in the Venetian lagoon
galleasses: 'Galleasse' is an obsolete form of 'gallias,' 'a heavy, low-built vessel, larger than a galley, impelled both by sail and oars, chiefly employed in war' [*OED*].
apes and peacocks of Holy Writ: a reference to the apes and peacocks of King Solomon [1 Kings 10.22]. Compare 'Bestiary,' 18 [*CP*, 1.282]: 'Gay peacock and glum ape.'
Tyre: principal city of Phoenicia, a wealthy centre of commerce in the biblical period
ways ... water-courses: Compare 'Who hath divided a watercourse for the overflowing waters, or a way for the lightning of thunder ...' [Job 38.25].

leviathan: Compare the description of the leviathan in Job 41.

sweet influence of the Pleiades: Compare 'Canst thou bind the sweet influences of Pleiades?' [Job 38.31].

whirlwind verses: Job 38–41 consists of God's answer to Job 'out of the whirlwind' [Job 38.1].

that first river ... onyx: the river of Pison, one of the four rivers of Eden, 'which compasseth the whole land of Havilah, where there is ... bdellium and the onyx stone' [Genesis 2.11–12]

Rialto: the quarter of Venice where the Exchange was located

Doge: the chief magistrate in the Republic of Venice

Asmodeus: Asmodeus was a demon who, according to legend, usurped King Solomon's throne. For Klein's own account of this legend, see the introductory explanatory note to '*In Re* Solomon Warshawer' [CP, 2.964–5].

Solomon's seal: According to legend, King Solomon possessed a seal ring on which the name of God was inscribed, which gave him the power to control demons.

Noah's rainbow: See Genesis 9.11–17.

Joshua ... Jericho: See Joshua 6.

Pentateuch and the Prophets ... Talmud: The Pentateuch and the Prophets comprise the first two of the three sections of the Old Testament (the third being the Hagiographa). They were traditionally studied by schoolboys before the Talmud, the compilation of Jewish law, which is more difficult.

sacred books ... Venezia the Renowned: Venice was an important centre for the publication of Hebrew books in the Renaissance.

Three Great Gates: *Baba Kama, Baba Meẓiah,* and *Baba Batra* (Aram., 'The First Gate,' 'The Middle Gate,' 'The Last Gate') are three Talmudic tractates dealing with various financial obligations associated with property. Talmudic study usually began with these tractates, and Klein himself had studied them in his youth under Rabbi Simcha Garber [S.H. Abramson, 'Abe Klein – In Person,' *Jewish Standard*, Sept. 1936, p. 23].

throwsters: A 'throwster' is 'one who twists silk fibres into raw silk or raw silk into thread, silk-throwster' [OED].

payttanim: (Heb.) composers of *piyutim*, liturgical poems

Gilgul: (Heb.) 'metempsychosis'

cocoon ... stanza: 'Stanza' is Italian for 'room.'

Azriel ... Archevolto: The article on 'Leon (Judah Aryeh) of Modena' in JE lists Azriel Bassola, Hezekiah Galico, and Samuel Archevolti as among 'Leon's masters.' On p. 153, the narrator says that he and Leon 'attended upon the same learned instructors.'

pepper-sharp, as pilpul: *Pilpul* (Heb.) is a method of Talmudic study involving sharp dialectical and often casuistic argumentation. Klein here relates it to the Hebrew word *pilpel*, pepper, but that is probably not its true etymology. The *pilpul* of the narrator's 'teacher Samuel Archevolto' is based on Klein's memories of his own childhood teacher Rabbi Simcha Garber. Compare 'Sophist' [CP, 1.137].

quillets and quiddities: A quillet is 'a verbal nicety or subtle distinction'; a quiddity is 'a subtlety or captious nicety in argument' [OED].

Betrothals ... Stripes: the Talmudic treatises *Ketubot* and *Makot*

elenchized: 'To elenchize' is 'to make use of the elenchus [a syllogism in refutation of a proposition that has been syllogistically defended]; to argue' [OED].

Tosfoth: (Heb., 'additions') famous commentary on the Talmud written during the twelfth to fourteenth centuries by Jewish scholars in France and Germany

Trani: a port in southern Italy, on the Adriatic coast, north of Bari (see next note). Its Jewish community was expelled during 1510–11.

Bari: a port in southern Italy, on the Adriatic coast. Its Jewish community was expelled during 1540–1.

Kingdom of Naples: The Kingdom of Naples at this time occupied the southern part of the Italian peninsula.

littoral: the Adriatic coast opposite the Italian peninsula

Serenissima: (Ital., 'the most serene') the Venetian Republic

made peace ... Murad: Murad III (1546–95) was the Ottoman emperor at the time of the events narrated. The peace referred to is probably the end of the fourth Turkish War (1570–3).

ocean of the Talmud: a translation of the Hebrew expression *yam hatalmud*

German ... unrelated to my own: As an Italian Jew, the narrator would not have been familiar with Yiddish, which was spoken in northern Europe and is closely related to German.

Leon da Modena: Leon (Judah Aryeh) of Modena (1571–1648) was an Italian scholar and rabbi. Klein's account is based on the article on him in JE, which Klein marked 'NB.' 'Leon' is the Italian translation of Modena's Hebrew name, 'Aryeh,' meaning 'lion.' Thus both of Sinai's mentors, Rabbi Löw and Leon, have names which mean 'Judah the Lion.' See note to 'Judah Leib ... Lion' [p. 240].

quarrels ... excommunicate: 'Leon ... developed a passion for all games of hazard ... This ... involved him, in 1631, in a struggle with the leaders of the community [of Venice], who launched an excommunication against any that should play cards, or take part in any game of hazard, within the period of six years. On this occasion, Leon wrote a brilliant dissertation, in which he demonstrated that the leaders had acted against the Law; the excommunication was accordingly revoked' [JE].

twenty-six callings: 'Besides preaching and teaching, Leon exercised not less than twenty-six professions (press-corrector, notary, bookseller, etc.)' [JE; marked '!' by Klein in margin].

grandson ... Golden Fleece: 'His grandfather Mordecai became distinguished both as a physician and as a philanthropist, and was raised by Charles V to the rank of Knight of the Order of the Golden Fleece' [JE].

forbidden learning: Leon 'was not only well versed in Hebrew and rabbinical literature, but was conversant with the classics' [JE].

poet ... orator: Leon 'was especially successful [as a preacher]; his addresses in Italian attracted large audiences, including Christian priests and noblemen. Leon's successes as an orator and poet won for him the consideration of the Christian scholastic world, and admitted him to the highest Venetian circles' [*JE*].

mathematic: Leon 'possessed a fair knowledge of mathematics' [*JE*].

King David: Compare 'And David danced before the Lord with all his might' [2 Samuel 6.14].

a dancer: 'His father ... gave him a complete education, not neglecting even such worldly accomplishments as singing and dancing' [*JE*].

expert in chess: 'Leo di Modena's work ("Ma'adanne Melek") was written for the purpose of teaching the author's two sons the game, and in the hope of inducing them to give up card-playing' [*JE*, 'Chess'; article marked by Klein].

astrologer: Leon 'attributed [his passion for gambling] to the astral influences under which he had been born' [*JE*].

Immanuel of Rome: Immanuel (ben Solomon) of Rome (c. 1261–after 1328) was an Italian poet, scholar, and physician. He composed a wide variety of poems in Italian and Hebrew, including erotic ones. Klein translated his 'The Prescription' [*CP*, 2.765–6].

many gentiles: 'He had among his pupils Louis Eselin (a nobleman of the French court), the Archbishop of Lodève, John Plantanit, Jacob Gaffarelli, and Giulio Morosini' [*JE*].

clinked canakins: Compare 'and let me the canakin clink, clink' [*Othello* 2.3.69].

wind ... vanity: Compare 'Vanity of vanities, saith the Preacher, vanity of vanities; all is vanity' [Ecclesiastes 1.2]. The Hebrew word for 'vanity,' *hevel*, also means 'fume, vapour, breath.'

Pietro Aretino: 1492–1556, Italian satirist. His *Sonnetti Lussuriosi*, a series of illustrated erotic sonnets, was the most famous work of pornography in the Renaissance.

Babel: See Genesis 11.1–9.

manna: the miraculous food which God provided for the Israelites in the desert [Exodus 16]

King Solomon ... concubines: 'And [King Solomon] had seven hundred wives, princesses, and three hundred concubines' [1 Kings 11.3].

Samson ... away: Compare 'the theologians, discussing the quantity of semen in mighty Samson's philistinish ejections' ['Of Hebrew Humour,' *LER*, p. 102]. The reference is to the Talmud, *Sotah* 10a.

midrashic: A midrash (Heb.) is 'an exegesis which, going more deeply than the mere literal sense, attempts to penetrate into the spirit of the Scriptures' [*JE*, 'Midrash'].

Zohar ... Sitra Achra: The *Zohar* (Heb., 'splendour') is the major work of the Kabbalah. For an account of the Kabbalistic concept of *sitra aḥra* (Aram., 'the other side'), the domain of demonic emanations paralleling the divine emanations, see Gershom Scholem, 'The Problem of Evil,' in *Kabbalah* (Jerusalem: Keter Publishing House 1974), pp. 122–8.

jactitated: 'To jactitate' is 'to toss restlessly about' [OED].

inamorata ... repulsive: 'We ... find among Immanuel's poems some where women, especially ugly ones, are spoken of derogatively and are the butt of his jests' [*Waxman*, 2.67–8].

casting his bread ... Qoheleth: 'Cast thy bread upon the waters: for thou shalt find it after many days' [Ecclesiastes 11.1]. Qoheleth is the Hebrew title of the Book of Ecclesiastes.

prayershawl, phylacteries and frontal: The prayershawl (*talit*) is a four-cornered shawl with fringes at each corner worn by Jewish males during morning prayers. Phylacteries (*tefilin*) consist of two black leather boxes fastened to leather straps, containing portions of the Torah written on parchment. They are affixed, one to the arm and one (the 'frontal') to the forehead, by Jewish males during weekday morning prayers.

Padua ... further studies: The University of Padua, founded in 1222, was one of the most prominent in Europe in the sixteenth century.

Knagged ... knurred and kinched: A 'knag' is 'a short spur or stiff projection from the trunk or branch of a tree'; a 'knur' is 'a knot or hardened excrescence on the trunk of a tree'; a 'kinch' is 'a loop or twist on a rope or cord' [OED].

white bread of his Sabbath: referring to braided egg-bread (Heb., *ḥalah*), eaten at meals on the Sabbath and holidays

Modena ... as great as mine: The account of the death of Leon's father is Klein's invention. However, according to JE, 'he had scarcely reached maturity when his father became impoverished, and Leon had to seek his own livelihood.'

The Perfect Crime: There is no evidence of actual blasphemy in the work of the historical Leon of Modena. However, he frequently attacked traditional Judaism, most notably in a pseudonymous work entitled *Kol Sakal*, in which he discussed, among other issues, 'the Creation, the purpose of the world' [JE].

corpus delicti: 'a collective name for the sum or aggregate of the various ingredients which make a given fact a breach of a given law' [OED]. Klein is using the term in the looser sense of the corpse in a murder case.

relicted ... heap: Compare 'the *relictae* of the camps, entire cairns of cadavers, heaped' [SS, p. 140].

shambles: used in the sense of 'a slaughter-house' [OED]

sage in Sanhedrin ... arrayed: 'According to R. Ḥiyya, the rending of garments was no longer required after the fall of the Temple ("He who hears blasphemy nowadays is not obliged to rend his garments, because otherwise his garments would be nothing but tatters," *Sanh.* 60a)' [JE, 'Blasphemy'].

pasquil: 'any circulated or published lampoon' [OED]

counsel of Job's wife ... desecrating of the Name: 'Curse God, and die' [Job 2.9].

arrogant blasphemy of Rab-shakeh: 'The Talmud bases the custom of rending the garments [on hearing a blasphemy] upon the Biblical precedent of II Kings xviii.37, where Eliakim and others rent their garments when they heard the blasphemy of Rab-shakeh' [JE, 'Blasphemy'].

Be not afraid ... heard: 2 Kings 19.6

quaeritating: 'To quaeritate' is 'to inquire or search into' [OED].

coronated iota: Special designs resembling crowns (*tagin* in Aramaic) are sometimes placed by scribes on the upper left-hand corner of certain letters including *yod*, the Hebrew equivalent of the Greek *iota*. These were frequently assigned mystical significance.

to foretell and hasten the End of Days: The Kabbalists sought evidence in the Torah for the precise time of the coming of the Messiah, and they also sought ways to hasten his coming.

Don Solomon Abenaish ... Don Joseph: Solomon Aben-Ayish (1520–1603) was a Jewish statesman, prominent at the Turkish court. He was created Duke of Mytilene. Joseph Nasi (c. 1524–79) was a Jew of Portuguese descent who acquired great influence with the Sultan of Turkey, and was appointed by him Duke of Naxos. He attempted, unsuccessfully, to establish a Jewish colony on the site of the ruined city of Tiberias. They are both discussed in *Roth*, pp. 277–82, for which there are notes in MS 3131.

macarized: 'To macarize' is 'to account or call happy or blessed' [OED].

Safed and Tiberias: Tiberias was the centre of religious life in Palestine for centuries after the destruction of Jerusalem in A.D. 70. Safed became the centre of Jewish mysticism in the sixteenth century. See *Roth*, pp. 282–4, cited in MS 3131.

Urim and Thummim: (Heb.) a priestly device in ancient Israel for obtaining oracles, kept in the breastplate of the high priest [Exodus 28.30]

foxes ... vines: Compare 'Take us the foxes, the little foxes, that spoil the vines' [Song of Solomon 2.15].

vineyard ... about: Compare 'My wellbeloved hath a vineyard in a very fruitful hill: And he fenced it, ... and planted it ... And I will lay it waste: it shall not be pruned, nor digged' [Isaiah 5.1, 6].

Messiah-ben-Joseph ... Messiah-ben-David: According to a Jewish tradition, the Messiah-ben-David is a descendant of King David who will rule over Israel in a golden age at the end of time. He will be preceded by the Messiah-ben-Joseph who will re-establish the Temple before being slain by his enemies.

letters ... Sefer Yetziroh: The *Sefer Yeẓirah* (Heb., *Book of Creation*), the earliest extant Hebrew text of systematic speculative thought on cosmology and cosmogeny, had a profound influence on the development of Jewish mysticism. The golem 'was supposed to be created by the aid of the "Sefer Yeẓirah," that is, by a combination of letters forming a "Shem" (any one of the names of God)' [JE, 'Golem'; marked by Klein].

shamash: (Heb.) 'caretaker, attendant'

Fire ... doves: '... during the fire which ravaged the Judenstadt in 1558, two white doves hovered over the roof of the Altneu and protected it from flames' [*Lowenthal*, p. 340; cited in MS 3134].

tallis & tfillin: See note to 'prayershawl, phylacteries and frontal' [p. 245].

attercop: 'a spider' [OED]

Debate re Coming of Messiah: This debate is based on the statement in the Talmud *Sanhedrin* 98a, that the Messiah will come only when the world is either totally pure or totally corrupt.

From the strong ... sweetness: See note to 'Sweetness ... fell' [p. 241].

Turkish War: See note to 'made peace ... Murad' [p. 243]

Responsa: replies to questions in Jewish law – a major form of rabbinic literature

causa causans: 'causing cause, i.e. primary or original cause' [OED]

catechism: For the catechistic structure of 'The Rationale of Pure Murder,' compare the 'Ithaca' chapter of *Ulysses* [pp. 650–722].

parasynthetic: 'formed from a combination or compound of two or more elements' [OED]

frustrate and non-avenu: from the French *nul et non avenu*, 'null and void'

Burke: William Burke (1792–1829), a Scottish murderer who, along with William Hare, suffocated his victims and sold their bodies to medical students for dissection. His name gave rise to the verb 'to burke,' meaning 'to kill secretly by suffocation or strangulation' [OED].

lapidation: 'the punishment of stoning to death' [OED]

noyade: 'the execution of persons by drowning' [OED]

Let x ... darkening: Klein's general intention is clear enough in this passage, but the expression is confused. He appears to have in mind a graph consisting of a line extending upward at an angle from the origin ('x'), so that the area ('y') underneath the line is triangular ('increasing triangularly in thickness'). Klein attempted to clarify his terminology in a revision, in which he changed the term referring to the area from 'y' to 'yz/2,' which would be the correct formula if the two axes of the graph were y and z. However, he did not complete the revision, and the confusion remains.

homologation: 'assent, ratification, confirmation' [OED]

pro tanto: (Lat.) 'for so much,' 'to that extent'; a legal term

crossed bar: Compare Tennyson, 'Crossing the Bar.'

devoutly to be wished: Compare 'a consummation devoutly to be wished' [*Hamlet*, 3.1.62–3].

antinomian: 'opposed to the obligatoriness of the moral law' [OED]

adiaphoric: 'Adiaphorism' is 'religious or theological indifference' [OED].

syllogism (Aristotelian): mode of argument defined by Aristotle, consisting of a sequence of three propositions, such that the first two imply the third

subjective idealism (Berkeleyan): See note to 'Bishop Berkeley ... mind' [p. 219].

to be is to be perceived: a translation of Berkeley's principle, *esse est percipi*

dialectic (Platonic): the logical method used by Plato for arriving at the Ideas underlying phenomena

dialectic (materialist): Dialectical materialism, the official philosophy of Marxism, argues that the basis of reality is material, and that change takes place through the struggle of opposites.

doctrines theosophical (eastern): Theosophy, in general, is 'any system of speculation which bases the knowledge of nature upon that of the divine nature' [*OED*]. Klein probably has in mind modern versions of theosophy which draw on eastern concepts such as reincarnation.

apocatastatic: 'Apocatastasis' is 'restoration, re-establishment, renovation' [*OED*].

dilemma: 'a form of argument involving an adversary in the choice of two (or, *loosely*, more) alternatives, either of which is (or appears) equally unfavourable to him' [*OED*]

categorical imperative (Kantian): Immanuel Kant (1724–1804) based his ethics on the categorical imperative: 'Act as if the maxim through which you act were to become through your will a universal law.'

hedonistic calculus (Benthamite): Jeremy Bentham (1748–1832), the founder of utilitarianism, argued that the fundamental principle of morality is the greatest happiness of the greatest number. 'The hedonistic calculus' is the moral arithmetic he devised for judging the value of pleasure and pain.

המקום ... כבוד: The Hebrew terms in the third column are the equivalents of the English ones in the first.

mandrake: a plant, also known as mandragora, with a short stem and thick, often forked roots, which is thought to resemble a human being and to have magic powers

2 Kings 2:11: 'And it came to pass, as they still went on, and talked, that, behold, there appeared a chariot of fire, and horses of fire, and parted them both asunder; and Elijah went up by a whirlwind into heaven.'

גילוי אליהו: 'According to talmudic tradition, the prophet Elijah never died, and many saintly persons in the period of the Talmud and thereafter, down to recent times, have been reputedly visited and taught by him. Such a privilege is called *gillui Elijah* – Elijah's self-revelation' [*Gordon*, p. 133; cited in MS 3009]. Gordon goes on to cite a comment by Rabbi Löw on the subject.

thirty six: According to a popular Jewish legend, there always exist thirty-six righteous persons, of unknown identity, on account of whose merit the world is preserved.

mandragora: See note to 'mandrake' above.

Job 33:14, 15: 'For God speaketh once, yea twice, yet man perceiveth it not. In a dream, in a vision of the night, when deep sleep falleth upon men, in slumberings upon the bed.'

custom of Talmudists ... text of the day: 'According to Talmudic legend God revealed His will through the mouths of school-children ... The way to obtain such guidance was by stopping a child and asking him, "Recite to me any *pasuk* (biblical verse) that comes to your mind." And the *pasuk* the child quoted was considered a significant omen' [*Gordon*, p. 150; referred to in MS 3009].

helpmeet: Compare 'for Adam there was not found an help meet for him' [Genesis 2.20].

emanations: the ten *sefirot* or stages through which God manifests his various attributes

Divisibility and adjustability of limbs: Compare 'Desideratum' [CP, 2.569].

vetus: (Lat.) 'old'

Creation of Golem: The ritual outlined in MS 3216–19 and MS 3231–2 is Klein's invention, although it draws on various sources, the most important of which are *Gordon, Müller*, and Yudel Rosenberg's *Niflaot Maharal im ha-Golem* (1909), reprinted in *Yenne Velt: The Great Works of Jewish Fantasy and Occult*, compiled, translated, and introduced by Joachim Neugroschel (New York: Stonehill 1976). MS 3237–8 contains notes to a number of passages in *Müller* which were incorporated into 'The Golem'.

Urim & Thummim: a priestly device in ancient Israel for obtaining oracles, kept in the breastplate of the high priest [Exodus 28.30]

Ezekiel's chariot: a reference to *maaseh merkavah*, the description of the Divine Chariot or Throne in the first chapter of Ezekiel, which was a major source text for Jewish mysticism

emeth ... אמת מארץ תצמח: (Heb.) 'truth.' The Hebrew letters spell out the words *emet meareẓ tiẓmaḥ*, meaning 'truth will out' (literally, 'truth will sprout from the earth'). The first letters of each of these words spell out *emet*.

aleph taken out of his forehead: *Müller* relates the story of Ben Sira and the prophet Jeremiah, who created a man 'on whose forehead was written "Emet" (truth), as on the forehead of Adam. Then the one whom they had created said to them: "God created Adam, and when He wanted to put him to death he erased a letter from the word *emet* and it became *met* (dead). So much the more reason is there why I should want to do the same, so that you may not again create a man and the world go astray through him like the generation of Enoch ..."' [p. 63].

אמת – מת: (Heb.) 'truth – dead.' See previous note.

Bezalel – in shadow of God: a reference to Rabbi Löw's full name, Judah Löw ben (son of) Bezalel. Bezalel was also the name of the artist who constructed the Tabernacle and its equipment [Exodus 31.1–11; 36–9]. 'Bezalel means then, "in the shadow of God"; but God's shadow is His Word which He made use of like an instrument, and so made the world. But this shadow and what we may describe as the representation is the archetype for further creation. For just as God is the pattern of the image to which the title of shadow has just been given, even so the Image became the pattern of other beings' [Philo Judaeus, *Allegorical Interpretations*, III, 96; cited in *Müller*, p. 34].

Aholiab, son of Ahisamach: an engraver and embroiderer who worked with Bezalel on the Tabernacle [Exodus 38.23]

homunculus, mannikin (See O.E.D.): The OED defines 'homuncule' as 'a little or diminutive man; a mannikin,' and cites passages from H. More and J. Edwards describing artificial homunculi. *Gordon* describes the golem as a '*homunculus* (little man)' [p. 168].

minyan: a *minyan* is the quorum of ten adult males required for public worship One rabbi was so convinced of the possibility of creating a golem that 'he raised the question as to whether a golem could be counted as one in a "minyan"' [*JE*, 'Golem'; marked '!' by Klein].

ps. 91: 'Especially mysterious is the power of "the soul which dwells in the shadow of the Highest," which in Psalm CXI is pictured as being borne on the wings of angels and treading fearlessly and harmlessly on adders and lions. Already in Talmudic times the Psalm was interpreted as referring to the soul nestling in God after death, and by mystics it was applied to kindred inner experiences also. In the Midrash and Zohar it is designated "Song of Afflictions" (*Shir shel Pega'im*), and it is included in the service for the dead' [*Müller*, p. 23]. 'Psalm 91 is recited every Saturday night in order to ward [devils] off' [*Gordon*, p. 137; cited in MS 3010].

אתה ... ישראל: According to one legend about the creation of the golem, Rabbi Löw prayed for help when the Jews of Prague were in danger, and received an answer consisting of these ten Hebrew words, which begin with the first ten letters of the Hebrew alphabet. In MS 3240 and MS 3263, Klein transliterates the words as *Ato Bra Golem Devuk Hakhomer V'Tigzar Zedim Chevel Torfe Yisroel*, and, in MS 3263, he translates them as 'Make a golem of clay & you will destroy the entire Jew-baiting company.' There is an account of this legend in *Gordon*, p. 172, giving slightly different versions of some of the words.

חצות: *Ḥaẓot* ('midnight'). *Tikun Ḥaẓot* ('midnight liturgy') are prayers at midnight in memory of the destruction of the Temple and for the restoration of the Land of Israel.

Walked seven times around clay figure: 'There, on a clay bank, we measured out a man three cubits long, and we drew his face in the earth, and his arms and legs, the way a man lies on his back. Then, all three of us stood at the feet of the reclining golem, with our faces to his face, and the rabbi commanded me to circle the golem seven times from the right side to the head, from the head to the left side, and then back to the feet, and he told me the formula to speak as I circled the golem seven times' [Rosenberg, p. 172].

ר״ח אברים: '248 limbs.' According to rabbinic teaching, there are 365 commandments and 248 prohibitions, each of which is associated with a part of the body. Compare 'Twelve score and eight the limbs, parts, and members of the body' [*SS*, p. 139].

Adar: a month of the Jewish calendar, usually occurring around March. Purim (see next note) is celebrated on the fourteenth day of Adar.

Purim ... appearances: Purim is a festival celebrating the deliverance of the Jews of Persia from Haman's plot to destroy them, as recounted in the biblical Book of Esther. It was an occasion for merrymaking, including masquerading. 'Father Tadeus drove home in a fury, like Haman, with his head downcast. And, like Shushan in ancient Persia when Queen Esther saved the Jews, the city of Prague "rejoiced and was glad"' [Rosenberg, p. 182].

Maaseh Breshith: narration of the mysteries of creation, which was one of the central topics of the Kabbalah

R. Oshaiah ... T.J. San. vii, 154: 'It will be sufficient here to refer to the legend mentioned in the Talmud that with its help [i.e., 'the Sefer Yeẓirah'] two scholars, R. Oshaiah and R. Chaninah, created a three-year old calf (San. 65*b* and 67*b*), and that R. Joshua b. Chananyah in the same way produced deer and fawn from cucumbers and pumpkins (T.J. San. [i.e., Jerusalem Talmud, tractate *Sanhedrin*] VII, 154)' [*Müller*, p. 48].

Maimonides: Legends about the creation of a golem grew up around the baseless claims (first recorded in the fourteenth century) that late in his life the great rationalist philosopher Moses Maimonides (1135–1204) turned to Kabbalistic thought and practices. Compare 'Talisman in Seven Shreds,' 48–50 [CP, 1.188]: 'Maimonides fed a wee / homunculus in a jar, a dwarf which he / created.'

בת-קול : 'A *bath kol* (small voice) was often heard in solemn moments and it was considered a divine oracle emanating from above' [*Gordon*, p. 149; referred to in MS 3009].

ob & yidonim Is 8.19: 'The *ob* was a spirit mentioned in the Bible, and was conceived as residing in a human being (Lev. 20, 27). The plural, *oboth*, may refer to women possessed of such spirits (Is. 8, 19) ... The *yideoni*, mentioned alongside *ob*, is related to the verb *yada*, "to know," and may signify that it was *familiar* to the magician, a *familiar* spirit, or that it *knew* information hidden from ordinary mortals' [*Gordon*, p. 138; referred to in MS 3009–10].

pitkas: 'Occasionally God used script to convey his will to men ... This form of divine notification continued through the talmudic period. It would come in the shape of an inscribed *pitka* (tablet). "A *pitka* fell down from heaven" is the usual talmudic expression' [*Gordon*, pp. 147–8; referred to in MS 3009].

Adam Kadmon: (Heb.) 'primordial man,' Kabbalistic concept of the spiritual man in whose image the physical Adam was created

elements 4 ... Israel: '... the four fabrics which were used in the sacred tent and in the priestly garments [correspond] to the four elements; ... the twelve precious stones on the breastplate of the High Priest, to the twelve signs of the zodiac and of their earthly counterpart, the twelve tribes of Israel' [*Müller*, p. 14].

Shedim ... Dumah: 'The evil angels or demonic beings also play in the whole of this literature ... a not unimportant role ... as ubiquitously roving spirits (*Shedim*). To the most prominent evil powers belong Asmodai, the opponent of Solomon, Lilith (Adam's first wife), Dumah, the angel of the stillness of death ...' [*Müller*, pp. 52–3].

shabriri ... Ben Nefilim: 'Some demons specialized in causing definite diseases in men: Shabriri – blindness; ... Ben Nefilim – epilepsy; Tezazith – insanity' [*Gordon*, p. 137; cited in MS 3010].

fimbriated ... cucullated: 'bordered with a narrow band or edge, ... fringed,' 'cowled, hooded' [OED]

capoched: Klein probably came across this word in the OED, which illustrates its meaning with a phrase which he cites in MS 7274: 'Capoched your Rabbins of the Synod.' The OED states that its meaning is uncertain, and quotes Dr Johnson, 'perhaps to strip of the hood,' a definition which is not relevant here. The context suggests 'hooded' as the intended meaning.

As he scanned ... balm: This passage alludes to the twelve signs of the Zodiac, although not in their proper order: Aries the Ram ('rammed'), Taurus the Bull ('bullying'), Gemini the Twins ('twin,' 'ambivalence'), Cancer the Crab ('crabbish,' 'in backward motion'), Leo the Lion ('lion'), Virgo the Virgin ('maidenhair,' 'virginal'), Libra the Scales ('unscaleable,' 'librated'), Scorpio the Scorpion ('scorpion'), Sagittarius the Archer ('fletched,' 'arched'), Capricornus the goat ('scapegoat,' 'capering'), Aquarius the Water Bearer ('water'), and Pisces the Fish ('fished').

maidenhair: 'the name of certain ferns having fine hair-like stalks and delicate fronds' [OED]

scapegoat Azazel: For an account of the scapegoat Azazel, see explanatory note to 'A Psalm or Prayer – Praying His Portion with Beasts,' 18 [*CP*, 2.974–5].

lion ... Torahs: In Jewish religious art, the Torah is often represented as being supported by two lions. For the lion of Judah, see note to 'Judah Leib ... lion' [p. 240].

homeopathics of the scorpion ... balm: a reference to the common belief that the scorpion's poison acts as an antidote to itself. Klein may have come across this belief in a passage from *Edmund* (1711) by Thomas Ken, cited in the definition of 'scorpion' in the OED: 'The Scorpion sucks the Poison he convey'd, / An antidote to his own Poison made.'

Sanhedrin 65b ... membrum virile: 'A baraitha (*Sanhedrin* 65b) gives further descriptions: "He talks from the joints [of his body] ... who brings up [a spirit], conjuring by means of a *membrum virile* or skull" ' [*Gordon*, p. 139 (passages in brackets added by Gordon); cited in MS 3610]. A *baraitha* is a statement from the Mishnaic period which was not incorporated into the Mishnah.

Creation ... Candles: 'Rabbi Liva [i.e., Löw] had given Abraham-Khaym, the old beadle, his permission to attend and told him to stay back a bit with two candles in his hands.

'When they reached the attic, the three men stood in positions opposite to the ones they had taken when creating the golem. First they stood at the head of the prostrate golem and faced his feet. Next, they began circling him along his left side to his feet and then along his right side to his head, where they stopped and said something. They did the same thing seven times.

'After the seven encirclements, the golem was dead' [Rosenberg, p. 224].

SELECTED NOTES AND FRAGMENTS

Modigliani tours the ghetto: Amedeo Modigliani (1884–1920), Italian-Jewish painter, known for his figure paintings characterized by elongated forms and languorous atmosphere. Compare 'Stranger and Afraid,' pp. 81–2.

letters out of Assyria: The modern Hebrew alphabet evolved out of the Aramaic alphabet, which the Jews adopted during the Babylonian (not Assyrian) exile, beginning in 586 B.C.

Flattery ... imagines: Compare 'Raw Material,' p. 13.

of the Mosaic Persuasion: an expression popular among assimilated Jews, particularly those of Germany, in the nineteenth and early twentieth centuries

coronated: 'furnished with a corona, or something resembling a crown' [OED]

stiffnecked: Compare 'And the Lord said unto Moses, I have seen this people, and, behold, it is a stiffnecked people' [Exodus 32.9].

mizrach wall: Compare 'Raw Material,' p. 20.

glory swims away in contraceptives: Compare 'Sonnet Unrhymed' [CP, 2.645].

arch of Titus ... gnat: The Arch of Titus in Rome commemorates the destruction of Jerusalem by the Roman general, and later emperor, Titus. In *The Second Scroll*, Klein describes the arch and refers to the 'miserable ending [of Titus], as reported by the rabbis, of the insect that through an orifice of his face had entered his brain and there had kept buzzing, buzzing, buzzing until he had gone mad and died' [p. 110].

God's itching powder – sex: Compare 'The Golem,' p. 169.

Violin ... in advance: Compare 'Raw Material,' pp. 20–1.

Is this our Canadian poet: Compare 'Writing in Canada: A Reply to a Questionnaire' [LER, pp. 216–21].

what is K to Hecuba or Hecuba to K: Compare 'What's Hecuba to him or he to Hecuba, / That he should weep for her?' [*Hamlet*, 2.2.559–60].

Ravitch: Melech Ravitch, a Yiddish poet and essayist, who was born in Galicia and settled in Montreal in 1941

shachris: (Heb.) the daily morning prayer

חללים חללים: (Heb.) 'orifices,' 'cavities'; a phrase from the *shachris* liturgy which Klein translates as 'grottoed and gutted' in 'Who Hast Fashioned,' 3 [CP, 2.706].

שלא עשני אשה: (Heb.) 'for not having made me a woman.' The *shachris* liturgy includes a benediction, from which these words are taken, in which Orthodox male Jews thank God for not having made them women.

קטרת: (Heb.) incense

Man ... stew: Compare 'Raw Material,' p. 8.

Along ... Unclejew: Compare 'Raw Material,' pp. 5 and 22.

Before the riesenrising ... Ap-hoch-ellipse: For another example of the influence of Joyce's *Finnegans Wake*, compare 'Stranger and Afraid' [pp. 88–9].

Yerushalayim: (Heb.) Jerusalem

The clamour ... destroy us: Compare 'Of the Making of Gragers' [CP, 2.707].

cere–brum: See note to 'Saxo cere- comminuit -brum' [p. 232].

Peter Shlemiehl: a reference to the tale *Peter Schlemiehl* (1813) by Adelbert von Chamisso (1781–1838) about a man who sells his shadow to the devil

A procession of Villon's daughters: Compare 'Ballade des dames du temps jadis' by François Villon (1431–63?).

shiksa: (Yid.) a non-Jewish woman

dibbuk: (Heb., literally, 'adhesion') the soul of a sinner which, after death, transmigrates into the body of a living person

Responsa ... requirement: Compare 'The Golem,' pp. 168–74.

aurea mediocritas: (Lat.) 'golden mean'

After ... genitalia: Compare 'The Golem,' p. 169.

con-sonant: a pun on the French word *con* ('cunt')

voyelles (from voyou): *Voyelles* is French for 'vowels'; a *voyou* is a street criminal.

ponce the lion: a reference to Ponce de León (c. 1460–1521), Spanish explorer and discoverer of Florida

The trouble ... race: Compare 'The Golem,' p. 175.

Envy ... disproportion: Compare 'The Golem,' pp. 152 and 169.

mezuzah: (Heb., literally, 'doorpost') parchment scroll with Torah verses in a container affixed to the doorposts in Jewish houses

gehenna: Hell, from the Hebrew word *gehinom*

epispasm: The OED defines 'epispastic' as 'a blister.' There is no entry for 'epispasm.'

matzo: unleavened bread eaten on Passover

Kaplan: probably Mordecai M. Kaplan, American rabbi, founder of the Reconstructionist movement

m'rachamim: (Heb.) 'showing compassion'

tenesmus: 'a continual inclination to void the contents of the bowel or bladder, accompanied by straining, but with little or no discharge' [OED]

Clough on Decalogue ... Churchill's poem to Roosevelt: In a broadcast to the American people in May 1941, Winston Churchill quoted the uplifting 'Say Not the Struggle Naught Availeth,' by Arthur Hugh Clough (1819–61). This was in response to 'lines of Longfellow which President Roosevelt had written out for him in his hand' [Winston Churchill, *The Grand Alliance*, vol. 6 of *The Second World War* (Boston: Houghton Mifflin 1950), pp. 236–7]. Clough's 'The Latest Decalogue' is, in contrast, cynical in tone.

marxists' ... peristalsis ... pendulum: two images of the Marxist dialectic. Compare 'Dentist' [CP, 2.568–9].

laocoön: a Trojan priest who was strangled, along with his sons, by two sea serpents when he counselled the Trojans against accepting the Trojan horse; the subject of a famous Hellenistic sculpture

cauchemar: (Fr.) 'nightmare'

Appendix: Klein's Inventory of His Literary Manuscripts

The manuscript of Klein's inventory of his literary manuscripts [MS 7606–10] consists of five sheets in the same ink throughout. There are a few later additions in that ink, and one item, which is listed twice, has been deleted in pencil at its first occurrence. The sheets are numbered, except for the last, which contains item 40.

The manuscript dates from the very end of Klein's career, since it lists several of his last works.

1. Second Scroll – correspondence

2. Poems – early mss. including Barricade Smith Series
   City of Slaughter – Bialik – mss.
   The Lord has not revealed
   Rachel
   Yehuda Halevi
   Rubaiyat

3. Adloyada – first chapter re Purim story
   Some Purim onomatopoeia

4. Of a Journey – Excerpts from Chronicle re trip to Israel
   Some pertinent photographs
   Tentative description of Rockies

5. American & British poetry notes
   Milton
   Some sixteenth century poets
   Modernism in the arts CBC – Nov. 29/50

Some Chronicle articles – Lady with a Lamp
Jerusalem the Golden
That Rank Picture
The Dybbuk
Notes on interview with [.....]

6. Some Chronicle – T.S. Eliot & Nobel Prize
And it shall come to pass
Of Jewish Existentialism
Isaak Babel
Songs of Zion – Yehuda Halevi
Review of Chassidic Anthology
Baedeker – Kasrilevke
Bernard Lazare – Job's Dungheap
Book-Reviewing in 7 easy lessons
Hershel Ostropolyer – Act 2 & Act 1
Dance of Despair – 1942 translation
Prayerbook – Agnon – translation
Some Praise the Lord – Pass the Ammunition
Hemlock & Marijuana – Kafka

6a. Of Hebrew Humour
Rabbi Levi Yitschok
Sinai, with stage directions
National Anthems
Three-fold Exile
Biography of Dictator
Heart of Europe
The Perfect Man
Karl Shapiro
Maimonides in Hollywood
Bella Chagall
On translating Yiddish folk songs
Deep in the Heart of Texas
Thirteenth Apostle

7. Some Jewish folk songs
The Last Jew of Danzig
Translation of the Ten Martyrs
Maimonides Prayer for Physicians
Captain Scuttle

7a. Some Jewish folk songs

8. Tricks of the Trade – Analysis of *South Wind*
Also some good notes from a Laski book; Auden, Stuart Chase

9. Jewish Themes in English Writing

10. Letter from Afar (The fate of the sixteen)
Shmelka
The Seventh Scroll
From whose bourne
And it shall come to pass

11. And the mome raths outgrabe

12. Marginalia: Bookreviewing in Seven Easy Lessons
Writing in Canada
The Gesture of the Bible
Robert Frost & the five senses. Apple-picking time
Towards an Aesthetic. Gens. Chap. 1
The Poem as Circular Force
Old Ez & his blankets
The Usurper
The poem of the age: the cliché
Of Japanese poets: Poems about Babies: Conversation (Interview re Jive)
Ballad of Sir Patrick Spens
Note on sonnets
Poetry & Clausewitz
The Classical Simile
Queen Mab & Mickey Mouse
Annotation on Shapiro
Cantabile – (E.P. Review)
Analysis of Sestina
$x^2 + 2xy + y^2$
The comma
Shakespeare's Dog
Man with the Hoe
Housman's figure eight
Hopkins & Rorschach
List of further subjects

List of jive slang
Milton's shibboleth
First lines
On translation

13. Sundry writing – Notes, ideas, philology
Notes on Sampson's English Literature
Some experimental poems
Note on satirical verse re Law
List of wines
Hapaxlegomenon

14. One More Utopia

15. O Canada – notes

16. British Poetry – Longer notes on Yeats, Eliot, Hopkins

17. Extra copies: Ballad of Yehuda Halevi & others
Some Segal translations
Gladstone
Seven Poems
& some unpublished

17a. Extra & unpublished

18. Reviews: Who should have been ours
Five Freedoms

19. Myriad-minded man
Arthur Ellis
Master of the Horn

20. Speeches: Argumentation & Refutation
Zionism & Dr. Rabinowitch

21. Some Raw Materials

22. Letters

23. Neilah in Gehenna

24. Villon's Ballads
Slang collection

25. The Trotsky play

26. Rite of Abraham

27. Some translations from Horace
Some free verse

28. The Bells of Sobor Spasitula

29. The Bells of Sobor Spasitula

30. The Book of Aggadah – first version

31. The Book of Aggadah

31a. The Book of Aggadah

32. Notes on Bible

32a. Notes on Bible

32b. Notes on Bible
Thirty Plots & Holy Writ
also article on Bible Manuscripts

33. Stories: We who are about to be born
Siamese Twins

34. Beggars of Bagdad & notes for other international stories

35. Idea for story by letters
Anthology of letters from Angry Men
Man who bought up all theatre tickets

36. Notes from Flaubert
Notes from Egon Friedell

37. Quotes from Chaucer

38. Blindfold Vision – Duplicates

39. Stories – Of Lowly Things
A Likely Story
Responsa

40a. The Golem – notes

40b. The Golem – characters

40c. Geography of Prague

40d. First chapter

40e. Notes

40f. Phrasing

40g. Debate on good & evil

40h. Rumphaeus

www.ingramcontent.com/pod-product-compliance
Lightning Source LLC
Chambersburg PA
CBHW082101090726
47910CB00008B/2547

* 9 7 8 1 4 4 2 6 2 3 0 5 7 *